D1391690

ENGLISH INTERIORS

Pictorial Guide and Glossary

Fully illustrated throughout by the author, an indispensable easy-reference book on a subject of immense interest and popularity.

The introduction, with 16 handsome illustrations of characteristic room settings, traces the historical development of the English interior from the fortified medieval house of AD 1300 to the easy-care apartment of the present day.

An extensive glossary illustrated with the author's thumbnail drawings, defines over 450 essential terms, from architectural and decorative features, through the means of heating and lighting, bathing and sanitation, and cooking and serving food, to furniture and furnishings: making up a book which presents its information in a concise, lucid and practical form.

Filmset in 11/12 Bembo (Introduction)
10/10 Bembo (Glossary of Terms)
by Nene Phototypesetters Ltd, Northampton

Printed in Great Britain by
Butler & Tanner Ltd, Frome and London

English Interiors

Pictorial Guide and Glossary

DOREEN YARWOOD

Illustrated by the author

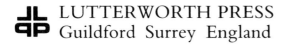 LUTTERWORTH PRESS
Guildford Surrey England

CONTENTS

INTRODUCTION

The intention in this book is to present a fully illustrated easy-reference account of the development of the English domestic interior from about AD 1300 until the present day.

As in my companion volume, *Costume of the Western World*, this introduction traces the important factors in this development and, for those who wish to study specific subjects in greater detail, provides cross-references to the alphabetically listed articles which form the major part of the book. These articles cover an extensive range of subjects from interior architectural and decorative features and furniture to cooking methods, toilet facilities and television.

The introduction is illustrated by monochrome interior scenes (each with a detailed caption), the glossarial section by a quantity of thumbnail line drawings. The illustrative material derives from my own drawings and photographs made during the past thirty years in houses and museums (acknowledgements, page 188). The introductory scenes display actual interiors (some, unfortunately, not now extant) though many are a blend of more than one room. In all cases, designs for heating, lighting, furniture and furnishings have been altered in order to depict an interior where everything is of the given date – not as in most houses open to the public, where these features necessarily illustrate the centuries of living which the house has experienced. This 'all-of-a-period' approach assists the student of domestic·history in identifying styles, artists, craftsmen and materials when visiting a historic house.

The factors which brought change and advance over the centuries to the character of the English house interior have come from three basic sources: social and political; artistic; and technological.

From the first of these came the expansionist changes in house-plan and layout which took place in the later Middle Ages. As the country became more peaceful and people felt more secure the fortified character of homes waned, giving place to a less severe and gloomy appearance, a greater number of rooms and a more open house-plan. In the 16th century, with a notable increase in population and trade, and greater wealth in the country, great landowners travelled abroad in Europe, returning to design larger and more imposing country homes to patterns which they had seen in their voyagings. Again, the tremendous increase in population resulting from the 19th-century advances in medicine and hygiene brought changes in house design, this time in city dwellings as towns were rapidly enlarged, seeking to cope with the unprecedented influx of families leaving the rural life which could no longer support them for the factory jobs which were becoming available. The suburb was born, giving rise to a type of house which had not existed before.

No less cataclysmic in its effect on home life and design of the house interior was one notable change brought about by the First World War. Women discovered that a wide and varied labour market had opened up to them and, almost overnight, the previously ample servant supply dwindled to a trickle. For the first time middle- and professional-class housewives had to organise cooking, washing and cleaning with little domestic help, and within a very few years the character of household surfaces, furnishings and equipment had radically altered to meet their needs.

Over the centuries England has been fortunate to have received an influx of artists and craftsmen from other European countries who have brought their skills to beautify English homes. Such craftsmen have introduced advances in many different trades, in glass-making, furniture-construction, silk-weaving, lace-making, ceramics and carpets, in painting, carving, terracotta work and stucco. In design, also, new concepts have been introduced which have completely altered the appearance of interior decoration. The most notable of these was the introduction of Renaissance forms of classical structure and orna-mentation to replace the Medieval Gothic ones, which came to England first in the 16th century in second-hand Flemish guise, then, by the 1620s, in purer Italian form. The studies abroad made on the 18th-century Grand Tour by aristocrats, architects and artists brought new versions of the classical mode; a few years later, artistic fashion changed once more and these were replaced by the different Gothic Revival forms.

The greatest overall influence upon the house interior has been, with-out doubt, technological. It was technical developments in glass-making which made possible larger window panes, advances in kiln design and clay mixing which gave us bricks to build homes and quality ceramics to make utensils. Improvements in the design of tools and machines made possible fine cabinet-making and veneering of furniture. The develop-ment of the blast furnace gave us cast iron, and Bessemer, Cort and Siemens made cheap good steel a reality for structure and equipment.

Most vital of all, without which no industrial advance would have been possible, was the development of power; first water, then steam, and eventually electricity – and electrical power is the basis of all modern life, no less in the home than elsewhere. Probably the single advance which has most radically altered life at home has been the development of electricity and, especially, the small electric motor to power so much of the household equipment which we take for granted.

The technical advances during the 19th and 20th centuries in the chemical industry have affected greatly the quality and production of many of our home needs: in textiles, glass-making, matches, soap and detergents, aerosols, to name but a few. A whole new range of materials has been evolved which has revolutionized both surfaces and articles: for example, plastics of infinite variety, fibreglass, bonding resins for laminated furniture, and non-stick surface coating for our pans.

The electronics industry is in the process of bringing about a new revolution. During the 20th century in home entertainment we have moved from singing round the drawing-room piano to listening to the phonograph, the gramophone or the wireless, and now to watching television. The microprocessor is being introduced into our household appliances: toasters, washing-machines, sewing-machines. It is not only the occupations and actions of the family which are being changed by these advances. The appearance of the rooms is being altered too. The open hearth used to be the focal centre of a room: it is now more likely to centre on the television receiver.

1.   THE MEDIEVAL INTERIOR: 1300–1500

By modern standards life at home in the Middle Ages was primitive and uncomfortable. Interiors were inadequately lit and heated: draughts were everywhere. The means and standard of cooking were equally unsatisfactory. Privacy was minimal. It is not surprising that the aristocracy wore fur-lined garments, even hose, in their own homes. The wealthier citizens fared better than the peasants; they were looked after by a retinue of servants and did not have to share their home with their livestock. Even so the standard of comfort and sustenance for everyone had sunk far below that experienced a thousand years earlier in Romano-British homes where people enjoyed underfloor and interwall heating by hypocaust (see CENTRAL HEATING) and a high quality of culinary expertise. Several centuries were to pass before such standards were reached once more.

During the Middle Ages most people lived in rural communities. Towns were small, each on an average having about 3500 inhabitants. Most medieval houses were built of timber, roofed with thatch, so few have survived. The danger of fire was great, especially so in town centres where houses were pressed close together and where the upper storeys projected outwards into the street, so giving only a narrow passageway between. It is understandable, then, that most houses still existing are those of the more important, wealthier members of the community who could afford to build in more permanent materials – brick, stone, flint or timber and brick – and these are mostly castles, manor houses and the smaller fortified houses.

By 1300 the country was becoming more peaceful and its citizens more secure but still defence was considered important in house design. Because of this the lowest floor of a house (the undercroft) was used for storage, its walls pierced only by narrow slit windows, allowing no ingress from the outside. Steps led up to the entrance to the house at first–floor* level where the living accommodation was to be found. This pattern was followed whether the home was a narrow-fronted town house or a more spacious country manor house.

During the 15th century the fortified aspect of houses gradually disappeared. Most houses were built round a courtyard approached through an entrance gatehouse. This had previously possessed a military function and appearance but now provided accommodation which usually included the house chapel.

The architectural style of medieval houses, both inside and out, followed the pattern set by ecclesiastical building and the successive forms of Gothic architecture could be discerned, adapted to a restrained version more suited to domestic structures. This was especially apparent in the design of window heads and tracery, door panelling and mouldings, staircases and interior roofing (see DOOR, GOTHIC ARCHITECTURE, STAIRCASE, TIMBER TRUSSED ROOF, TRACERY, WINDOW).

The most important apartment in a medieval house, whether large or small, was the hall (**1†**). Particularly in the earlier centuries this was where everyone, from the lord and his family downwards, lived, ate and, in many cases, slept. The main entrance led into a passage known as the screens and from this passage were doorways giving ingress to the hall. By this design the draughts from the front door did not blow directly into the hall (see SCREENS PASSAGE).

The hall was nearly always two storeys high and, until the later 15th century, covered by an open timber roof, the designs of which

---

*In American usage, second-floor level.
†Numbers in bold type refer to illustrations in the Introduction.

1. Fourteenth-Century Great Hall

Timber trussed roof with collar beams and curved braces. Moulded wall plate with carved wood life-size figures as corbels. Central hearth with andirons. Smoke escaped through vent in roof timbers. Carved wood screen with screens passage behind: the two doors led to the buttery and the pantry. Windows have appropriately Decorated Gothic style of tracery. Woven woollen wall hangings. Lighting by iron hanging candlestands and wall sconces. Furniture of oak comprising decoratively pierced food cupboard, boarded chest, benches and trestle tables.

developed over the centuries to become complex and beautiful (see TIMBER TRUSSED ROOF). The walls of this large apartment (up to about 50 feet, or 15 metres, in length) were gaily painted or, for warmth, covered with wool hangings or tapestry (see TAPESTRY, WALL HANGINGS). The floor was strewn with rushes which were renewed at intervals. At one end of the hall, over the screens passage, was a gallery which could be used for musicians or other entertainers and at the other was a raised area, the dais, on which the high table was set for the lord, his family and guests. Here was a high-backed bench and, for the lord himself, usually the only chair (see CHAIR, DAIS).

Windows were generally set along both long sides of the rectangular room. At first these were small but became larger as glass was more readily available and as knowledge of building structure increased so that it was deemed safe to weaken the wall by greater openings (see WINDOW, WINDOW GLASS). Gothic tracery appeared in the window heads and, for decoration, coloured heraldic glass also (see TRACERY). The dais end of the hall was often illuminated by an impressive bay or oriel window (see BAY WINDOW, ORIEL WINDOW). Wooden shutters were fitted to be bolted across at night and, in the early Middle Ages when little glass was available, the stark choice for the inhabitants was to close the shutters to keep out the cold air but also exclude the light or leave them open for illumination but suffer the draughts.

Heating was by log fires, the logs piled up against massive metal andirons (see ANDIRON). In some halls the hearth was placed centrally, the smoke escaping (when the wind was in the right direction) through a louvre in the roof timbers above (see LOUVRE). As time passed, wall fireplaces became more common. These had hoods to contain and direct the smoke which escaped up a chimney shaft to the outside wall or a roof chimney stack. An iron fire-back protected the rear wall of the hearth from the heat of the burning logs (see FIRE-BACK) (**2**).

There was little privacy in life in the great hall. Seated on benches, people ate at trestle tables set up for meals, and slept round the fires at night. In later houses there were more private rooms; the lord and his family had their parlour or withdrawing room, called the solar (see SOLAR) reached by a staircase from the dais end of the hall (**2**). Staircases in these houses were simple structures, taking up minimal space. They were either of a newel design or a straight flight of stairs – or even just a wood ladder type (see FLIGHT, LADDER STAIR, NEWEL, STAIRCASE). From the solar a small window made it possible to keep an eye on the activities below.

2. Solar 1485–95

Tie beam and king post timber trussed roof. Oriel window with stone mullions and transom. Stone fireplace with four-centred arched opening and carved spandrels. Iron andirons, brick hearth. Wooden boarded floor, plaited rush mat in front of hearth. Bronze wall sconces. Wooden hanging candlestand (candle beam). Chair, bench and cupboard of oak, carved with linenfold panelling. Oak ambry for holding food, carved in Gothic design with pierced holes.

15th-century houses possessed several bedchambers. These were passage rooms, one leading directly into another, and since the entrance and exit doors were lined up with one another, the rooms were apt to be draughty. Not surprisingly beds were designed with canopies and enclosing curtains. At this time the canopy was still supported from the ceiling beams while the curtains hung from side rails attached to the walls (see TESTER).

Washing and toilet facilities were limited and primitive. Cold water had to be carried from an outside pump and heated in a cauldron over the kitchen fire. Jugs and bowls for washing were available in bedchambers; bathing was infrequent and took place in a tub in front of the kitchen fire or in greater privacy in the bedchamber (see BATH). Chamber pots were provided and some houses were fitted with garderobes which drained into a moat or cesspool below (see GARDEROBE).

The level of artificial illumination was extremely low. Rushlights, candles and oil lamps were the traditional means of providing such interior lighting and all, at this time, were smoky, smelly, needed constant attention and were a fire hazard (see CANDLE, OIL LAMP, RUSHLIGHT). One of the greatest problems was to create a flame in order to light one's candle or make a fire to warm oneself. The tinder box was an essential household article for this but it was not easy to use. The kitchen fire was, therefore, always kept burning and at night was banked down and covered with a curfew so that the flames could be coaxed back in the morning (see CURFEW, TINDER BOX).

In the early Middle Ages the kitchen was often a separate building kept away from the timber house-structure for fear of fire. When more permanent building materials came into wider use, the kitchen became part of the house interior and led off the opposite side of the screens passage from the hall doorways. Cooking was by means of the open hearth where pots were suspended over the fire or set beside it, and in front of it spits were continually turned to roast meat and fish. Large baking ovens were built into the walls beside the fire (**7**). Most of these kitchens were only one storey so the smoke and steam could find an exit through the louvre boards in the roof above (see CHIMNEY-CRANE, LOUVRE, SPIT).

Most houses, especially those in country areas, had to be self-sufficient throughout the year in their needs for food, clothes and cleaning materials. In consequence, any house of fair size would have a dairy, where cheese and butter were made, a brewery, a laundry room and various larders and store-rooms to keep food in good condition for several months at a time. Such rooms were accommodated near the kitchen and were also reached from the screens passage (see BUTTERY, PANTRY).

There was very little furniture in a medieval home and the pieces were all of basic, utilitarian design. The most valued item was the wooden bed on which lay the feather mattress, supported on boards or a rope mesh. There were ample layers of bed covers and fur rugs which, with the bed curtains, kept the sleeper warm.

After the bed the chest was the most important article of furniture. It was a multi-purpose item, used for storing linen and other possessions as well as for seating (see CHEST). There were also cupboards for food and plate (see CUPBOARD), solid and trestle tables, benches and stools (see STOOL). Most furniture was made of oak, boarded for the most part and decorated by carving and painting. The introduction of joined furniture towards the end of the 15th century made possible stronger and lighter articles as the new craft was gradually developed (see JOINERY, PANEL-AND-FRAME CONSTRUCTION) (**1, 2**).

2. THE TUDOR INTERIOR: the sixteenth century

During the Middle Ages priority in building resources had been allocated to ecclesiastical architecture. In contrast, in the 16th century, great wealth and energy were devoted to the design and construction of houses, both in town and country and for the yeoman and middle classes as well as the aristocracy. The initial impetus for this stemmed from the Dissolution of the Monasteries in the 1530s when Henry VIII re-allocated the monastic wealth and properties to chosen recipients. The high level of building activity of the years 1530–50 was continued in Elizabethan times as the country became more populous and wealthy.

With this energetic construction drive came also new ideas in archi-tectural style, in building materials used, in house-plan and in the use and layout of rooms. The Renaissance in architecture and decoration came late to England, partly because the country was, geographically, so far away from the source of the movement in Italy, and partly due to further delay resulting from Henry VIII's break with the Roman Catholic Church which hindered the easy flow of Italian craftsmen into England (unlike what happened in France) to teach the new style to the indigenous builders (see CLASSICAL ARCHITECTURE, CLASSICAL ORDER).

All this not only caused delay in accepting the Renaissance styles of building but resulted in the type of decoration and structure which was finally adopted in the second half of the 16th century in England being different from the pure Italian Renaissance form. Elizabethan interpretation of Renaissance design was based mainly upon the Flemish and French versions of Italian classicism; this was second-hand and one which was less correct and more ornate than the original. The knowledge of English builders was derived from the books of drawings and designs produced in Flanders and France (based on Italian prototypes) and from wealthy English landowners who had visited the Low Countries and northern France, particularly the Loire Valley, then returned to sketch out the house which they wanted built and to instruct their master mason upon the design, supporting these instructions with the drawing pattern books from which the English craftsmen could work. The results of this new decorative classical medium being imposed upon the traditionally English asymmetrical gabled manor house created a national style, different from European origins. An original English architectural form of great vitality and interest had been born and this can be seen in the considerable numbers of fine Elizabethan houses – large and small – which survive in many parts of the country.

To discern how the English 16th-century interpretation of Italian Renaissance forms differed from the original it may be said that the English incorporated the classical orders in their building design (both exterior and interior) but largely employed them decoratively rather than structurally and, not properly understanding their purpose, used them incorrectly and mistakenly. The English also adopted with enthusiasm Flemish Renaissance ornamental forms such as cresting, gabling, strapwork and cartouches (see CARTOUCHE, CRESTING, STRAPWORK).

The English professional architect, on Italian Renaissance pattern, had not yet emerged but we can trace the designers and leading craftsmen of some of the great Elizabethan houses. John Thorpe and Robert Smythson were two of these; the latter is thought to have been connected with the direction of three such houses: Longleat (Wiltshire), Wollaton (Nottinghamshire), Hardwick (Derbyshire). Typical of the aristocratic architectural dilettanti of the time was Lord Burghley who absorbed ideas for Burghley House from his travels in Europe, returned to instruct his master mason about the house design he envisaged, and gave him books of drawings of classical detail and orders to work from.

Towards the end of the 16th century a more symmetrical form became apparent in the English country mansion and the 'E' and 'H' ground plans began to replace the medieval courtyard one. The house ground-plan was a rectangle. In the 'E' plan side wings projected forward forming the end strokes of the E and the entrance porch was the central stroke. Symmetry was stressed by a balance of doorway and window design on each side of the central porch. Window matched window, as did also dormers and chimney stacks. Classical symmetry was slowly being accepted.

Inside the house there was, during the century, a gradual trend towards greater privacy expressed by a larger number of smaller rooms. The use of the great hall as a sleeping- and living-room for everyone was abandoned. Bit by bit it became a smaller entrance or staircase hall. Various family reception rooms replaced the medieval solar; chief of these was a main or great chamber (3) but also there were parlours and a dining-room. More bedrooms were introduced with the top-floor attics or dormers being designed for servants (see DORMER).

A particularly Elizabethan innovation was the long gallery. A very few such apartments existed before 1550 and, in general, they were characteristic of the years 1560–1660. They were extensively used for a variety of occupations (see LONG GALLERY).

Another advance in Elizabethan times was in staircase design where the first step was taken towards the spacious open well staircase (see OPEN WELL STAIRCASE). The usual Elizabethan pattern was the heavy, carved oak, dog-legged design where flights returned alongside one another (see DOG-LEGGED STAIR, FLIGHT, STAIRCASE).

In the 16th century the decorative plaster or plaster panel and carved oak beam ceiling largely replaced the open timber roof (see CEILING). Elizabethan ceilings and friezes were ornately decorated in ribbed and pendant form with heraldic, animal or plant motifs ornamenting the panels between. This profusion of precise decoration was made possible by the new plasterwork techniques introduced by Italian craftsmen (see PENDANT DECORATION, PLASTERWORK) (3, 4).

Although some walls were still decorated by painting and others covered by hangings, embossed leather or tapestry, or even small pieces of wallpaper (see TAPESTRY, WALLPAPER, WALL HANGINGS), the most characteristic wall covering of the 16th century was wood panelling or wainscoting. Linenfold panelling was most typical of the first half of the century (see LINENFOLD PANELLING) while Elizabethan panels were more commonly decoratively carved or inlaid with coloured woods in patterns with Flemish Renaissance motifs (see PANEL-AND-FRAME CONSTRUCTION, WAINSCOTING) (3, 4).

Although the home was becoming more spacious and comfortable the

3. Elizabethan Main Chamber 1585–95

Decorative plaster ceiling, cornice and frieze; strapwork design on ceiling, the floral frieze pattern incorporates figures and heraldic beasts. Oak panelled walls and chimneypiece with inlay ornamentation of differently coloured woods. Panelling scheme incorporates classical pilasters. Wood boarded floor. Stone carved window frame, iron casements and diamond-shaped leaded lights. Iron candlestand and hanging candelabrum, pewter candlesticks. Stone fireplace with four-centred arch and carved spandrels; cast-iron fire-back and andirons. Carved walnut court cupboard inlaid with holly and bog wood. Oak armchair.

floors, of tile, wood or stone, were as yet largely uncovered though the introduction of plaited rush mats to replace the insanitary loose rushes was a marked improvement.

Oriental and Arab carpets had been made for centuries. Because of its occupation by the Moors, Spain was the first European country to possess knotted oriental carpets and to learn how to make them. Spanish carpets were made from sheep and goat wool and these were exported to other European countries from early in the Middle Ages. When Eleanor of Castile came to England in 1255 to marry Prince Edward (later Edward I) she brought eastern and Spanish carpets with her which were greatly admired.

By the 16th century wealthy English homes possessed some imported oriental and Turkish carpets and the English were beginning to hand-make their own. Some were woven in Turkish manner with wool on linen ground but most were needlework carpets embroidered on canvas using a frame (see CARPET).

Doors were panelled in keeping with the room's wainscoting scheme. The design was so similar that the opening was not readily discernible.

As the quality and supply of window glass improved and the under-standing of building construction became greater, the window area increased. Each window was divided by mullions and transoms, and iron-framed casement sections were made to open and close. Panes of glass were still small; they were framed in lead and often of diamond shape. Window curtains were now usually provided (see CASEMENT WINDOW, MULLION, TRANSOM, WINDOW, WINDOW GLASS) (3).

The wall fireplace had become the focal centre of each room. In early Tudor times it was in late Gothic style, carved in stone or wood with a four-centred arch inside the square-headed frame, so leaving a spandrel to be decoratively carved (3) (FOUR-CENTRED ARCH, SPANDREL). The Elizabethan chimneypiece was an imposing two-storeyed affair, the lower part flanked by carved columns or caryatid figures (see CARYATID) and the upper ornately decorated all over with a variety of Flemish-style Renaissance motifs. Such chimneypieces displayed the essential character of the Elizabethan form of Renaissance art and architecture, using a variety of materials from stone and marble to wood and plaster, the ornament picked out in colour or gilt (4).

Furniture was slowly becoming more varied in design and greater in quantity. Oak continued to be the wood most in use and decoration was by carving and inlay. In the first half of the century linenfold panelling was extensively carved to decorate panels for chests and cupboards (see

4. Elizabethan/Jacobean Bedroom 1590–1615

Plaster ribbed, pendant ceiling fashionable about 1580–90. Decorative plaster frieze. Oak panelling. Boarded wood floor. Needlework wool, fringed bedside rug. Carved marble and decorative plaster chimneypiece of Jacobean style with Flemish-influenced ornamental motifs. Brick fireplace opening, cast-iron fire-back and andirons. Carved oak bed (c. 1600) with wool hangings and bedcover decorated with coloured wool embroidery. Carved oak chest and cradle. Pewter candlestick and candleholder.

BUFFET, CHEST, COURT CUPBOARD, CUPBOARD). Elizabethan furniture is characterized by the bulbous leg, carved with acanthus leaf decoration, seen in beds, tables, court cupboards and buffets (see BULB, TABLE). The four-poster bed made its appearance in this century; the framework of tester, posts and headboard was richly carved over the entire surface (see FOUR-POSTER BED, TESTER). Though still not common, chairs were more numerous than in the Middle Ages (see CHAIR) (**3**, **4**).

Metalware of good quality was being produced for home use, in iron, brass, copper and pewter and for more valued items, silver (see BRASS, BRONZE, IRON, NON-FERROUS METALS, PEWTER). Home-produced pottery was still of simple, utilitarian design but the more decorative delftware and majolica were being imported (see CERAMICS, DELFTWARE, MAJOLICA). Similarly the home product in glass was plain and useful with the high-quality ornamental glass being imported from Venice (see GLASS).

3. THE STUART INTERIOR: 1600–1714

Two very different factors exerted a lasting influence upon 17th- and 18th-century homes: the depletion of timber stocks and the introduction of Italian/Roman classical styles of architecture.

When William of Normandy invaded Britain in 1066 the country was heavily afforested. During the Middle Ages this timber, mainly hardwood, was felled in a profligate manner for ship-building, iron smelting, construction of buildings of all kinds, and all heating and cooking purposes. It has been estimated that when the 16th century opened, up to four million acres of Britain were still afforested but by its end concern was being felt for the loss of supplies which had not been replaced by planting schemes.

From the early years of the 17th century various forms of legislation were passed to restrict, for specific purposes, this indiscriminate felling. One result was the increased use of brick as a domestic building material to replace timber construction, another was to change the equipment used when burning fuel at an open fire for heating and cooking. Gradually coal replaced wood as fuel and, as it is difficult to kindle and burn coal on a flat hearth and the material could not be contained by andirons (see ANDIRON), the domestic fire-grate evolved (see BASKET GRATE) (**7**).

It was in the 1620s that Inigo Jones introduced the Italian Renaissance building style to Britain, a style which had appeared almost a century earlier in French chateau design. Despite, or probably because of, this long delay the movement quickly gathered momentum in Britain and this purer form of ancient Roman classicism before long superseded the Elizabethan version derived from Flemish sources (see CLASSICAL ARCHITECTURE, CLASSICAL ORDER).

Inigo Jones took advantage of an opportunity offered to him to spend 18 months in Italy and France to study at first hand, making detailed drawings and measurements, both antique Roman buildings and Italian and French examples based upon them. He was particularly interested in the work of the Italian architect Andrea Palladio, who had closely followed the building structure and decorative characteristics of the early years of ancient Rome, and Jones' Queen's House at Greenwich (1616–35) shows a clear affinity with Palladio's villa designs at Vicenza. Inigo Jones was the first English Palladian architect, designing in true classical form, constructively as well as decoratively (see PALLADIAN).

By and large, from the 1630s until the 19th century, the classical style of building remained paramount, though it appeared in various guises and interpretations during these years. The Flemish decorative influence was still apparent in the 1630s and 1640s, though now in less ornate and more muted and classical form, while from about 1650–90, the Dutch Palladian pattern, initiated by such English architects as Sir Roger Pratt and Hugh May, was the model both for medium-sized and larger houses. The limited and, in England, somewhat short-lived Baroque movement was to be seen between about 1690 and 1715 when some magnificent large houses were built such as Sir John Vanbrugh's Castle Howard and Blenheim, Nicholas Hawksmoor's Easton Neston and Thomas Archer's work at Chatsworth (see BAROQUE).

The layout and disposition of rooms inside the house was changing, partly in response to the desire for greater privacy and more varied room functions, and partly because of the symmetry of the architectural design. The entrance door or porch was set in the centre of the main façade, approached up a flight of steps. It led into the hall which, by the 17th century, was becoming simply an entrance staircase hall, and no longer a reception room. The main staircase (most larger houses had more than one staircase) had advanced from the Elizabethan dog-legged design to the open-well type (see OPEN WELL STAIRCASE), providing an easy ascent up short, straight, broad flights (see FLIGHT). The 17th-century staircase was still solidly and heavily built of carved wood (usually oak) on closed string pattern. There were two chief types, the richly carved panel balustrade design, and that with spiral-twisted balusters (see BALUSTER, BALUSTRADE, STAIRCASE) (6).

The reception rooms were to be found on the principal, first floor*, the *piano nobile* (see PIANO NOBILE); these would include a withdrawing-room, dining-room, card room, library and private parlours. The long gallery, fashionable until about 1660 (though one or two fine examples,

---

*In American usage, the second floor.

5. Caroline Long Gallery 1630–40

Decorative plaster ceiling. Oak panelling with carved Ionic pilasters. Double-stage chimneypiece is very ornate in Flemish Renaissance design. Door is at the far end on the right-hand side. Windows, of casement type, with stone mullions and transoms, iron casement openings and lead frames to small panes of glass (curtains omitted on the long left-hand side of the gallery in order not to obscure the pilasters and panelling). Wooden floorboards. Brass hanging candelabra. Furniture: pair of oak back stools with columnar legs with stretchers, turkeywork upholstery and fringe decoration, matching settee, oak draw-top table, joint stool and chest.

Sudbury Hall, for instance, were built after this) might be on this floor or the one above (see LONG GALLERY) (**5**).

Bedchambers would be on the second floor. By mid-century these were no longer passage rooms but the door to each led off the staircase landing. Each room had its own fireplace and more items of furniture than hitherto. Apart from the four-poster bed (see FOUR-POSTER BED), there would be chairs, stools, a table with dressing-box and mirror upon it (see TOILET GLASS) and a chest-on-stand which, later in the century, developed into a chest-of-drawers (see CHEST). There would be a mirror over the fireplace and a rug on the floor in front. In houses with adequate servants, bedchambers would also contain close stools for convenience of family and guests (see CLOSE STOOL).

In the kitchen methods of cooking had changed little from medieval times but the equipment had developed a greater efficiency and was easier to handle. The boy turnspit was replaced by the power of a dog turnspit or mechanical jack: both were innovations of the late 16th century (see MECHANICAL SPIT, TURNSPIT). The chimney-crane had become a complex piece of equipment which made possible the easier handling over the fire of the many different pots and pans at one time (see CHIMNEY-CRANE). A kettle tilter eased the pouring of hot liquids (see KETTLE TILTER). As with the heating fire-grate, the kitchen hearth was also gradually adapted to burn coal, the fire being contained within a basket grate and the spit turned in front of it, resting upon cob irons (see SPIT). It was now possible to use different kinds of toaster as some could be made to stand in front of the fire-bars and others hang upon them (see TOASTER). Furniture, as elsewhere in the house, had become more adequate and convenient. In addition to the kitchen table there was also generally a settle, a dresser and chairs (see DRESSER, SETTLE) (7).

The design of Jacobean plaster ceilings was similar to, though more ornate than, Elizabethan ones, all-over strapwork pattern predominating (see STRAPWORK) (3, 5). Towards mid-century the ceiling more usually had a high-relief centrepiece, oval, circular or rectangular in shape, and was ornamented with naturalistic classical motifs of fruit, flowers, putti and festoons (see PUTTO, SWAG). In large houses the centrepiece panel was painted with allegorical or historical scenes. By 1700 ceiling designs were in lower relief once more, and less richly ornamented (see PLASTERWORK).

The walls of a room were usually wood panelled but, instead of the all-over, small, rectangular or square, inlaid or carved panels of the 16th century, the whole room was designed as one unit in the form of a classical order (see CLASSICAL ORDER). Using the proportions suited to the individual order, the lower part of the wall from dado rail to the floor (see DADO) represented the plinth of the order and the entablature encircled the room immediately below the ceiling (see ENTABLATURE). Between these two bands of carved woodwork, pilasters with capitals

6. Restoration Stuart Staircase 1670–80

Painted, carved pinewood staircase with panel balustrade. Oak stairs and floors.
Decorative plaster ceilings. Casement window. Painted and carved wood
doorcases and doors.

and bases were set round the room at intervals with panels between (see
CAPITAL, PILASTER). The panels were now large and generally raised
above the level of the wall surface by use of bolection mouldings (see
BOLECTION MOULDING). Doors and windows were part of the complete
scheme, being flanked by pilasters. Doorcases were of classical design
often surmounted by pediments (see PEDIMENT). Smaller doors had two

large panels, larger double doors usually six. Until about 1675 wood panelling was usually painted white or in a light colour; after this the natural wood was just waxed (**5**).

In the second half of the 17th century the carving of woodwork reached an exceptionally high standard of craftsmanship. Mouldings were carved with classical ornament, most commonly egg and dart, bead and reel, and acanthus foliage (see ACANTHUS, BEAD AND REEL, EGG AND DART). A new style of decorative carving for mirror and picture frames and to surround the upper stages of chimneypieces was initiated by Grinling Gibbons. This was a freer, more naturalistic form than hitherto, depicting flowers, fruit, drapery and birds almost in the round and displaying such delicacy as to appear intensely realistic. Gibbons preferred lime or fruit woods which were suited to this type of work.

By 1685 the sash window, of Dutch origin, had begun to replace the casement type. Early sashes had to be wedged open before a weight and pulley control system was evolved (see SASH WINDOW). Window curtains were long and full, of heavy rich fabrics: a valance above concealed the curtain rail (see VALANCE). Panes of glass were now larger; they were rectangular, generally six panes per sash (see WINDOW GLASS).

Floors were covered by tiles or stone flags on the lower storey and were of polished wood boards elsewhere. Rugs were now much more common and, in wealthy homes, there were carpets (see CARPET): many were imported, especially from Persia, Turkey and Spain. The establishment during the 17th century of the French State manufactories of Savonnerie and Aubusson led to importation of these carpets and rugs also. Hand-made English rugs and carpets of turkeywork or needlework were in use too.

The Restoration of the Monarchy in 1660 represented a turning-point in English furniture design and making. Until that time furniture, though steadily becoming more varied and greater in quantity, was still heavy and utilitarian, carved and mainly in oak. Charles II and his fellow exiles returned to England from years of living in France and the Low Countries where they had found furniture regarded as a decorative as well as a useful adjunct to a home. They had also seen and appreciated the methods of making this furniture, the using of the different woods and means of ornamentation. Craftsmen from these countries were persuaded to come to England to demonstrate these skills and techniques and when, in 1685, the Revocation of the Edict of Nantes led to a Huguenot exodus, many skilled French cabinet-makers came to work in England permanently.

7. Kitchen *c.*1700

Stone-flagged floor, stone walls thinly plastered, wood beam and board ceiling. Wooden bread car hung by chains from ceiling beams. Fireplace (left) has a basket spit, supported on posset dogs, powered by a weight-driven mechanism attached to the wooden chimneybreast. Also attached there is a candleholder. Fireplace of brick, cast-iron fire-back, iron coal-burning grate. Iron chimney-crane, cauldrons, skillet, down-hearth toaster, salamander, dripping tray and camp oven. Fireplace (right) has a spit powered by a dog turnspit. Hot cupboard at left-hand side with iron door. Copper kettle, brass dripping tin. Propped against the wall a besom broom, bellows, poker and tongs. Furniture: wooden settle and table. On the table: earthenware bowl, wooden milk luggie, sugar loaf and cutters.

The period from 1660 until the mid-18th century is known in furniture history as the 'age of walnut'. This became the fashionable wood though, due to its cost, it was not until about 1680 that its use became general. During these years furniture became more delicate in construction and more varied in design. Legs were turned, in bobbin, vase or columnar form, or, as the quality of lathe design improved, in spiral twist (see TURNING). More chairs were available, also settees, and the day bed appeared (see CHAIR, DAY BED, SETTEE). There was a greater variety of pieces to contain pottery, linen and books. Different types of table were in use from solid dining-tables to the gate-leg design and small side or card tables (see CARD TABLE, GATE-LEG TABLE, SIDE TABLE). Upholstery was in more general use for seating furniture. It was covered with turkeywork, velvet or embroidery and edged with fringe and tassels. New decorative techniques were developed: veneering, marquetry, japanning, gesso (see GESSO, JAPANNING, MARQUETRY, VENEER).

With the improved quality of glass from the Duke of Buckingham's manufactory, mirrors were becoming more common in houses and were also of larger size. Beautiful frames were made for these, some of decorative silverwork, some of marquetry-ornamented wood and many elegantly carved in wood in Grinling Gibbons' style (see GLASS, MIRROR).

Better quality, more attractive and durable pottery was becoming available for the home. Majolica and delftware were being imported and, from the 1670s, stoneware was being produced in England (see CERAMICS, DELFTWARE, MAJOLICA, STONEWARE).

The application of the pendulum to clock design brought about a much greater reliability in all types of clocks whether weight- or spring-driven; the long-case clock with long pendulum appeared in the home (see CLOCK).

The 17th-century introduction of tea- and coffee-drinking into Europe (see CADDY) brought into use a range of suitable equipment: tea tables, tea kettles, tea and coffee pots, sugar bowls, cream jugs.

4.   THE GEORGIAN INTERIOR: 1714–1837

The 18th century was the 'golden age' of the English house. The quality of design and craftsmanship in architecture and the decorative arts had been steadily improving since Elizabethan times and this reached its zenith in the years 1760–90.

It is not easy to explain why such fine workmanship was achieved at this time. It is true that 18th-century England was wealthy and comparatively peaceful but this might also be said of much of Victoria's reign; yet no art historian would equate the architecture of William Kent, the decoration of Robert Adam, the furniture of Thomas Chippendale or the pottery of Josiah Wedgwood with the products of the 1870s.

Apart from the fact of a steady progression in the classical art forms over two centuries, it was the aristocratic patron who helped to make such beautiful craftsmanship possible. The members of most aristocratic families and landowners were knowledgeable. They travelled widely and long in Europe, studying both the antique classical world and its modern equivalent. They knew clearly what they wished to create in England and they had the wealth to employ the best of architects, artists and artisans in all fields of domestic building. They demanded the highest standards and, as one style of classical architecture followed another, they built and rebuilt in order to reflect the latest fashion in their town and country houses.

This high standard set an example to others lower down the scale of wealth and position. A professional man could not afford a Holkham or a Kedleston, and he did not possess a large estate to be laid out by Capability Brown, but he could follow the examples of his betters and insist upon a fine quality, though smaller, house of good taste and craftsmanship. The aristocratic patron would employ one of the great contemporary architects, himself trained by two or three years of study in Europe; the local builder of a less pretentious house would carefully follow the designs for windows, doorways, chimneypieces, etc., shown in the architectural handbooks of the day produced by the well-known architects. Every detail of design, proportion and ornament was shown, the fruits of 150 years of English classical research.

The form of classicism followed by architects during this long period changed markedly. Paramount in the years 1714–60 was Palladianism (see PALLADIAN), a characteristically English style, restrained and almost austere on the exterior, correct in its classical design and detail, richer, warmer and bold within. The country houses of this type were set in carefully selected, ideal positions in beautifully laid-out parkland. Town houses, whether terrace or individual, were naturally restricted by the site and tended to have narrow frontages but were extended rearwards and upwards to provide comparable spacious interiors.

In the second half of the 18th century the travels of aristocracy, architects and artists became more extensive. Research showed the

8. Palladian Bedroom 1740–60

Plaster ceiling and frieze, gold decoration on white ground. Walls hung with blue silk to dado rail, dado painted white with gilt moulding ornament. Wood board floor with two Turkish rugs. Chimneypiece: white marble lower stage; above, wood painted white with gilt decoration. Steel grate, brass fender, iron fire-back. Door painted white with gilt decoration. Chippendale bed with fringed silk hangings (c. 1755). Commode chest of drawers veneered in mahogany (c. 1760). Wall mirror with gilded carved pinewood frame (c. 1735). Mahogany washstand with stoneware jug and bowl (c. 1760). Mahogany armchair with cabriole legs (c. 1740). Carved mahogany wardrobe (c. 1750). Carved and gilded chandelier (c. 1735).

originator of antique classicism to be Greece, not Rome, and homes were built both in Greek and Roman forms while several of the leading architects of the day (for instance, Robert Adam and James Wyatt) adapted both forms into their work, producing a blend which was a personal interpretation rather than a carbon copy (see NEO-CLASSICISM).

The years 1790–1837 are usually referred to in this context as 'Regency' though the actual Regency (that of the Prince of Wales, later George IV) only lasted nine years, 1811–20 (see REGENCY). This was a time of transition from the comparatively rural Georgian England to the increasingly industrial Victorian one. Regency domestic building marked the tail-end of the classical era (though a minority of houses were being built in a variety of styles – rustic, literary Gothic, a flavour of imagined Indian and Chinese) but it also displayed a hint of things to come. There was, for example, a tendency to hide one material under a veneer of another, as in covering a brick house with stucco and painting it to imitate stone (e.g., the Regent's Park terraces by Nash). There was a trend in furniture and furnishing design to follow a rapidly changing variety of different source material – Greek, Egyptian, Gothic, for instance. Hand-craftsmanship survived but the industrial age was making it possible to save time, and so cost, by mass-producing decorative parts or whole items and, inevitably, the standard of workmanship suffered. The faster rate of population increase meant an extension of building activity and many new houses were constructed of inferior materials as well as to inferior designs. In total, the time and patience required to train a craftsman and the money to pay him to produce over a long period a superb piece of furniture or porcelain, or a plaster ceiling, were running out and the decay of taste was imminent.

In the later decades of the 18th century the size of towns and cities was beginning to increase quickly as the Industrial Revolution created unemployment in rural areas, forcing families to migrate to the towns in search of work available in the new factories. Much of the housing provided for these workers was poor but at the same time a new form of high quality, though speculative, town planning was developing where houses were being designed in classical dress in terraces. Such houses were joined together in a long block, these being laid out in complete streets, squares and crescents, all in one symmetrical scheme. Bath was one of the first cities where such terrace architecture was constructed. Soon followed London, then spa towns like Cheltenham and Tunbridge Wells, and the idea spread to seaside resorts along the south coast.

The layout and disposition of rooms in these years had not changed greatly. Especially in architect-designed houses convenience took second place to artistic priorities so, while the beautifully proportioned and furnished reception rooms were symmetrically arranged on the *piano nobile*, the kitchen was relegated (in large country houses) to a separate block, while in a town terrace house it would be at the rear, probably in a semi-basement. In both cases it was inconveniently far from the dining-room but, in an age where more than adequate servant labour was available, this was not too serious a problem.

In the 1730s and 1740s William Kent set the pattern for an architect to design everything in a house interior, not just the ceiling decoration, the general interior scheme and the chimneypiece, but all the furniture and furnishings, down to door handles and fire-irons (**8**). This lent interiors a fine quality of homogeneity which had not been present before. His example was followed by others, notably Robert Adam who made a practice, for instance, of creating a carpet design to echo that of the ceiling above; several survive, as in the Music Room at Harewood House.

Throughout these years ceilings were decorated in classical design in stucco (see PLASTERWORK). The Palladian interiors displayed a heavy, richly ornamented Roman influence, the background generally being white and the ornament picked out in colour and gilt. Around mid-century lighter, freer Rococo motifs became paramount (see ROCOCO) and from about 1765 Robert Adam's influence led to more delicate classical decorative forms in low relief. Adam preferred a pastel shade of colour for the ceiling ground rather than white which he considered to be glaring and unsympathetic. His decoration was usually white and he used gilt sparingly except in his richer interiors which he based on Imperial Roman ones – Syon House, for example. His favoured motifs were arabesques, anthemion and mythical animal forms (see ANTHEMION, ARABESQUE, GRIFFIN). Most of his ceiling designs incorporated circular or oval panels which were painted with mythological scenes by painters such as Angelica Kauffmann (see NEO-CLASSICISM). By 1800 ceiling design became plainer though still in low relief and classical in form (**9**).

In the larger rooms of wealthy homes, walls were also ornamented with stucco, the designs following schemes similar to those of the ceilings (**9**). In smaller homes, wood panelling was still used; it was now generally made from deal or pine rather than oak and was painted to harmonize with the interior scheme. Carving was restricted mainly to the chimneypiece, door cases and window frames.

9. Adam Dining-Room 1765–75

Walls, alcove and ceiling decorated in low relief white stucco design in neo-classical forms upon coloured grounds. Painted ceiling lunettes. Carpet designed to echo ceiling pattern. White marble fireplace, steel grate and fender. Urns on stands flank side-table in alcove; knife boxes on table, wine cooler beneath. Carved and gilded candlestands. Mahogany dining-table and chairs. Mahogany doors with ormolu door furniture.

For bedchambers, hangings from cornice to dado rail were thought appropriate. These might be of velvet, brocade, silk or other rich fabric. Wallpaper was becoming more popular as time passed and was especially to be seen in Regency interiors (see WALLPAPER) (**8**, **11**).

From the second half of the 18th century carpet manufactories were set up in England and these gradually took over from the existing cottage industry. Among the best-known were those of Axminster, Wilton, Moorfields, Exeter, Kidderminster and Kilmarnock. A number of architects created their own designs and had the carpets made at manufactories of their choice. Carpets were also still widely imported from the Orient and from France (see CARPET) (**9, 11**).

Technical advances stemming from the Industrial Revolution were influencing the supply of building and decorative materials and the gradual adoption of steam power in the later 18th century made significant advances possible in textile production for furnishing materials and in the making of iron (cast and wrought) and glass. Wrought iron was widely used for staircase balustrades (**10**); cast iron became more and more important with the development in design of hob grates and the cooking range (see CAST IRON, HOB GRATE, IRON AND STEEL, KITCHEN RANGE). The adoption of the French system of cast plate glass in the 1770s made possible larger panes of window glass and mirrors (see MIRROR, PLATE GLASS) (**11**).

Technical advances were also improving standards of artificial illumination and of home heating (see HOB GRATE) (**11**). Expansion in the fishing industry brought candles made from sperm whale oil; these could be purchased (instead of having to be made at home) and were a marked improvement on tallow candles (see CANDLE). Meanwhile the Swiss chemist Ami Argand introduced his new burner which immensely enhanced the level of artificial illumination from oil lamps (see ARGAND BURNER).

For actually making a light the tinder box and tinder pistol continued to be the staple method (see TINDER BOX). From about 1775, however, various, somewhat dangerous, chemical methods were also introduced to make the process easier. These were based upon the interaction of one chemical upon another and the hazards stemmed from their highly inflammable nature. Typical of these methods were the chlorate and phosphorus matches and the instantaneous light box (see PHOSPHORUS BOX, INSTANTANEOUS LIGHT BOX). Fortunately these methods were not widely used as they were expensive.

In the kitchen technical improvements were slowly making the housewife's life easier. The hob grate, which gradually came in about mid 18th century, decreased the fireplace aperture and increased the draught. The fire burned better and it was possible to keep food and liquids hot on the hobs which flanked the grate (see HOB GRATE). Hot cupboards were now also built into the wall at either side of the fireplace in which plates could be warmed and drinks mulled. The use of bottle

10. Late-Eighteenth-Century Staircase Hall

Marble staircase with wrought-iron balustrade and mahogany handrail: the ironwork painted and gilded. Top natural lighting from lunette windows above. Cut-glass chandelier with many branches for artificial lighting. Galleries at first-floor level ★ supported on console brackets. Stone flagged floor. Woodwork of door frames painted, the doors of polished mahogany. Gilt wood settee, silk-covered upholstery.

★ *In American usage, second-floor level*

jacks and hasteners helped in roasting food and the smoke jack and roasting range were important assets in larger homes where considerable numbers of people had to be catered for (see BOTTLE JACK, HASTENER, ROASTING RANGE, SMOKE JACK). Finally, the kitchen range was introduced in the later 18th century. It was a coal-devouring monster, temperamental and difficult to control and clean, but greeted as a considerable advance on cooking by means of the open fire (see KITCHEN RANGE).

Home water supplies had changed little and until mid-century, cold water had usually to be pumped from an outside supply into a pail, then brought indoors and heated over the kitchen fire. After this, however, with the introduction of the ball valve, the water supply was brought into the house and, though still intermittent, was available for much of the time. In larger houses, the introduction of washstands and shaving-tables into the bedchambers made washing more convenient (see SHAVING-TABLE, WASHSTAND).

Home sanitation and toilet facilities had improved only negligibly since the Middle Ages, and throughout the 18th century, in stark contrast to the quality of the interior decoration and furniture, sewage disposal remained primitive and insanitary. The usual toilet facilities consisted of an outside privy with wooden seat built over a small pit. Such pits had to be emptied by household staff who carried the contents in buckets through the house to larger, communal cesspools which were regularly emptied by the professional night-soil men. Night commodes (see COMMODE) and chamber pots sufficed for indoor use.

It was, therefore, a great relief, at least to the wealthier homes, when the WC, patented in 1775 by Cumming and improved three years later by Bramah, was introduced. These water closets were not very efficient by today's standards but were a great improvement, lasting for a century before being superseded. However, they ranked high as a health hazard because they were sited in corners or cupboards where ventilation was inadequate – it was rare for a WC to be built into a room designed for the purpose – and, as the waste pipe emptied into a cesspool similar to that of the earlier privy, there was nothing to prevent the foul gases from ascending the pipe back into the house (see WATER CLOSET).

No less than in architecture and the decorative arts was this the 'golden age' for furniture. The names of many of the designers – Chippendale, Vile and Cobb, Linnell, Adam, Hepplewhite, Sheraton – are household words. This was primarily the 'age of mahogany' although walnut continued in use until mid-century and, in the later years, other woods were employed also. After the abolition in 1721 of

11. Regency Drawing-Room 1810–20

Floral striped wallpaper. White painted woodwork. Sash windows with silk, fringed curtains. English-made carpet upon polished wood floorboards. Carved white marble chimneypiece, cast-iron hob grate, brass fender and fire-irons. Carved, gilded, convex circular mirror with candleholders. Silk embroidered mahogany panel fire-screen. Cut-glass chandelier. Rosewood chiffonier with glass panels; cupboards fronted by brass lattice over pleated silk. Rosewood sofa with brass inlay, striped silk covering. Carved, gilded X-frame stool. Painted and gilded armchair.

the import duties on West Indian timbers, mahogany began to enter the country in quantity. It was a superb wood for furniture making. It was immensely strong; suitable for delicate carving, as in ribband- and lyre-back chair splats and cabriole legs terminating in claw-and-ball feet (see CABRIOLE LEG, CHAIR, CLAW-AND-BALL FOOT, LYRE-BACK CHAIR, RIBBAND-BACK CHAIR, SPLAT); and available in much greater widths than walnut, making it ideal for veneered surfaces of large area and for table tops (see VENEER). It had a beautiful patina and a resistance to woodworm and warping.

All kinds of pieces of furniture were introduced and perfected in these years. Many new designs of table appeared, also chairs, stools, settees, bureaux, dumb waiters, china and corner cabinets, mirrors, candle-stands, desks and commodes (see BUREAU, CANDLE, CHAIR, CHINA CABINET, COMMODE, DUMB WAITER, MIRROR, SETTEE, STOOL, TRIPOD TABLE). In general, the designs of the first half of the century were large-scale, richly carved in classical manner and notable for superbly veneered surfaces. Around 1750 the Rococo motif appeared in furniture design and, soon after, the Chinese and Gothic forms (see CHINOISERIE, GOTHIC-STYLE CHAIR, LATTICE-BACK CHAIR, ROCOCO) (8).

With the 1760s came the Adam neo-classical influence, seen in the more delicate designs of furniture, sometimes in carved mahogany but also painted and gilded beech, harewood and satinwood veneers, ormolu mounts and a revival of 17th-century marquetry and brass inlay (see INLAY, MARQUETRY, ORMOLU, VENEER). The neo-classical furniture was varied, displaying the same type of motifs as the Adam ceiling and wall stucco and painted work (see NEO-CLASSICISM). Hepplewhite con-tinued and advanced the Adam tradition, his furniture becoming even more delicate (the tapering square-sectioned leg having replaced the cabriole one) and using a variety of methods of decoration. The shield-back chair is associated with him, and the ornamental Prince of Wales' feathers (see PRINCE OF WALES' FEATHERS, SHIELD-BACK CHAIR). New items of furniture in the 1770s and 1780s included the Pembroke table and the sideboard (see PEMBROKE TABLE, SIDEBOARD). At the end of the century came the Sheraton era, generally thought to represent the height of technical achievement in furniture-making, displaying simultaneously strength, function and delicacy (9, 10).

Much of the Regency furniture was still well made and designed. It was plainer and, on the whole, derived and copied from antique originals, from Greece, Rome and Egypt. Decoration was restrained in painting, inlay and veneer, often with gilt linework and metal inlay and mounts. Chairs were characterized by horizontal shoulder backs rather than vertical splats, and legs which often curved in sabre design (see EGYPTIAN CHAIR, ETRUSCAN CHAIR, TRAFALGAR CHAIR). The sofa table evolved from the Pembroke form (see PEMBROKE TABLE). The long dining-table was revived, standing on pillared supports with curving legs. Typical of mirror design was the circular convex type. Some furniture of lower quality was also beginning to appear, though mass production and mechanization had not yet shown itself in this field as it had in textiles and others (**11**).

The 18th century was a vital one in the development of the ceramics industry. Chinese-type porcelain was finally produced in Germany and the soft-paste version was developed at Chelsea. This was expensive but Wedgwood and, later, Spode, put attractive, durable yet delicate ware on the market at much lower prices, bringing it within reach of most families (see CERAMICS, CHINA, JASPERWARE, PORCELAIN, QUEEN'S WARE).

5.   THE VICTORIAN INTERIOR: 1837–1901

The interiors of Victorian houses were in marked contrast to those of the previous century. One of the major reasons for this was that the unprecedentedly rapid growth of population – doubling between 1850 and 1911 from 18 millions to 36 millions – made necessary a tremendous building drive to provide homes. Also, the process of urbanization – the migration of people from country to city – accelerated enormously so that much the greater percentage of houses were of speculative building constructed closely packed in towns.

This building boom affected houses of all prices and social levels but, inevitably, the general aesthetic standard fell appreciably. A second vitally important cause of change in home life was the quickening trend towards factory production methods and mechanization of processes stimulated by an ever greater demand for building materials, interior decorative features, furniture and furnishings. Mass-production methods of supplying these needs led to a greater similarity in their design so that the interior of one dining-room greatly resembled that of another, and overall resulted in a poorer level of design and work-manship. The individual craftsman decorating a plaster ceiling or panelling a wall *in situ* was disappearing, to be replaced by a workman attaching ready-made lengths of cornice or dado rail to a plain plaster wall.

The architectural style of house building varied very much according to the social status of the occupier. This was the age of eclecticism when all past styles were regurgitated endlessly. In domestic building the large country house and the high-quality town terrace house tended still to be of classical design. The middle-class suburban house, semi-detached or standing alone, was more likely to have Gothic gables, window and door heads, coloured glass and ornament. The working man's home,

12. Victorian Kitchen 1850–60

Stone flagged floor, plastered stone walls. Painted wood dresser. Gas chandelier with glass-covered burners. Painted wooden chimneypiece enclosing black-leaded cast-iron kitchener which is equipped with oven, open fire, hob and hot-water boiler. Chimney-crane fitted at side of hob. Hanging from chimneypiece: brass bottle jack, oven holder, toasting fork and ladle. Polished steel fender with flat surface for standing vessels upon to keep food hot. Bellows. Oak settle with cushion. Painted wood chair. Scrubbed wood table with bread bin beneath. Roller towel. Other equipment: meat tenderiser, sugar sifter, colander, pans and steamer, sugar jar, pestle, coffee grinder.

one of a row in a long street, was unlikely to be dignified by any architectural style at all: it was reduced to the lowest basic level.

Most houses, and the middle range in particular, due to lack of space and rising land values in towns occupied a comparatively small ground-plan but rose four or five storeys from a basement or semi-basement level. There were innumerable stairs, and coal fires in every room, but with more than enough servants available, this was no problem. Many servants spent their working days in the basement and slept in the attics.

Interior decorative schemes were in great contrast to the earlier Regency ones. White or light-coloured painted woodwork had been replaced by dark brown tones. Wallpaper, carpets, furnishing fabrics were all darker and richer in hue and most often strongly patterned (see CARPET, LINCRUSTA, WALLPAPER). There was a strong tendency to drape material over everything: lace and chenille curtains over the windows, tasselled velvet covers to tables and chimneypieces, antimacassars on chair and sofa backs (see ANTIMACASSAR, CHIMNEYPIECE). Upholstery was heavy and bulging; buttoned designs were very fashionable (see UPHOLSTERY). The fireplace and grate were of black-leaded cast iron, surrounded by dark shiny tiles and potted-meat marble chimneypieces. The whole interior was over-furnished and over-decorated, a profusion of stuffed birds, framed photographs, lace mats and wax fruit (13).

In the last 20 years of the century the rebellion of such men as William Morris, Norman Shaw, Philip Webb and Charles Voysey, combined with the efforts of the Arts and Crafts Movement, had some effect upon the scene just described. Colours became lighter again, patterns less vivid; and overall, fewer pieces of furniture were placed in a room.

Parallel with the general decay of taste and lowering of standards of craftsmanship, there took place a series of technical advances in many fields of work which greatly affected the Victorian interior. These advances were partly responsible for the loss of quality and individuality but they also brought considerable benefits to the home occupant.

The textile industry was the first to be affected by and to benefit from industrialization. Power from steam, factory methods and mechanization of all the processes gradually transformed the industry. An important result of this was to increase the range of fabrics, to make all kinds of woven patterns possible and to reduce the price, so making textiles available to a much wider section of the public.

The 19th-century development of the chemical industry affected a wide range of materials needed in the home. In textiles the new ways of producing sulphuric acid and chlorine were vital to bleaching processes.

13. Victorian Parlour 1860–70

*Sash window covered with cream lace curtains and cut-velvet long curtains.
Richly patterned heavy wallpaper. Carpet in dark colours. Dark brown grained
paintwork. Gas lamp wall bracket. Carcel oil lamp on piano. Papier mâché table
in window with glass-covered bird and floral decoration on top. Carved wood
fire-screen with painted panel. Satinwood pianoforte decorated with gilding and
inlay. Turned mahogany piano stool with velvet-covered seat. Satin-covered
horsehair ottoman-type buttoned sofa with cord and tassel trimming. Chair to
match. Papier mâché chair and work-table, both inlaid with mother-of-pearl and
painted with scenes of famous buildings.*

In dyeing, the introduction of aniline dyes in 1856 was somewhat of a mixed blessing. The new dyes were strong and brilliant; they became very popular but, in comparison with the earlier vegetable dyes, the colours were strident. It was (perhaps) fortunate that several of them were fugitive to light (see ANILINE DYES).

Among other important domestic improvements brought about by chemical developments was the 19th-century commercial manufacture of soap, made possible by the new soda processes (see LYE). Research into the different types of phosphorus made safety matches possible. The electroplating process for silver was developed to replace the 18th-century Old Sheffield Plate method (see ELECTROPLATING, SHEFFIELD PLATE). By the second half of the 19th century rubber was being produced in sheets, tubing and thread, and early plastics, such as celluloid, were being manufactured from natural polymers (see PLASTICS).

Technical progress in other fields was even more relevant to home needs. The production of sheet glass, combined with the final abolition of the window tax, made possible sash windows with panes of much greater size, no longer subdivided by glazing bars. Sadly, this opportunity for letting more light into the rooms was more than offset by the Victorian fondness for shutting it out by lace curtains (see PLATE GLASS, SASH WINDOW, SHEET GLASS, WINDOW GLASS). The immense progress in producing iron more cheaply and in vast quantities made this the 'age of iron'. Cast iron, in particular, was manufactured into all kinds of fittings and articles for the home (see CAST IRON, IRON AND STEEL) (**13**).

Technical progress revolutionized lighting, heating and cooking methods. This was the 'age of gas', though coal also continued to be used all the century for cooking and heating and, by the later decades, electricity was beginning to make a small contribution (see ELECTRIC LIGHTING, GAS COOKING, GAS HEATING, GAS LIGHTING, INCANDESCENT FILAMENT ELECTRIC LAMP). Running water was being laid on in many homes and, by the end of the century, heated baths, gas geysers and even fitted bathrooms were becoming available (see GEYSER, HEATED BATH, LOUNGE BATH, SHOWER BATH, SLIPPER BATH) (**14**). In home entertainment the phonograph and the gramophone were introducing exciting (if scratchy) new sounds (see GRAMOPHONE, GRAPHOPHONE, PHONOGRAPH).

The kitchen too was changing rapidly. To modern eyes it would represent drudgery in cleaning, polishing and cooking but it was a tremendous advance on that of the previous century and there was an army of domestics to do the work. Piped water had arrived here also.

14. Bathroom 1889

Up-to-date bathroom design and fittings as advertised in contemporary catalogues. Decoratively tiled walls and floor. Carved wood framework to bath, washbasin, cupboards, dressing-table, pull-out bidet and separate chamber for water closet. Brass taps fitted in vertical panel at side of bath to control hot and cold water and shower fitting. Marble top to washbasin, brass taps to basin and bidet. Two wall mirrors. Electric light fittings on wall and over washbasin.

The kitchen range would cook, heat the room and produce hot water (see KITCHEN RANGE). There were ice boxes to keep the food fresh (see REFRIGERATION). Early washing-machines appeared (see WASHING-MACHINE); at the least, there was a wash boiler and a mangle (see BOX MANGLE, DOLLY STICK, POSSER, WASHBOARD). A wide variety of irons made the immense task of ironing in a Victorian household much easier (see ELECTRIC IRON, GAS IRON, IRONING, SLEEVE IRON, SPIRIT IRON) (**12**).

Furniture was now less attractive; it was heavier in design and often over-elaborately decorated. Late in the century, particularly, the whole gamut of 18th-century and earlier styles were reproduced for a mass market. Among characteristically Victorian features was the extensive use of papier mâché (see PAPIER MÂCHÉ) and, to a lesser degree, Tunbridge ware (see TUNBRIDGE WARE), the balloon-back design of chairs (see BALLOON-BACK CHAIR), bentwood furniture (see BENTWOOD FURNITURE) and the introduction of brass and iron in the construction of bedsteads and other items, such as rocking chairs (see CHAIR, PRIE DIEU, ROCKING CHAIR, TENT BED, TUBULAR METAL FURNITURE, UPHOLSTERY). Plainer, more traditional furniture was made in the last quarter of the century by a number of designers and craftsmen working for such groups as the firm of Morris & Co., the Cotswold School and the Arts and Crafts Movement (see ADJUSTABLE CHAIR) (**13**).

6.   THE TWENTIETH-CENTURY INTERIOR

It is arguable that the interior of the English home has altered more during the 20th century than in any previous age. The reasons for this are social and technical.

The rapid increase in population engendered during the previous century continued, though at a decreasing speed, and Britain steadily became a more urbanized community. Concurrently the ideas which had emerged from the 19th-century arousal of the nation's social conscience were gradually translated into action. The rise and acceptance of socialist principles brought about a fairer distribution of wealth which, in turn, led to a raising of standards of living for millions of people and, thus, to a higher level of expectation in housing.

The two world wars of the 20th century were not in themselves responsible for the changes in society which followed them: most of these would have taken place eventually anyway. The wars did, however, act as catalysts, giving impetus to the changes and greatly speeding up the process. Because of this the wars became divisive barriers between domestic life before and after the years of struggle and there could be no return to the previous existence. Not only was the situation afterwards different but so was the attitude of people towards it.

After each war the position and function of women in society had altered fundamentally. Before 1914 an immense pool of feminine labour was tapped to service the labour-intensive Edwardian home: to clean and polish, to scrub and scour, to cook and serve. During the First

World War this servant army began to melt away. For the first time in England jobs of all kinds opened up for girls of great or little education and intelligence and it was accepted that there was no social stigma attached to their helping the country in its hour of need. After 1918 only a minority returned to the hard restrictive life of domestic service. Middle- and upper-class housewives, finding themselves without sufficient labour to run their homes as before, lost no time in demanding more labour-saving equipment and finishes. Interiors quickly became plainer, there was far less furniture in a room, cleaning aids were introduced and heating became easier (see CARPET SWEEPER, ELECTRIC HEATING, GAS HEATING, VACUUM SUCTION CLEANER).

This process received another boost after 1945 when more and more women, not only single girls but also married ones, adopted careers and full-time work outside the home, only giving this up for a few years while their children were very young. The home gradually became more easy-care and labour-saving than ever as technical advances made this possible.

Also, after each war, a rapid expansion of house building was needed, partly to replace those destroyed during the war and partly to make up for the years when no building had taken place. To cut corners and speed up the programme new methods were adopted: prefabricated building structures, high-rise blocks built from steel and concrete, modular construction (see MODULE). A tremendous range of new materials was developed, some synthetic and some the result of recent processes of manufacture (see FIBREGLASS, PARTICLE BOARD, PLASTERBOARD, PLASTICS, PLYWOOD). Different ways of planning housing were tried to accommodate people in different areas as work patterns changed; these were first in garden cities, later in new towns.

The two world wars divide the century into three periods and it is easy to appreciate the changing character of the English interior by studying and comparing them.

Between 1900 and 1918 there was a slow reaction from the mid-Victorian interior, over-furnished and over-decorated, in dark colours; this reaction had begun in the 1880s. The patterns of carpets and wallpaper became daintier and less strident, and colours were lighter. There were fewer pieces of furniture and ornaments. Soon after 1900 the brief decorative movement known as Art Nouveau showed itself in Britain but by 1914 it had burnt itself out (see ART NOUVEAU).

The interiors of the inter-war years illustrated a much stronger reaction against Victorianism. Fashionable interior decorative schemes

15. Lounge 1933–38

Distempered walls in fawn colour. Cream paintwork. Wooden sash window. Woven wool curtains. Plain wool carpet. Fur hearth rug. Tiled fireplace in brown and cream. Wooden fender. Belling electric fire. Electric standard lamp and table lamp, silk shades. Polished oak dinner wagon on castors, occasional table, and bureau-bookcase. Oak veneered radiogram cabinet. Sprung and hair-stuffed settee and armchair with chromed tubular steel frame and woven wool covering.

reflected the functionalist architectural mode, so displayed a clinical severity. Though this represented only a minority of homes, most interiors were affected by the mood of the time. Colour schemes were light and neutral, walls were distempered or covered with wallpaper of indeterminate pattern, floors were plainly carpeted or of parquet, ceilings were undecorated and mouldings were few. Fireplaces, doors and windows were severely plain and seating furniture was chunkily upholstered (**15**).

There was a boom in furniture production to supply all the new homes. Machine production had now been established but the standard of commercial manufacture was not good and a modern revival of past styles – for 'traditional' popularly meant an imitation of the past – was much less successful than the late-Victorian one had been. Some excellent modern designs in machine-made furniture were being manufactured in Scandinavia, and in the 1930s were gradually influencing the English product for the better.

The coal fire survived but many homes were now heated by gas or electric fires, though these still stood in the hearth or were fixed to the fireplace so that it remained the focal centre of the room (see ELECTRIC HEATING, GAS HEATING). Lighting was gradually transferred from gas to electricity (see ELECTRIC LIGHTING, INCANDESCENT FILAMENT ELECTRIC LAMP). In home entertainment this was the age of the gramophone and the wireless (see GRAMOPHONE, RADIO).

In the years after 1945 the modern style of architecture and decoration became established. Despite this, except in high-rise flats, many homes were still being built in a fairly traditional fashion, using brick construction, though decoration was kept to a minimum and there was general simplification of design. The interiors had altered much more: they were comfortable, convenient and more colourful than in the 1920s.

Convenience and time-saving became more important to the whole family in the decades after 1945. Gradually central heating was adopted, replacing the heating of individual rooms. These two factors, together with a rising standard of living for many people and a desire for greater privacy amongst members of the family (especially the young) to 'do their own thing', led to a redisposition and new décor of rooms. The recognition (sometimes unwilling) that with a central-heating system there was no longer need for a fireplace in a room led to a general rearrangement: in many homes the television receiver replaced the fireplace as focal centre. There were more, if smaller, individual bedrooms. The two-bathroom house became less of a novelty. During the years 1955–65 the open-plan house was received with grudging approval but, as in offices, experience revealed more drawbacks than advantages.

Probably the two most important causes of change were the development of the very small electric motor and that of a wide range of plastics and synthetic textiles. It was the technical achievement of making an

16. Kitchen/Diner 1980s

Vinyl washable wallpaper on walls. Carpet-tiled floor covering. Worktops, kitchen units and dining-area faced with decorative plastic laminate. Chairs of aluminium tubing, the seats and backs covered in white vinyl. Fluorescent ceiling strip lighting. Fitted equipment includes electric cooker, washing-machine, dishwasher, double stainless-steel sink and waste disposal unit and (out of view) fridge-freezer.

electric motor small enough to power household cleaning and cooking equipment which made housewifery so much easier in the early 1920s (see VACUUM SUCTION CLEANER, WASHING-MACHINE). After 1950 a new generation of even smaller motors made all kinds of kitchen and bathroom equipment possible, from food mixers to shavers. In recent times the microprocessor has been introduced into a selection of such equipment and promises to open a new era in their control and efficiency (see ELECTRONIC CONTROL OF DOMESTIC APPLIANCES) (**16**).

In the field of plastics an extensive range of new materials has become available to produce colourful, attractive, easy-care surfaces in the home and these, together with the simultaneous development of synthetic textile fibres, have revolutionized almost every decorative and utilitarian feature from gramophone discs to carpets, from plate racks to furniture (see DECORATIVE PLASTIC LAMINATES, PLASTICS).

A number of other technical advances have had their effect. The establishment of new processes for window glass (see FLOAT GLASS, SOLAR CONTROL GLASS, WINDOW GLASS); the development of refrigerators and deep-freeze cabinets (see REFRIGERATION), of soapless detergents, aerosol sprays and fibreglass for roof cavity insulation (see FIBREGLASS), of new materials and production methods for furniture-making (see CANTILEVER, CHAIR, LAMINATED FURNITURE, PLASTICS, PLYWOOD, TUBULAR METAL FURNITURE, UPHOLSTERY) and, probably, most widespread of all, of television and video-recording (see TELEVISION, VIDEO-RECORDING): these have brought further benefits and improvements to every aspect of home comfort, convenience and activity.

GLOSSARY OF TERMS

Greek classical
acanthus leaf

ACANTHUS: a hardy, perennial plant with ornamental leaves, native to southern Europe. Used widely since early times as a foliate motif but especially in classical architecture where formalized acanthus leaves encircle the bells of the Corinthian and Composite capitals and enrich various mouldings (see CAPITAL, CLASSICAL ORDER). In general, the spiky leaves of the *acanthus spinosus* are depicted in Greek architectural ornament while the Roman inspiration derived more from the rounded leaves of the *acanthus mollis*.

ADJUSTABLE CHAIR: an easy chair with a back whose angle could be altered from an upright to reclining position. The best-known model of this type was the one made by the firm of **William Morris** from about 1866.

ALUMINIUM: although the third most common element in the world (after oxygen and silicon), aluminium does not occur in nature as a metal but in various compounds, so it could only be manufactured commercially after the development in the 1880s of the successful electrolytic process of reduction. The name derives from the Latin word *alumen*, the term given by the Romans to salts then found in volcanic coastal areas of the Mediterranean. They used these salts, which it is believed were sulphates of iron and aluminium, in medicine and dyeing processes.

The aluminium industry developed early in the 20th century and by the 1920s the metal had become a popular material for cookware because of its lightness in weight and resistance to attack by a variety of chemicals. By the 1930s the development of extrusion processes made it suitable as an architectural material. At the same time aluminium alloys were introduced such as Duralumin (which is 4.5% copper, 0.6% manganese and 1.5% magnesium); these were harder and possessed a greater

Adjustable chair
of the type made
by Morris & Co.
from about 1866

tensile strength than pure aluminium but despite this and the rustless quality of the metal, the high cost meant that it was only used on prestige building work until after 1945.

In the post-war years aluminium alloys have been widely used in domestic building for structural needs, cladding, window and door framing as well as for furniture. Since 1945 the use of the metal in the kitchen equipment and the food processing industries has increased markedly.

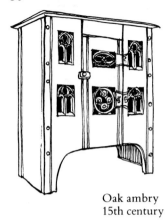

Oak ambry
15th century

AMBRY, ARMOIRE, AUMBRY: a term used from the Middle Ages onwards for a cupboard to store things, a pantry or a storehouse. Used primarily to store food when, as a piece of furniture, it was often decoratively carved; a design feature was made out of the need to provide air holes (see also LIVERY CUPBOARD).

Andiron
15th century

ANDIRON(S): iron supports used in pairs to hold in place logs burning on an open hearth. Each andiron had a horizontal bar terminating in a foot at the rear while the front part which faced the room extended upwards in a vertical pillar; at the lower end this divided into two feet which stood on the hearth.

Andirons were also known as **fire dogs** because the horizontal bar and foot resembled the hind leg of a dog.

ANILINE DYES: the many years of research aimed at producing synthetic dyes resulted in success when **Sir William Perkin** made in 1856 the first aniline dye, which became known as mauveine. European research soon produced several more synthetic aniline dyes, notably magenta, alizarin and fuchsia.

The chemical base, aniline, had first been obtained in 1841 by C. J. Fritzche who distilled indigo with caustic potash; he named it 'aniline' from the Sanskrit word for the indigo plant. Since then aniline has been made chiefly from coal-tar and the dyes are also known as **coal-tar dyes**. The colours produced in the second half of the 19th century were brilliant and achieved great popularity both for clothes and furnishings but, unfortunately, tended to be fugitive to light.

Anthemion
ornament

ANTHEMION: an ornament widely used in classical architecture which is a formalized version of the honeysuckle flower.

ANTIMACASSAR: a decorative cover placed over chair and sofa backs, particularly in Victorian times, to protect the upholstery from the macassar oil used by men as a dressing for the hair.

Fringe and crochet antimacassar 1870

ARABESQUE: ornamental design composed of interlaced curling scrolls and foliage incorporating figures of realism and fantasy. An Arabian and Saracenic form of decorative surface ornament but also characteristic of classical architecture, in particular, in Renaissance and neo-classical work (see NEO-CLASSICISM, RENAISSANCE).

Arabesque decoration Robert Adam 1765–70

ARCH: from the Latin *arcus*, 'arch, vault, or bow'. A curved structure of wedge-shaped blocks which are supported only at the sides and maintain their position by mutual pressure. Such a structure is capable of bearing considerable weight or may (if constructed in wood, for instance) be purely ornamental.

Building by the structural use of arches (**arcuated construction**) is of ancient origin. The Etruscans built true arches of radiating **voussoirs** (the wedge-shaped blocks composing the arch) and the Romans extensively developed this method of building. The classical arch is usually round and the medieval (Gothic) one pointed; there are many variations in both forms, the chief of which are shown in separate entries (see EQUILATERAL, FOUR-CENTRED, LANCET, OGEE, POINTED, SEMI-CIRCULAR). The principal structural parts of an arch are illustrated (see also EXTRADOS, IMPOST, INTRADOS, KEYSTONE, RELIEVING ARCH, SPRINGING).

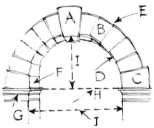

STRUCTURE OF
AN ARCH:

A = Keystone
B = Voussoir
C = Springer
D = Intrados
E = Extrados

F = Soffit
G = Impost
H = Spring-
    ing Line
I = Rise
J = Span

ARCH BRACE: in a timber trussed roof a curved piece of timber which helps to strengthen the structure; for example, the piece which braces the hammer beam in this style of roof (see COLLAR BEAM, HAMMER BEAM).

ARCHITRAVE: the lowest member of the classical entablature resting upon the column capitals (see CLASSICAL ORDER, ENTABLATURE). The term also refers to the moulded frame surrounding a door, window and arch.

ARGAND BURNER: in 1784 the Swiss chemist **Ami Argand** made an important contribution towards improving artificial lighting from oil lamps which, until then, had given a very low level of illumination: only one candlepower for each wick burning. Argand devised a tubular wick in

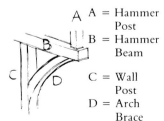

TIMBER
ROOF

A = Hammer Post
B = Hammer Beam
C = Wall Post
D = Arch Brace

Double Argand lamp
early 19th century;
two burners fed with oil
which flows under gravity
from a central reservoir

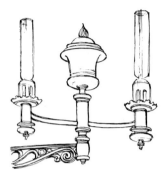

the form of a hollow cylinder and enclosed this in a metal chimney. The wick was attached to a tube which passed through the oil reservoir into the base of the lamp so providing oxygen to make the flame burn brightly and creating sufficient heat to consume all the carbon and avoid smoking. This improved combustion increased the level of illumination ten-fold. Before long it was found that the replacement of the metal chimney by one of glass further enhanced the light. Many further improvements were later made to oil lamps (see CARCEL LAMP, OIL LAMP) but a majority of designs continued to make use of the principle of the Argand burner.

ART NOUVEAU: an ephemeral movement, more decorative than architectural, which appeared in several European countries, including Britain, from the 1880s but which had burnt itself out by 1914. It represented a deeply felt conviction of the need to break away from 19th-century dependence upon past styles towards something different and original. In decoration Art Nouveau design is characterized by flowing, undulating lines and shapes, either abstract or natural, resembling waves, flames or flowers. In domestic interiors in Britain it appeared decoratively in coloured window glass, furniture design, textiles and furnishings, wallpaper and many items of equipment and fittings such as coal boxes, fire-screens and chimneypieces.

Art Nouveau
metal coffee pot

Different countries applied different names to the movement. For instance, in Italy it was *Lo Stile Liberty* (an expression derived from the textiles of London's Regent Street store), in Germany *Jungendstil*, in Spain *Modernismo*. The term used in England and America derived from the decorative arts shop opened in Paris in the 1890s, Maison de l'Art Nouveau, to sell articles of a non-derivative design.

Art Nouveau bed

ASTRAGAL: a narrow moulding of semicircular section found in classical architecture where it encircles the top of the column, so dividing it from the capital above (see BEAD AND REEL MOULDING). The term is also used more loosely in furniture design for a similar moulding placed at the junction of doors to keep out dust.

BACK STOOL: a chair without arms introduced in the mid-16th century. As the house-plan
and way of living gradually changed from the
medieval custom of everyone eating in the great
hall to the Renaissance concept of a private dining-
room for the family and guests, it became desirable
to provide a back support for the benches and
stools on which, previously, everyone except the
head of the family had been seated, leaning against
the wall of the hall dais. In the private dining-room
the table was placed in the centre of the room so
backs were added to stools to be occupied by
important guests and members of the family.

By the 17th century the back stool was becoming known as a **back chair** to distinguish it
from the **elbow chair** which had arms. Broad-
seated armless chairs of this type dating from the
years 1570–1625 are often known as **farthingale
chairs**, presumably because it would be easier to sit
down wearing a farthingale skirt on a chair which
had no arms to get in the way. This term seems to
have originated in the 19th century, perhaps because the crinoline skirts of this period reminded
people of the similar problems which were en-
countered by their ancestors 300 years earlier.

Early-17th-century
walnut back stool
(farthingale chair)

BAIN-MARIE: a utensil employed from Roman
times onwards for keeping food hot without its
drying or losing flavour. **Mrs Beeton** tells us in the
1861 edition of her *Book of Household Management*
that the bain-marie is an open vessel filled with hot
water, almost at boiling point, in which smaller
vessels and pans containing food may be placed.

The utensil was referred to more than once by
Apicius, the famous Roman epicure of the 1st
century AD. It is believed to have acquired its name
because of the gentleness of this method of retain-
ing heat in the food. It could also be used for slow
cooking.

BAKESTONE, BAKSTONE: in early times a
flat stone or piece of slate used for baking at an open
fire or in a primitive oven. The word survives in

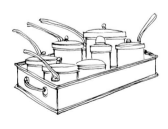

Metal bain-marie
as illustrated in
Mrs Beeton's *Book of
Household Management* (1861)

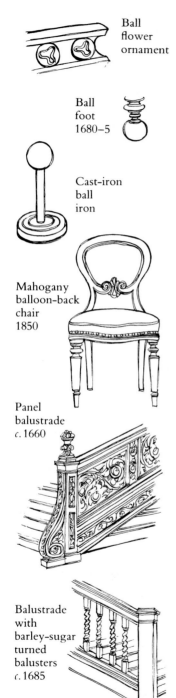

Ball flower ornament

Ball foot 1680–5

Cast-iron ball iron

Mahogany balloon-back chair 1850

Panel balustrade *c.*1660

Balustrade with barley-sugar turned balusters *c.*1685

many dialects to describe the later iron **griddle** or **girdle** (see GIRDLE); a Scottish version is **bannockstone**.

BALL FLOWER: carved ornament of the 14th century (Decorated) period of Gothic architecture (see GOTHIC ARCHITECTURE). Set in a hollow curved moulding, it is a sphere contained within a three-petalled flower.

BALL FOOT: spherical terminal to a turned leg of, for example, a cabinet or table of the late 17th century.

BALL IRON: a special-purpose iron used widely in the 19th century to smooth and finish the complex garments of the time which were difficult to handle on a flat table. The rounded ball of the metal iron was heated and the fabric drawn over it (see IRONING, SLEEVE IRON).

BALLOON-BACK CHAIR: a style which was characteristic of early Victorian design from the years 1835–50. The back is waisted and the cross-rail at that point forms a continuous curve with the uprights.

BALUSTER: in a staircase or gallery the vertical posts which support the handrail (see STAIRCASE).

BALUSTRADE: the complete side unit of a staircase or gallery comprising the handrail, balusters, newels and string. Some designs of balustrade are panelled, carved or plain (see NEWEL, STAIRCASE).

BANNER SCREEN: a standing fire-screen made of a heavy embroidered or painted material hung from a pole and cross-bar.

BARLEY-SUGAR TURNING: a twisted form of wood turning for furniture legs and balusters fashionable especially in the 17th and early 18th centuries (see TURNING).

BAROQUE: a late form of Renaissance art and architecture (17th and 18th centuries) which also stemmed from Italy (see RENAISSANCE). It was characterized by a free use of curves within the classical framework of orders and ornament. The three arts of painting, sculpture and architecture were blended into one exuberant creation; lighting effects were dramatic and spatial concepts complex. The keynote of Baroque work in all media was a richly ornamented sensual vitality.

Several theories have been put forward for the origin of the word 'baroque'; it is thought that the most likely is its derivation from the Portuguese word *barocco*, meaning an ill-formed imperfect pearl. This is a reference to the curving bulbous shapes of some of the orders and ornament. The term was first applied in a derogatory sense – a parallel here to the earlier coining of the word 'Gothic' to describe medieval architecture (see GOTHIC ARCHITECTURE) – for in the 19th century Baroque design was designated as being simply a decadent form of Renaissance classicism: for less than a century has it been recognised as a style in its own right.

English Baroque was more reserved and ornamental than its Continental counterpart. In domestic architecture **Sir John Vanbrugh** was its greatest exponent and the two finest of the gigantic residences which he designed survive: **Blenheim Palace** in Oxfordshire, built between 1705–22, and **Castle Howard** in Yorkshire, built between 1700–26 and later.

Silver wall sconce Baroque style 1703

Baroque design of side table of carved and gilded wood with marble top 1735

BASKET GRATE: during the 16th century it became apparent that the supply of timber available from the once dense forests which had covered much of Britain, was not infinite; for centuries wood had been used up in a profligate way, in particular for domestic needs, ship-building and charcoal-burning for smelting purposes, without any planting replacement schemes. Gradually it became necessary, especially in towns, for coal to replace wood for domestic use.

This posed a problem. The open hearth design, traditional for centuries (see OPEN HEARTH), was unsuited to the burning of coal. A draught of air was required underneath the fuel both for kindling and burning. Also, the andirons which had traditionally supported the burning logs (see ANDIRON), would not serve to hold lumps of coal. It was found easiest to place the coal in an iron fire-basket, with bars in front and a slatted floor beneath, which was still flanked by the andirons.

By the later 17th century, the fire-basket had developed to the next stage where the andirons were attached to it so that it stood on legs, raising it well above the level of the hearth and so creating a better draught. This type of design was called a

Dog grate *c.* 1690

Polished steel basket grate Robert Adam 1765–70

55

Basket spit

Bay leaf garland

16th-century bay window

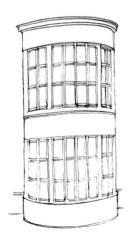

Regency bow window

dog grate from its use of the andirons or fire-dogs. Before long the cast-iron fire-back (see FIRE-BACK), which had been in traditional use with the open hearth, was also incorporated, making a sturdy iron basket, standing on legs and with a solid iron back. This was a self-contained unit which could be moved about within the fireplace. It was called a **basket grate**.

During the 18th century, such grates were made in many beautiful designs, following closely the architectural and decorative styles of the day. Of particular interest are the steel, iron and brass grates which were designed by **Robert Adam** in the neo-classical period of 1760–90.

BASKET SPIT: also known as a **cradle spit**. A straight spit (see SPIT) was adapted in order to roast small animals and birds. Removable metal bars were added so that the meat could be inserted, enclosed securely, and then taken out when cooked.

BATH: because of a lack of running water, and the difficulties of heating a sufficient quantity and disposing of it afterwards, domestic bathing before 1850 was confined to small bath tubs which had to be hand-filled using jugs. With the coming of better water supplies and drainage systems, the invention of the gas geyser (see GEYSER) and the extension of hot-water systems from the kitchen boiler to upstairs bathrooms, various types of bath were manufactured and sold (see HEATED BATH, HIP BATH, LOUNGE BATH, SHOWER BATH, SITZ BATH, SLIPPER BATH).

BAY LEAF GARLAND: an ornament seen in classical architecture which depicts the leaf of the bay tree. It is usually designed in rows to decorate torus mouldings; these are the bold convex mouldings used on the bases of columns (see CLASSICAL ORDER).

BAY WINDOW: a window projecting outwards, set on the ground and extending upwards through one or more storeys. It may be multi-sided or may be curved. In the latter case, the curved style, it is referred to as a **bow window**, a style which was particularly favoured in Regency housing.

BEAD AND REEL MOULDING: a classical ornament applied to a narrow round moulding such as an astragal (see ASTRAGAL) which resembles a string of beads interrupted by reels.

Bead and reel

BENTWOOD FURNITURE: originally a method of bending wood to make curved furniture, particularly chairs, by the use of steam heat. The Viennese designer **Michael Thonet** experimented with a method using birchwood which he perfected by 1850. These chairs with curved backs became very popular in the mid–Victorian period. Inexpensive designs in upright and rocker types with cane seats were soon in use in every home.

Bentwood continued to be widely used in furniture design during the rest of the 19th century and the idea was resurrected by the modern architects and designers of the 1920s to make original high-quality articles as well as providing designs for less costly furniture. Laminated woods and plywood were used as well as solid wood (see LAMINATED FURNITURE, PLYWOOD). Among the famous designers from different countries who adopted bentwood and moulded wood techniques should be mentioned **Le Corbusier**, **Marcel Breuer**, **Alvar Aalto**, **Eero Saarinen** and **Charles Eames**.

Bentwood chair 1870

BOBBIN TURNING: a form of turning which resembled bobbins (see TURNING), common in 17th-century furniture.

Bobbin-turned chair stretcher *c.* 1650

BOLECTION MOULDING: a curved moulding used to raise one surface, such as a panel, above the remainder. Seen especially in 17th-century doors.

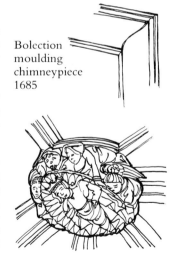

Bolection moulding chimneypiece 1685

BOSS: an ornamental projecting block, usually carved and painted, placed to cover the intersection of ribs in a stone vaulted ceiling (see STONE VAULTING) or wooden roof (see TIMBER TRUSSED ROOF).

BOTTLE JACK: 'a jack' is a traditional term for an odd-job man and, in kitchen usage, was applied to any mechanism which turned the spit for roasting meat (see SMOKE JACK, MECHANICAL SPIT). The bottle jack came into use at the beginning of the 19th century. So-named because of its resemblance to a bottle, it was spring-driven, the mechanism being wound up with a key. The joint to be roasted was suspended from a wheel under the jack which made the joint turn; first one way for a given length of time, then back again in order to cook the other side. Often the bottle jack was

13th-century carved boss from south porch of West Walton Church

Brass
bottle jack
19th century

Oak
box chair
1574

Box iron

Charcoal iron

clamped to the mantelpiece above the fire (see MANTELPIECE) or it could be suspended inside a hastener (see HASTENER).

BOULLE, BUHL: a form of marquetry (see MARQUETRY) which was developed and made famous by the French cabinet-maker **André-Charles Boulle** (1642–1732), and in which a variety of different materials such as tortoiseshell, mother-of-pearl and horn were combined in the veneer with certain metals (usually brass or pewter) to form elaborate decorative designs.

BOW WINDOW: see BAY WINDOW.

BOX CHAIR: one of the earliest forms of surviving chairs in Britain. Most of the examples seen today date from the late 15th or the 16th century. The design shows the chairs to have evolved from the panel-and-frame construction used for chests (see CHEST, PANEL-AND-FRAME CONSTRUCTION), with the addition of a back, and sides to provide arm rests. A drawer or cupboard could be incorporated in the base.

BOX IRON: also known as **slug irons**, box irons were in general use from the 17th century until replaced in the later 19th century by self-heating irons. The design included a large hollow container to hold the heating agent, which was often a cast-iron slug of similar shape to the iron. Slugs were provided in pairs: one was made red hot in the fire and then was placed in the iron with the aid of a pair of tongs (a hinged gate at the back of the iron was lifted up or swung open to allow the slug to be inserted); the second slug was put to heat while the first was in use.

An alternative heating agent was burning charcoal or coal. A plate at the top of the iron was opened and the charcoal was inserted with tongs. In order to assist the charcoal to burn well and provide escape for the smoke, a draught of air was created by a row of holes along each side of the iron and a chimney was set in front of the top plate. A 19th-century improvement to this **charcoal iron** was a hole made at the back into which the nozzle of a small pair of bellows could be inserted to pump in more air to improve combustion. A drawback, when an unskilled hand was operating this iron, was that a shower of smuts could easily and inadvertently be ejected through the chimney on to the clean linen about to be ironed.

BOX MANGLE: a large machine used during the 18th and 19th centuries to press linen. Measuring some 6 feet in length, 3 to 4 feet in width and 3 feet in height (approximately $1.75 \times 1 \times 1$ metre), this cumbersome apparatus was suited only for use in large houses where washing was done for a considerable number.

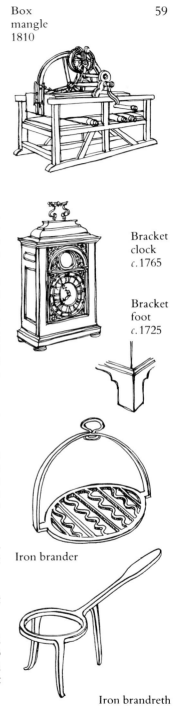

Box mangle 1810

The mangle was in the form of a wooden box, usually filled with stones, though some models were metal-lined to contain water instead. This box was incorporated into a stout wooden construction which stood on the floor. Below the box were several wooden rollers which ran on a flat bed of stone, wood or slate.

The linen was carefully wound round the rollers, with the smaller items inside the larger ones, and an outer layer of brown Holland mangling-cloths to keep the washing clean. A lifting device in the machinery raised the rollers into position under the box. The mechanism was then turned by handle, so that the box full of stones (or water) was trundled slowly and heavily to and fro over the linen. It was hard work to overcome the inertia and get the machine moving, but once this had been achieved, a flywheel at the back kept it going easily. To prevent the machine under this momentum running off its bed and crashing to the floor, an elaborate system of stops was incorporated into its design.

Bracket clock c.1765

Bracket foot c.1725

BRACE: see ARCH BRACE, TIMBER TRUSSED ROOF.

BRACKET CLOCK: a portable, spring-driven pendulum clock introduced during the 17th century to stand on a piece of furniture or a wall bracket. Later designs were often fitted with handles on top so that they could be carried easily around the house.

BRACKET FOOT: a squared type of termination used from about 1680–90 to support bureaux, bookcases and cabinets.

Iron brander

BRANDER: a type of girdle made from straight or twisted iron bars (see GIRDLE).

BRANDRETH: a long-handled iron tripod which could be placed in or near the open fire to hold an earthenware cooking vessel. Its position could be adjusted so that the food contained in it would cook or keep warm, as desired.

Iron brandreth

Wooden bread car
16th century

Bulb leg 1610

Bun foot 17th century

BRASS: a copper-base alloy known in ancient Greece where it was probably made by a cementation process using zinc ore and charcoal. Since then brass has been widely employed as a domestic metal material for articles such as candlesticks, candelabra, decorative inlay for furniture and architectural ornamentation as well as for kitchen and dining-room utensils.

BREAD CAR: from the Middle Ages until the 19th century, bread and similar food was generally stored in a wooden box suspended by cords or chains from the kitchen ceiling, well above the reach of vermin.

BROAD GLASS: see CYLINDER GLASS.

BRONZE: originally an alloy of tin and copper, believed to be the first metal alloy made (accidentally) by man; this probably occurred in the Middle East, about 3500 BC, when smelting impure ores, which as well as copper contained tin. The resulting metal proved to be harder, stronger and more durable than copper.

Two thousand years later it had become an everyday metal cast into all kinds of articles from weapons to cooking pots. During the Middle Ages in Britain, and until at least the 17th century, bronze became the most widely used domestic metal.

BRUSSELS CARPET: a term generally applied to a carpet with uncut pile surface and linen-thread back.

BUFFET: a cupboard or cabinet for the display of silver and pewterware, china and glass, which may be free-standing or of wall-recessed design. The display may be open or fronted by glazed doors.

BULB: the bulbous form of carved, turned support, seen especially in bed posts and table legs, in Elizabethan and Jacobean furniture. Typical of the architectural and decorative Renaissance designs used in England especially between 1570 and 1620 which were derived not from Italian original sources but from Flemish and German pattern-book interpretations of these.

BUN FOOT: a late-17th-century type of flattened ball leg termination.

BUREAU: a word of French origin applied broadly to a type of furniture used for writing, such as a desk or chest, which contained drawers. A **bureau-bookcase** would also include enclosed shelving for books and a **bureau-cabinet**, similarly, cupboards.

BUTTERY: a store-room for provisions. From the Middle Ages until the 18th century this was of particular importance since large supplies of food had to be kept in good condition throughout the winter months: it was, therefore, usually situated on the north side of the house.

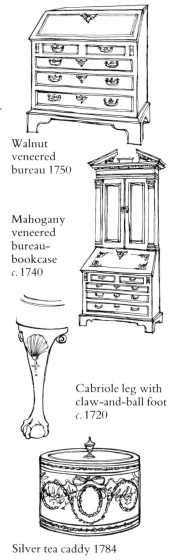

Walnut
veneered
bureau 1750

Mahogany
veneered
bureau-
bookcase
c. 1740

CABRIOLE LEG: a style of chair and table leg fashionable for much of the 18th century, notably between 1715 and 1770. The leg curved outwards at the knee; then, becoming slenderer, turned inwards; and turned outwards once more at the foot, which was terminated in a variety of ways (SEE BUN FOOT, CLAW-AND-BALL FOOT, CLUB FOOT, HOOF FOOT, SCROLL FOOT).

Cabriole leg with
claw–and–ball foot
c. 1720

CADDY: a container for tea, a beverage which, from its introduction into Britain until well into the 19th century, was so expensive that the caddy was kept locked: the key was held only by the housekeeper or mistress of the house. Tea was first brought to Europe in 1609 by the Dutch East India Company. On the London market it then sold at £3 10s. 0d. per pound (£3.50 per 450 grammes). The price fell slowly but by 1689, despite its popularity, tea still cost £1 per pound. The term 'caddy' is believed to be a corruption of a Malay word, *kati*, which is a measure of weight equal to about 1⅓ pounds (600 grammes).

Silver tea caddy 1784

CAMP OVEN: a portable oven usually made of cast iron. It was round or oval in shape and stood on short legs; it had handles at the sides and a lid on top. Such an oven could be placed in the hot ashes of an open fire; cooking could be hastened by piling hot embers on to the lid.

Iron camp oven 19th century

Grease pan

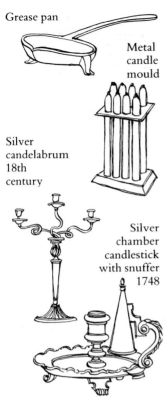

Metal
candle
mould

Silver
candelabrum
18th
century

Silver
chamber
candlestick
with snuffer
1748

Iron candleholder
c. 1810

Tray
to catch
dripped
wax

Cut-glass
chandelier
c. 1770

CANDLE: though the origin of the candle is not known, it was in use in ancient Egypt. In Britain, until the coming of gas and electric lighting in the 19th century, candles were one of the important means of providing artificial illumination at home (see also OIL LAMP, RUSHLIGHT). For centuries most candles were home-made using tallow (animal fat) melted down in the kitchen and collected in a greasepan. The fat was then coated on to a wick in the same manner as for rushlights. Later, candles came to be made in single or multiple tube-shaped metal moulds. The wicks were inserted first and the moulds were then dipped into a pan of melted tallow until the tubes were filled. When they had cooled the candles could be withdrawn. They were stored by being hung up in bunches by their wicks. A **candle-box** was hung on the wall holding candles ready for use.

Tallow candles were anything but ideal for burning. Because the fat burned faster than the wick they needed constant trimming while alight. They gave off smoke and unpleasant odours; they also dripped constantly. Much more satisfactory were beeswax candles which gave a better light, smelt less unpleasantly and needed less attention, but they were much more expensive and also incurred a heavy tax.

From the late 18th century, with expansion in the fishing industry, sperm whale oil was used for making candles, to be purchased, not made at home. Later, better still, was the paraffin wax candle which was introduced after the process for the solidification of paraffin from petroleum was developed in the mid-19th century. After this it was found that a blend of the two oils produced a candle which burned with a better, less offensive flame. A further improvement at the end of the century was the stearine candle, manufactured as a result of earlier research into the chemical nature of fats; this burned yet more brightly and without any acrid odour.

Over the centuries a variety of means were designed to hold one or more candles in order to supply artificial lighting at the point where needed. There was always the single **candle-stick** which for bedroom use was set in a saucer-like holder; this usually incorporated a means of lighting, and **snuffers** and **trimmers** (see INSTANTANEOUS LIGHT BOX, SNUFFERS, TINDER BOX, TINDER PISTOL). Some candlesticks were branched (**candelabrum, candelabra**) to accommodate several candles. There were elegant and ornamental

candlestands, also **wall sconces** (see SCONCE) and hanging **chandeliers** (see CHANDELIER). In the 18th century, in particular, large, elaborately framed wall-mirrors were designed as part of the room decor which, by means of reflection, enhanced the level of illumination (see MIRRORS).

CANTERBURY: a piece of furniture, a stand with partitions, designed to hold, for example, sheet music, books, plate or cutlery.

CANTILEVER: a projecting member supported securely at one end, and either carrying a load at the other free end, or having a load distributed uniformly along it. Such a member (for example, a staircase tread) is not braced externally, so appears to be self-supporting. A **cantilever bracket** may be used to support a cornice or balcony of considerable projection. The use of tubular steel in furniture design of the 1920s led to the **cantilever chair** with only two supports instead of the traditional four legs (see CHAIR).

CAPITAL: the crowning feature, usually decoratively moulded or carved, of a column or pilaster. In classical architecture it may carry an entablature (see ENTABLATURE) or arcade, in Gothic architecture the arch springing of a vault or arcade (see CLASSICAL ARCHITECTURE, CLASSICAL ORDER, GOTHIC ARCHITECTURE).

CAQUETOIRE (CAQUETEUSE) CHAIR: a wooden, joined, panel-back chair of French 16th-century origin. The word derives from the French verb *caqueter*, 'to chatter', and it was used because the design of the chair, with narrow back panel and open sides below the arms, was thought to lend itself to conversation.

CARCEL LAMP: a mechanical oil lamp with a spring-driven pump which supplied fuel under pressure from a reservoir in the base. Invented in 1800 by a Frenchman named **Carcel**.

CARD TABLE: small, circular, oval or rectangular tables in use particularly between about 1680 and 1850 for playing cards and gambling at home. Most designs had baize-covered, hinged and folding tops and a movable fourth or fifth leg. In the corners were depressions to hold candlesticks and between them were scoops for counters or coins.

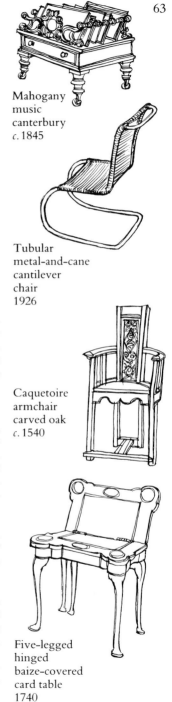

Mahogany music canterbury c.1845

Tubular metal-and-cane cantilever chair 1926

Caquetoire armchair carved oak c.1540

Five-legged hinged baize-covered card table 1740

Caroline
temp. Charles I

Carved and turned
oak chair *c.* 1645

Caroline
temp. Charles II

Chimneypiece:
wood-carving by
Grinling Gibbons 1678

CAROLINE: in Britain, of the period of Charles I (reigned 1625–49) or of Charles II (reigned 1660–85).

CARCASE: the body of a piece of furniture to which a veneer is applied (see VENEER).

CARPET: the making of carpets by flat weaving, and later by knotting, dates from the early centuries AD in the Middle East, Central Asia and the Far East, but in Britain home-produced rugs and carpets were rare before about 1700.

Until the 18th century, rushes and rush mats were the normal floor-covering and, though small carpets were imported in the 16th century, chiefly from Persia and Turkey, these were so expensive that they were used as wall-hangings and as covers for pieces of furniture or window seats. They were thought to be far too valuable to be walked upon. In very limited numbers, small carpets were made in England from about 1575. These were **cross-stitch needlework** and **embroidered** designs, or **turkeywork**, which meant a pile carpet made with wools knotted on a canvas base in imitation of those produced in Turkey. Not until the later 17th century were these, too, set upon the floor.

It was after the Revocation of the Edict of Nantes by Louis XIV of France in 1685, when many Huguenot carpet weavers fled to England from France to escape religious persecution, that the craft was established in this country, with the aid of royal patronage, in towns such as Wilton and Axminster. These names became synonymous with fine-quality carpets, each noted for the different weaving techniques which evolved there. Even in the first half of the 18th century, however, many oriental carpets were still imported and were so prized and costly that, though used on the floor, they only covered the centre of the room; stair-carpets were rare until the early 19th century.

By 1800 many British manufactories were producing carpets, notably **Wilton**, **Kidderminster**, **Axminster**, **Moorfields** and **Kilmarnock**. Several architects in the neo-classical period of the years 1760–90 (see NEO-CLASSICISM) designed carpets especially for specific rooms, often to echo the ceiling pattern. **Robert Adam** was the chief of these and, amongst other examples, original specimens can still be seen in the Music Room at Harewood House, Yorkshire, and the Dining-Room at Saltram House, Devon.

The steam-powered carpet loom devised in 1839

in America by **Erastus B. Bigelow** was a great advance. At first the equipment would only make a flat-weave carpet but within a decade Bigelow had adapted his design; his new machine was able to produce a Brussels carpet (see BRUSSELS CARPET). Soon other machines were being designed in America and in Britain to suit alternative types of carpeting, for example, the **Wilton cut-pile** and the **Axminster** and **Chenille carpets**. The **Jacquard** attachment was adapted for patterned carpet weaving. In more recent times processes have been developed to mechanize both **tufted** and **knitted carpets** (see TUFTED CARPET).

Bissell
Grand Rapids
carpet sweeper
1895

CARPET SWEEPER: a machine to sweep floors was patented as early as the beginning of the 19th century, and by 1865 a number of carpet sweepers were available. These were not very efficient as they consisted of cast-iron boxes running on two rollers and containing roller brushes rotated by a belt pulley attached to the back roller. This belt drive was not powerful enough to counteract the frictional resistance of the brush as it moved over the carpet.

   Melville R. Bissell, the owner of a china shop in Grand Rapids, Michigan, USA, was allergic to dust and suffered greatly when unpacking his china from its straw and sawdust wrappings. This encouraged him to design the first really satisfactory and effective carpet sweeper (patented 1876). Though less streamlined than a modern one, it worked on the same principles. The brush was rotated by means of the friction of four rubber-treaded carrying wheels against the drum to which it was fitted. Frictional carpet resistance was minimized by setting the brush spirally in tufts around the drum so that only a few bristles at a time could be in contact with the carpet. By 1880 the Bissell carpet sweeper was a success: it still is.

   In Britain, Ewbank was probably the best-known make of sweeper: by 1911 it was selling well, at 10s. 6d. (52½p).

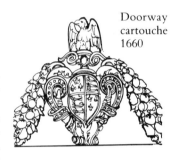

Doorway
cartouche
1660

CARTOUCHE: an ornamental tablet, usually inscribed, framed by scrolls and other decorative features.

CARYATID: a sculptured female figure in the form of a support or column. Caryatides are chiefly used in classical architecture, a famous example being the south porch of the Erechtheion on the Acropolis of Athens where six figures support

Marble
chimney-
piece
caryatid
1760

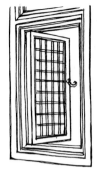

Casement window 1620

Cast-iron cooking vessel
traditional design

Cast-iron lavatory
(washbasin) stand 1895

Cast-iron
gas fire
c. 1890

the porch entablature. In domestic architecture, caryatid supports are generally to be seen in chimneypiece design. Also used, but less often, are male figures which are called **atlantes** or **telamones**. Characteristic of 17th- to early-19th-century design are female figures carrying baskets on their heads, known as **canephorae**, or three-quarter-length figures, the lower parts of which merge into pedestals, which are **herms**.

CASEMENT WINDOW: a metal or wooden window hinged along one vertical side to enable it to be opened inwards or outwards.

CAST IRON: contains a higher proportion of carbon than wrought iron and is hard and brittle, so it cannot be shaped by hammering, but may be made liquid to pour into moulds. It is strong in compression but weaker in tensile strength than wrought iron.

Iron is extracted from iron ore by smelting, a process in which the ore is fused or melted. This process was developed in Asia and introduced into Europe by 1200 BC. Early furnaces were simple, usually holes in the ground where charcoal and iron ore were burned together, a sufficiently high temperature being attained by blowing in a draught of air with a pair of bellows. The smelted ore became a partially melted metallic lump which was called a bloom. By hammering this bloom while it was still hot, the smith beat out the impurities. The iron made in this way was **wrought iron**. The temperature obtained by this method was not high enough to melt the ore fully, so cast iron could not be produced.

During the Middle Ages better furnaces were developed and water power was harnessed, both to drive the bellows for the furnace and to power the hammers. By 1400 the blast furnace had evolved. This was a tall construction fuelled by charcoal. Iron ore was fed in at the top. As the ore gradually penetrated to the bottom of the furnace it absorbed a greater quantity of carbon from the charcoal fuel. The increased carbon content lowered the melting point of the iron sufficiently for it to be liquidized and poured into moulds. (The melting point of pure iron is 1535°C, 2795°F, but of this cast iron about 1185°C, 2165°F; that is, 350°C, 662°F, lower). From the time of its becoming possible to produce cast iron in quantity, it was to be an important metal for domestic use. By the later Middle Ages this chiefly meant fire-backs, andirons, and utensils and containers for cooking (see ANDIRON, FIRE–BACK).

At the end of the 16th century a shortfall in timber supplies for conversion into charcoal meant that coal had to be used more often as a furnace fuel. This was not satisfactory as, due to its sulphur content, it produced iron which was too brittle and lacked strength. It was only when the ironmasters of Coalbrookdale, led by **Abraham Darby**, discovered that the answer was to use coked coal that, once more, cast iron began to be made in quantity. Manufacture was further vastly increased by the introduction of steam power in the later 18th century and, at the same time, the process called 'puddling' introduced by Henry Cort in 1784. In this the molten iron was stirred in order to free it more rapidly from impurities and so reduce its tendency to brittleness.

The 19th century was the age of iron, both wrought and cast, but especially the latter. The improved processes and furnace design, the availability of power and, soon, railway transport, made it into a cheap material which the Victorians utilized for all kinds of purposes, from building needs to lamp standards, from gates to railway stations. Nowhere was it in greater evidence than in the home. It could be seen in the coal-burning kitchener, the copper, baths of many shapes and sizes, furniture for both house and garden, grates and fire-irons, lamp fittings, bedsteads and ornaments of all kinds (see BASKET GRATE, BATH, COPPER, GAS LIGHTING, HOB GRATE, IRON AND STEEL, KITCHEN RANGE, OIL LAMP).

CAVETTO MOULDING: a concave moulding which, in section, is a quadrant arc of a circle.

CEILING: a term derived in the Middle Ages from the verb 'ciel', which was used to describe the process of lining the roof or walls of an apartment with plaster, wood beams and boarding or a canopied hanging.

Until the late 15th century, interior roofing for larger apartments was by the open timber roof or stone vaulting (see STONE VAULTING, TIMBER TRUSSED ROOF). Smaller rooms were timber-boarded. From about 1470 onwards, a flat wood or plaster covering began to replace the open design and the word 'ceiling' was used to describe it. Until about 1540 most of these ceilings were supported by massive wood beams which could be plain, or moulded, or decoratively carved; these were

Cast-iron kettle 1860

Cast-iron kitchen scales 1895

Cast-iron 'Tortoise' room-heating stove 1920

Cavetto moulding

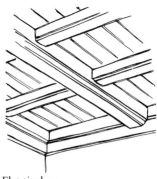

Flat timber
ceiling 1475

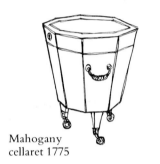

Mahogany
cellaret 1775

ROMAN HYPOCAUST

A = Ceramic wall flue
B = Tesserae floor covering
C = Concrete layer
D = Tile layer
E = Hypocaust pier
F = Base
G = to Furnace

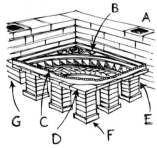

generally augmented by smaller cross rafters. The panels between the beams were wood-boarded or of plaster. After this most ceilings were decoratively plastered all over the surface (see PLASTER-WORK).

When the First World War ended in 1918 there was a shortage of plasterers, and plasterboard was more generally used as a replacement material (see PLASTERBOARD). The Second World War, ending in 1945, created an even greater shortage of plaster craftsmen, since when a variety of materials have been developed which may be applied directly to brick, concrete and wooden surfaces.

CELLARET: a cabinet or container, usually metal lined, for storing wines in the dining-room (also termed a wine cooler). The word is also applied to similar storage in a sideboard.

CENTRAL HEATING: the Romans heated their houses by the hypocaust system in which hot air from a furnace in the basement was passed through ceramic wall flues to heat all the rooms. The hypocaust was the underfloor chamber; the word derives from two Greek words meaning 'the place heated from below'.

After the collapse of the Roman Empire the idea of heating a building from one central source was forgotten, and was only revived in the late 18th century with the development of steam power. But, though successful systems were designed for industrial and civic use, no serious attempt was made to adapt them to domestic needs. Indeed, in Britain, central heating for the home is a recent development only realized on a wide scale since 1945. Now the range of possible means of central heating is considerable, powered by solid fuel, oil, gas or electricity.

CERAMIC HOB: an electric cooker development introduced in the 1970s in which the hob is made of toughened heat-resistant glass. The heating areas are incorporated beneath this surface and glow yellow or red when heated, while the surrounding area remains cool. Such hobs are easy-care and, especially those fitted into the modern electronic ovens, possess highly accurate temperature controls (see ELECTRONIC CONTROL OF DOMESTIC APPLIANCES).

CERAMICS: a term originally applied to vessels, utensils and artistic products made from natural earths moistened with water, then dried and fired to make them durable. In the present day the term has acquired a wider, technological meaning and can now embrace a range of products which includes glass, enamels, cements and plasters, but domestically the original meaning is still apposite.

Since the Stone Age, pottery (that is, earthenware) vessels and utensils have been made for cooking and storage. Earthenware clays contain many impurities and can only be fired at comparatively low temperatures (up to 1000°C, 1832°F) and so produce a soft pottery (see POTTERY). The traditional method of making such vessels was to press the worked clay into a mould or to build up a pot by coiling ropes of the material round and round, then smoothing it to the desired shape. With the invention of the potter's wheel in the Middle East, about 3000 BC, the art of pottery took a great step forward.

Throwing a pot on the wheel

In order to make such porous earthenware impervious to liquids it was coated with a glaze. The art of glazing is an ancient one in which, as in ancient Egypt, a surface layer of clear or coloured glass was fused to the pot in a second firing. Later, a variety of chemicals were added to the glaze to improve its practical qualities, also to make it more attractive.

Gradually the knowledge of how to produce more durable pottery was acquired in Europe, first as stoneware and later porcelain. At the same time great advances took place in kiln design, understanding of the chemical nature of clays and their treatment, means of decoration and, finally, the introduction of various ways of powering the mechanization and mass production processes which would make attractive ceramic products available to all at a reasonable price (see CHINA, DELFTWARE, FAIENCE, JASPERWARE, MAJOLICA, PORCELAIN, QUEEN'S WARE, STONEWARE).

Stacking earthenware saggars (containing the pots) in a kiln for firing

CHAFING DISH: a method of keeping food hot by means of one vessel placed over another, the lower one containing burning charcoal or hot water (see BAIN-MARIE).

CHAIR: until nearly the end of the 16th century, movable chairs with backs, designed to seat one person, were rare pieces of furniture, their use reserved for the heads of households and important guests: a chair was a symbol of authority as evidenced by the term 'chairman'. The usual seat-

The lower vessel (to contain charcoal or hot water) of a chafing dish

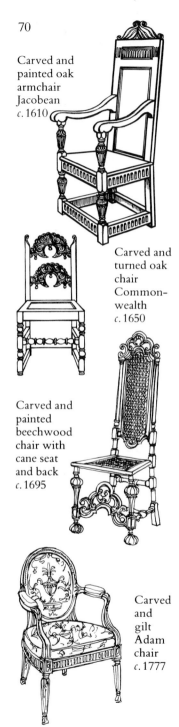

Carved and
painted oak
armchair
Jacobean
*c.*1610

Carved and
turned oak
chair
Common-
wealth
*c.*1650

Carved and
painted
beechwood
chair with
cane seat
and back
*c.*1695

Carved
and
gilt
Adam
chair
*c.*1777

ing for everyone else was in the form of settles, stools and benches (see SETTLE, STOOL). We can gain an impression of medieval chairs from illuminated manuscripts which show several forms, notably imposing, throne-like, ecclesiastical designs, or the more common X-framed shape, or the turned wood chair, often with triangular seat: examples survive of later versions of these (see TURNING, X-FRAMED CHAIR). The box chair, its panelled form derived from chest construction (see CHEST, PANEL-AND-FRAME CONSTRUCTION), was characteristic of 16th-century designs (see BOX CHAIR), as was also the lighter, panelled conversation chair which came originally from France (see CAQUETOIRE CHAIR).

By the end of the 16th century chairs became more numerous and varied in design. The panel-back, joined chair with arms, and stretchers linking its four legs, was most usual, decoration being by carving or inlay with different coloured woods (see INLAY, STRETCHER). Upholstery became more common in the early 17th century and chairs with silk- or velvet-covered padded seats and backs, and no arms, accommodated the wide farthingale skirts (see BACK STOOL, CAROLINE, JACOBEAN). With the Restoration in 1660 (see RESTORATION) the elaborately turned chair with richly carved stretcher and cresting, cane seat and back, was introduced. Towards the end of the century, very tall chair backs echoed the contemporary lofty head-dresses and periwigs (see BALL FOOT, BUN FOOT).

The great age of furniture design, the 18th century, was clearly reflected in the high quality and immense variety of chairs which were made. This was the period of the famous architect-designers, **Kent** and **Adam**, for example, and the cabinet-maker-designers – **Chippendale**, **Sheraton**, **Hepplewhite** and many others. There was great variety in the woods used (particularly walnut, mahogany, satinwood), in the means of decoration (carving, painting, inlay, veneer and gesso) and in the design where all phases of fashionable style were represented from Baroque to Rococo, neo-classicism, Chinese, Gothic (see CABRIOLE LEG, CLAW-AND-BALL FOOT, CLUB FOOT, GOTHIC-STYLE CHAIR, HEART-BACK CHAIR, HOOF FOOT, LADDER-BACK CHAIR, LATTICE-BACK CHAIR, LIBRARY CHAIR, LYRE-BACK CHAIR, PALLADIAN, PRINCE OF WALES' FEATHERS, QUEEN ANNE, RIBBAND-BACK CHAIR, ROCOCO, SHIELD-BACK CHAIR, SPLAT, WINDSOR CHAIR, WING CHAIR).

Regency chairs were eclectic in design, the inspiration drawn chiefly from a revived classicism based on the styles of Greece and Rome, and also ancient Egypt. They were still admirably proportioned and displayed fine craftsmanship, using quality mahogany, rosewood and satinwood decorated in a restrained manner with metal inlay, painting and carving (see EGYPTIAN-STYLE CHAIR, ETRUSCAN, REGENCY, TRAFALGAR CHAIR).

Regency beechwood chair japanned and gilded c. 1810

Victorian chairs were noted for an increase in upholstered (often buttoned) seats and backs and a revival of past styles from medieval to classical but several designs were particularly characteristic of the age, for example, the balloon-back chair and the kneeling-chair or prie-dieu. Also often seen, though not solely of this time, were the rocking chair and adjustable chair (see ADJUSTABLE CHAIR, BALLOON-BACK CHAIR, PRIE-DIEU, ROCKING CHAIR). The Victorians also used a number of different materials for making their furniture and this applied especially to chairs, for instance, cast iron, papier mâché and wickerwork (see CAST IRON, PAPIER MÂCHÉ, UPHOLSTERY, WICKERWORK CHAIR).

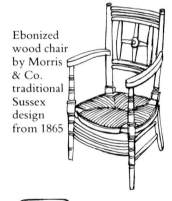

Carved walnut upholstered Victorian chair c. 1855

Design and manufacture in the 20th century have varied between extremes of excellent craftsman-designed and -made chairs in traditional materials, good and bad machine-made examples based upon many past styles and, especially since 1930, the development of new means of shaping and using known materials and the appearance of new ones.

A revival of hand-craftsmanship was initiated in the 1860s by **William Morris** and his colleagues, and this was taken up after 1880 by the architects, artists and designers of the **Arts and Crafts Movement**. Distinctive, yet simple, well-made chairs were produced by, for instance, **Mackmurdo** and **Gimson**. This type of work was quickly succeeded by that of **Art Nouveau** designers such as **Voysey** and **Baillie Scott** (see ART NOUVEAU). The trend was continued in the early years after 1900 by **Ambrose Heal** whose famous Tottenham Court Road store in London marketed his simple, well-designed chairs.

Ebonized wood chair by Morris & Co. traditional Sussex design from 1865

In the early 1920s the improvements and development of metal tubing, lamination and stainless steel led to innovatory designs from the Continent, notably **Breuer**'s cantilever chair of 1925 (see CANTILEVER) and **Aalto**'s laminated birch chair of 1929 (see LAMINATED FURNITURE) followed by **Mies van der Rohe**'s solid, stainless steel chair. Research during and after the Second World War made possible the production of new

Modern chair with light metal alloy frame and bent plywood 1948

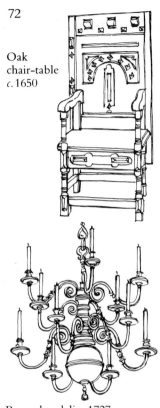

Oak
chair-table
c. 1650

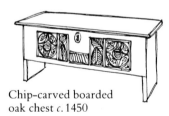

Brass chandelier 1727

Chip-carved boarded
oak chest c. 1450

Linenfold panelled
oak chest c. 1520

materials for making chairs: a wide range of plastics, moulded plywoods, chipboard and aluminium alloys. These are materials and processes which lend themselves to modern manufacture, novel designs, toughness and convenience of storage (see ALUMINIUM, PLASTICS, PLYWOOD).

CHAIR-TABLE: a combination piece of furniture, made from medieval times, in which the back of the chair was hinged or pivoted to come forward when needed, resting on the chair arms to form a table.

CHAISE LONGUE: an elongated chair for reclining (see also DAY BED, SOFA).

CHAMBER CLOCK: a weight-driven clock based on the larger public clock adapted for domestic use in the 14th century: such clocks were rare and expensive. In the home they had to be set upon a bracket or shelf projecting from a wall so that the weights could hang freely.

CHANDELIER: a decorative branched candle-holder made of wood, metal or glass, usually hung from the ceiling (see CANDLE).

CHARCOAL IRON: see BOX IRON.

CHEST, COFFER: during the Middle Ages and the 16th century the most important piece of furniture, used for storing linen, plate and clothes; also acting as a seat. A bride possessed a **dower chest** in which her belongings were brought to her new home. Early chests were made from solid oak boards, often bound with iron bands; the lids were hinged and iron locks were fitted. In the 14th century carved and painted decoration was increasingly found on these heavy chests. Such boarded chests continued to be made until the 17th century but from about 1490–1500 were gradually replaced by joined panel designs (see PANEL-AND-FRAME CONSTRUCTION). Most chests were on legs and some of them had back rests.

Early Tudor chests were often decorated by linenfold panelling (see LINENFOLD PANELLING) but those of the years 1550–1620 were richly carved and/or inlaid with Elizabethan and Jacobean Renaissance motifs (see INLAY, RENAISSANCE). During this period drawers were introduced into chest design. At first a single large drawer was added at the bottom, to make heavy blankets and linen more accessible: these were known as **mule chests**. By about 1650 two or three drawers were fitted, the lid above them still being hinged, and the whole chest was supported on a decorative stand. The true **chest of drawers**, also set on a stand, was well established by the end of the 17th century and in the Queen Anne period the chest-on-chest or **tallboy** became fashionable (see QUEEN ANNE, TALLBOY).

Oak chest of drawers
on a stand c. 1690

CHEVAL GLASS: a mirror which swung between two vertical supports mounted to stand upon the floor, in which a person's full height could be reflected (the stand was termed a 'horse'). A design especially to be seen in the Regency and early Victorian period (see REGENCY).

CHEVAL SCREEN: a fire-screen similar to and contemporary with the cheval mirror (see above) in which a painted or embroidered screen panel hung from a stand. The height of the panel could be adjusted as desired.

CHEVRON ORNAMENT: a French word for rafter, particularly stressing where two rafters meet at an angle, given to a zig-zag form of ornament which was used notably in Norman (Romanesque) architecture.

Cheval glass
painted
satinwood
c. 1790

Chevron
ornament
(Norman)

CHIFFONIER: a piece of furniture originating during the Regency. The top part comprised a series of receding shelves on which to display porcelain and plate while the lower part was devoted to drawers and to a cupboard fronted by drawers. It was named from the French word for 'rag-picker' because the drawers were often used by women for their pieces of needlework and lengths of embroidery silks. Mid-Victorian chiffoniers were large ornate pieces of furniture, usually including a mirror above, and hardly distinguishable from a sideboard.

Rosewood
chiffonier
with back mirrors,
cupboards fronted by
pink pleated silk
and brass latticework,
c. 1820

CHIMERA: a fire-breathing monster of Greek mythology reputed to have a lion's head, a goat's body, an eagle's wings and the tail of a dragon or serpent; used in classical ornament.

CHIMNEY-CRANE: an iron contrivance which was employed with the open fire to suspend cooking pots at the desired height and distance from the heat.

During the early Middle Ages the domestic

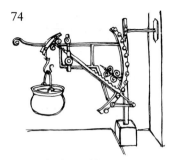

Wrought-iron chimney-crane
with three movements
17th century

Carved and gilt pinewood
chimney-glass c. 1774

Carved chimneypiece c. 1650

hearth was, in many homes, moved from the central position in the room (see ANDIRON) to a wall fireplace and various means were adopted to hang cooking vessels over the fire; hooks were fixed into the chimney walling and chains were suspended from these to hold the pots. There were two chief drawbacks to this system: only one or two vessels could be suspended at once and any attempt to adjust their position during cooking could result in a nasty burn.

Improvements took place only slowly, first by the introduction of ratchet hangers, finally the fully fledged chimney-crane. In this contrivance a vertical post was sunk into the hearth floor at the side of the fire. To this was attached a horizontal iron bar, making a bracket which could be swung like a gate through an angle of 90° so that pots hanging from the bar could be pushed or pulled towards or away from the fire. In addition sophisticated cranes of the 17th century were fitted with a mechanical means of raising and lowering suspended pots or moving them along the bar, so making possible a three-dimensional movement. Chimney-cranes were of iron, generally made by the local blacksmith, and later examples were often richly ornate.

CHIMNEY-GLASS: a decorative mirror set on the chimneybreast over the chimneypiece, a feature especially fashionable in the 18th century.

CHIMNEYPIECE: the ornamental carved structure, of stone, marble or wood, designed over and around the open fireplace recess: also known as a **mantelpiece**. The complete scheme may include a mirror or picture above the fireplace, a mantel-shelf and, often in the 18th and 19th centuries, candle-fittings and small brackets and shelves to display ornaments.

CHINA: a delicate, translucent pottery called porcelain. The word 'china', referring to china-ware or porcelain which originated in China, is generally used to describe English bone china. It was **Josiah Spode II** who improved his father's best-selling, inexpensive cream pottery in 1797 by making it into a harder ware with the addition of bone-ash and felspar, so producing a tough material of delicate, expensive appearance but yet cheap enough to be available to all. This English bone china became world famous during the 19th century (see CERAMICS, PORCELAIN).

CHINA CABINET: an elegant, beautifully made piece of furniture which adorned reception rooms in the 18th and 19th centuries; it had glass-fronted doors to display fine ceramic ware.

CHINOISERIE: a term used to describe the European adoption of Chinese decorative motifs and craftsmanship, particularly in vogue during the later 17th and the 18th centuries. Such adaptations were widespread, from pagodas and tea pavilions to porcelain, textiles and wallpaper, as well as having a marked influence on furniture design displayed in, for example, lacquerwork and bamboo-fret chair-backs (see LACQUERED FURNITURE, LATTICE-BACK CHAIR, PORCELAIN, ' WALL-PAPER).

Mahogany china cabinet c.1800

CHIP CARVING: shallow carving carried out with chisel and gouge on early oak furniture (see CHEST).

CINQUEFOIL: see FOIL.

CLASSICAL ARCHITECTURE: the style of building practised in ancient Greece and Rome, then revived nearly a thousand years later in Renaissance Italy, whence it gradually spread over almost all of Europe and survived until finally supplanted by modern architecture (see BAROQUE, NEO–CLASSICISM, PALLADIAN, REGENCY, RENAISSANCE, ROCOCO).

Japanned chair decorated in the Chinese manner c.1675

The Greeks initiated the classical style of building which is based upon the trabeated form (from the Latin *trabes*, 'a beam'). This is a post-and-lintel type of construction which consists of vertical supports (the columns) and horizontal blocks (the entablature). The early structure of a lintel stone supported on two vertical blocks to form an opening soon led to a colonnade in which a row of columns could carry an extended lintel, and this became the elevation of a building. The colonnade gave much-needed shade in a sunny climate and rectangular openings for windows were suited to an open-air life. There was little snow to contend with, so roof pitches could be low and the development of the end gables as moulded pediments filled with sculpture was logical and attractive.

The beauty of Greek architecture derives not from its variety and complexity of form, for these are essentially simple, but from its subtle and detailed attention to line and proportion. The Greeks developed a system of orders (see CLASSICAL

CLASSICAL TEMPLE

Greek trabeated structure
5th century BC

A = Acroteria
B = Roof tiles
C = Antefixae
D = Pediment
E = Entablature
F = Column
G = Capital

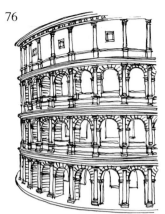

Different classical orders
one per storey in conjunction
with arcuated construction
The Colosseum in Rome
AD 70–82

Aqueduct
arcuated structure
Roman AD 14

Arcuated construction
in vaulted roofs
Roman 4th century AD

ORDER) wherein the proportions of the individual parts were balanced and interrelated. In each order the types and decoration of mouldings, and the relation of the height of column to the width, to the capital and to the horizontal members, are strictly regulated. The system developed gradually over centuries from the archaic beginnings in about 700 BC to the zenith of the style at the time of the building of the Parthenon in Athens in 447–432 BC, when a perfection of quality had been achieved. This quality in Greek building varies from the ordinary to the magnificent according to the architect's subtle interpretation of the rules so carefully established.

The Romans, too, built in a trabeated style and used the orders but they went on to experiment also with the arcuated form of construction, combining both arches and orders in a single building as in, for example, the Colosseum in Rome. The Roman civilization lasted many centuries, overlapping the Greek one for a long time and achieving its best architectural work between the 1st and 3rd centuries AD. Roman orders are coarser than the Greek, they are more varied and the ornament is richer. The Romans were also great engineers, world-famous for their vaults (see STONE VAULTING), public baths, bridges and aqueducts. The two different styles (Greek and Roman) are both represented in English classical structures and in English interior decorative schemes over the centuries: all three forms – Greek, Roman, English revival – are classical architecture (see ACANTHUS, ANTHEMION, ARABESQUE, ARCHITRAVE, ASTRAGAL, BAY LEAF GARLAND, BEAD AND REEL MOULDING, CAPITAL, CAVETTO MOULDING, CHIMERA, CONSOLE, CORNICE, CYMA, EGG AND DART ORNAMENT, FLUTE, FOLIATED, FRET, FRIEZE, GRIFFIN, GROTESQUE, GUILLOCHE, MANNERISM, MODILLION, PALMETTE, PATERA, PEDIMENT, PILASTER, TYMPANUM, VOLUTE).

CLASSICAL ORDER: the basis of the design of classical architecture (see CLASSICAL ARCHITECTURE). Each order consists of a **column**, generally a **base**, a **capital** and an **entablature**. Each of these parts is regulated in proportion and design according to its order and to the other parts. The entablature comprises the structural lintel, that is, the horizontal mouldings (see ENTABLATURE); the column, the vertical support (see COLUMN, ENTASIS, FLUTE, PILASTER); and the capital, the larger block upon which the entablature rests (see CAPITAL).

The Greeks used three orders: Doric, Ionic,

Corinthian. The most distinctive features are the capitals but each order has specific characteristics throughout its parts. The Greeks preferred the Doric Order, especially in mainland areas (the Ionic is more often to be seen on the islands and in Asia Minor), and their most important buildings (the Parthenon in Athens, for example) were erected in this style. The **Greek Doric Order** has no base, its sturdy, fluted column stands directly on the temple steps. The capital is simple, consisting of a square top member – the **abacus** – and below this a curved moulding – the **echinus** – below which narrow rings encircle the capital to mark the junction between it and the column. The entablature has a plain **architrave** (see ARCHITRAVE), a deeply projecting **cornice** (see CORNICE) and, between, a **frieze** (see FRIEZE) decorated by alternate triglyphs and metopes. **Triglyphs** are blocks of stone with vertical channels cut in them, and **metopes** plain panels in which may be set sculptural groups. Some of the Parthenon metope sculptures may be seen in the British Museum in London.

The **Greek Ionic Order** has a slenderer column which stands upon a moulded base. Its capital is distinguished by curving side scrolls called **volutes** (see VOLUTE), between which a band of **egg and dart** moulding encircles the capital (see EGG AND DART MOULDING). The frieze of this order is usually decorated along its full length by relief sculpture.

The **Corinthian Order** was not often used by the Greeks. It is similar to the Ionic design except for the capital which is shaped like a bell and clothed by one or more rows of leaves, mainly of acanthus (see ACANTHUS). At the top the capital becomes four-sided and at each corner is a small volute.

The Romans used all three orders, most often preferring the Corinthian, and they added two more, the **Tuscan** and the **Composite**. The **Roman Doric Order** has a slenderer column than the Greek version and stands on a base. The **Tuscan Order** is similar to this but plainer; its column is never fluted. The **Composite Order** is like the Corinthian except for its capital which resembles a blend of Ionic and Corinthian features. There is a band of egg and dart moulded ornament encircling the capital between large volutes while below two rows of acanthus leaves sheathe the capital bell.

The Greeks used one order only on the exterior of a building though they sometimes preferred

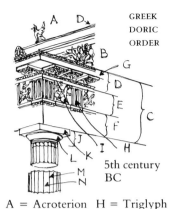

GREEK
DORIC
ORDER

5th century BC

A = Acroterion   H = Triglyph
B = Pediment   I = Metope
C = Entablature J = Capital
D = Cornice   K = Abacus
E = Frieze   L = Echinus
F = Architrave   M = Arris
G = Mutule   N = Flute

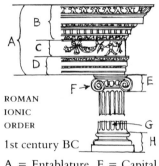

ROMAN
IONIC
ORDER

1st century BC

A = Entablature E = Capital
B = Cornice   F = Volute
C = Frieze   G = Flute
D = Architrave   H = Base

Roman Corinthian capital
2nd century AD

Earthenware
(cloam) oven

Set of sand glasses
in brass container

Spring-driven table clock
of drum type *c.* 1595

a different one inside. The Romans often used several on a single façade, one above the other, as on the Colosseum exterior walling. In Renaissance, Baroque or neo-classical revivals of the orders all versions can be seen, utilized in a variety of ways, both structurally and decoratively.

CLAW-AND-BALL FOOT: a termination for chair and table legs of oriental origin representing a claw or paw holding a sphere. Fashionable particularly during the first half of the 18th century (see CABRIOLE LEG).

CLOAM OVEN: a simple, often primitive oven, made of earthenware.

CLOCK: before the introduction of the first mechanical clocks for domestic use in the late 14th century, people told the time at home by means of a water clock or by candle and oil-lamp clocks. A simple design of **water clock**, used in Britain before the coming of the Romans, was in the form of a bowl (usually made of bronze) which had a small hole bored in the bottom. It was placed on the surface of a reservoir of water, and the unit of time measured was that which passed before the bowl sank. **Candle** and **oil-lamp clocks** were used from about the 10th century. Time scales were marked on the candle or oil reservoir and the passing of time could be measured by the diminution of the candle or the quantity of oil.

    Sand glasses were in use from the 14th century. These were in the form of two glass bulbs joined by a narrow neck. The upper bulb was full of sand, and time was measured in terms of how long it took for the grains to empty, by means of gravity, into the lower bulb. The sand glass was then up-ended for continued use.

    The first **mechanical clocks** were weight-driven, the **chamber clock** being the domestic version copied from the larger public clocks (see CHAMBER CLOCK). In these the mechanical motion of the geared wheels was achieved by the slow descent of a weight. Though chamber clocks were smaller than public ones, they were still cumbersome and expensive, and not portable.

    A more convenient motive force was then utilized: this was the coiled spring. **Spring-driven clocks** were introduced in the later 15th century. At first there were problems because the drive was not constant; the pull (or torque) was greater when the spring was fully wound than when it had been

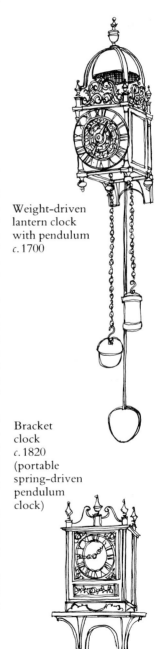

partly released. Control of the drive was provided by a device called a fusee which equalized the force of the uncoiling spring. Early portable clocks of this type were called drum clocks; this was due to their shape. They were metal drums designed to stand on a table and the dial was on the top surface. By the middle of the 16th century upright spring-driven clocks were being made with the dials on one side.

The **lantern clock** was also made, from the later 16th century onwards. This was weight-driven but designed to hang on a wall; so-called because it resembled a ship's lantern, it was a great advance on the early-14th-century designs. The weights took much longer to descend so it only needed winding about once in 24 hours.

Most clocks prior to the 17th century were not accurate time-keepers. They generally had only an hour hand but this was adequate in the circumstances. More accurate time-keeping resulted from the introduction of the pendulum to regulate the speed of rotation of the clock wheels. A pendulum has a definite period of swing depending on its length so a repeated unit of time may be calculated. Towards the end of his life, the Italian **Galileo** tried to apply the principle of the pendulum (which he had studied in Pisa Cathedral in 1582) to clock design, but he died (1642) before his work was completed. It was the Dutch scientist **Christiaan Huygens** who, working independently, made the first successful model of a **pendulum clock** in 1656. The application of the balance spring to the balance wheel was a further notable advance, also first successfully achieved by Huygens. The pendulum was applied both to weight-driven and spring-driven clocks, and their reliability was greatly improved. During the 18th and 19th centuries such clocks of many different types and sizes were made for the home (see LONG-CASE CLOCK).

The idea of using **electricity** to replace both weights and springs as motive power for clocks was experimented with in England as early as 1840 and a number of inventors worked on different designs during the remainder of the 19th century. By 1920 highly accurate electric time-keeping was available. The **quartz crystal clock** was developed in the 1930s to achieve an even higher degree of accuracy.

CLOCKWORK SPIT: see MECHANICAL SPIT.

Weight-driven lantern clock with pendulum
c. 1700

Bracket clock
c. 1820
(portable spring-driven pendulum clock)

Velvet-
covered
close stool
c. 1620

CLOSE STOOL: a toilet facility used between about 1500 and 1750 in well-to-do homes where it was emptied and cleaned by servants. It consisted of a bowl within a lidded box. Some designs were elaborately made, well upholstered for comfort, and shaped like armchairs; the padding was covered by a rich fabric such as satin or velvet usually fastened by brass studs.

CLUB FOOT: an 18th-century termination to furniture legs shaped like the curved end of a club. An alternative to the claw-and-ball foot used with the cabriole leg (see CABRIOLE LEG, CLAW-AND-BALL FOOT). In later years the club foot stood on a flat disc and was known as a **pad foot**.

Club foot
c. 1710

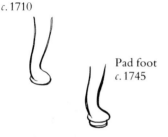

Pad foot
c. 1745

COADE STONE: a stoneware material fired in a kiln (see STONEWARE). Made by Coade's Artificial Stone Manufactory (a business started in 1769 and run by **Eleanor Coade**) this ceramic material was widely used by many of the leading architects of the later 18th and early 19th centuries, notably Adam, Chambers, Nash, Soane and Wyatt. The material closely resembled stone and was particularly hard and resistant to weather, so was ideal for decorative sculpture and ornament as it retained its sharpness of form better than the natural substance. Coade stone was manufactured until the mid-19th century by which time the fashion for darker, richer colours sharply reduced demand.

COAL SCUTTLE: a receptacle for a supply of coal to be kept beside the fireplace.

COFFER: see CHEST.

COLLAR BEAM: a horizontal tie beam in an open timber roof connecting a pair of rafters at high level (see TIMBER TRUSSED ROOF).

Painted cast-iron
coal scuttle 1850

COLUMN: a vertical support, circular in plan and generally tapering towards the top, surmounted by a capital and standing upon a base (see CAPITAL, CLASSICAL ARCHITECTURE, CLASSICAL ORDER, GOTHIC ARCHITECTURE). The part between the capital and the base is known as the **shaft**. An **engaged column** is one attached to a wall. A **demi-column** is one sunk into the wall so that only half the column is visible.

Mahogany veneered
commode c. 1755

COMB-BACK CHAIR: see WINDSOR CHAIR.

COMMODE: there are two distinct meanings to this term:

1. A chest, cabinet or chest-of-drawers particularly favoured in the 18th century when bombé or serpentine fronts were fashionable (p. 80).

2. A piece of bedroom furniture, also known as a **night commode** or **night stand**, which had the same function as a close stool (see CLOSE STOOL); it took various forms, sometimes being combined with a washstand, but always contained some kind of chamber pot.

COMPANION STAND: a metal stand of the late 19th and early 20th centuries which held a matching pair of tongs, a poker and a hearth brush. It stood beside the fire-grate and was used to tidy the hearth after making up the coal fire.

CONSOLE: a scrolled bracket (taller than it was wide) which supported an architectural cornice, or such a moulding on a piece of furniture.

CONSOLE TABLE: a term often applied to a table designed to be supported partly by standing against a wall and partly by two front legs.

COPPER:

1. A metal first mined in Asia Minor nearly 6000 years ago and of great importance for kitchen and dining-room utensils.

2. In the 18th century, a cauldron into which hot water was poured in order to wash household linen and personal garments; so-called because early examples were made of this metal.
   By the mid-19th century, coppers were mostly made of cast iron and had become wash boilers, a fire being lit beneath the vessel to heat the water. When gas was piped into homes gas-heated coppers became available, and soon these were fitted with a tap for emptying the water, though they still had to be filled by hand. With the 20th century appeared the galvanized copper coated with zinc to resist rust and, by the 1930s, enamelled coppers, later powered by electricity or gas.

CORBEL: a projecting block, usually of stone and decoratively carved, which supports a beam or other member.

Child's wooden commode chair

Copper companion stand 1905

Carved wood console 1625

Carved and gilt console table with marble top c. 1735

Metal gas-heated copper c. 1910–15

Carved stone corbel 1490

Window cornice 1725

Jacobean court
cupboard c. 1610

Doorway cresting c. 1612

Iron and brass
crimping machine
late 19th century

A **corbel-table** is a row of corbels supporting balcony, parapet or cornice.

CORNICE: the top member of the classical entablature (see ENTABLATURE); also used to refer to the projecting mouldings crowning a doorway, window or wall.

COURT CUPBOARD: a piece of furniture characteristic of Elizabethan and Jacobean times (c.1550–1630), consisting of three open shelves for the display of the household plate. The supports for the two upper shelves were decoratively carved, most often in bulbous form (see BULB). In some court cupboards a closed section with a door was incorporated into the upper part (see also CUPBOARD).

COVING: a deep concave moulding most typical of ceiling design. The coved section extends from the cornice upwards to the horizontal area of the ceiling.

CRESTING: the decorative finish to the top member of a wall, roof, window or door frame, or piece of furniture.

CRIMPING MACHINE: a piece of equipment introduced during the 19th century which resembles a miniature mangle, the purpose of which was to goffer or crimp material. So many of the garments worn at this time had decoratively frilled or flounced edges (aprons, blouses, petticoats, etc.) that the crimping machine, which was faster and more efficient, took over, at least in well-to-do households, from the earlier goffering stack (see GOFFERING STACK).

The rollers of this little mangle were made of brass, corrugated to crimp the fabric, and hollow because heated iron cylinders were inserted in them. When the handle of the machine was turned, the damped fabric passed between the rollers and was instantaneously crimped. The idea was the same as that used earlier in the box and tally irons (see BOX IRON, TALLY IRON).

CRISTALLO: a colourless, crystalline glass of then exceptional clarity, made in Venice from the 15th century.

CROCKET: an ornamental form in Gothic architecture, carved usually in flower or leaf shapes, decorating the edges of mouldings (see GOTHIC ARCHITECTURE).

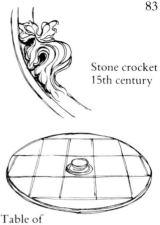

Stone crocket
15th century

CROWN GLASS: a method of making window glass introduced into England in the 16th century from Normandy where the craft had been practised in the Middle Ages; in England it was commonly known as **Normandy glass** (see GLASS).

The crown method was expensive, so it did not replace the cylinder process (see CYLINDER GLASS) until, in the 18th century, larger panes were needed for Georgian windows. Glass made by the crown method was much more suited to the fine mansions of the 18th century because it did not come into contact with any surface while molten, so retained a natural lustrous finish and was brilliantly transparent. It was costly to make because the process produced a flat circle of glass – known as a **table of crown glass** – and much of the material was wasted when it was cut up to fit into rectangular window frames.

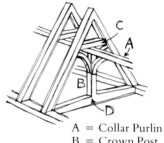

Table of
crown glass
marked for
cutting

To make crown glass the glass-worker blew a globe of molten glass with his blowpipe. He then attached an iron rod, called a punty, to the 'eye' at the opposite end of the globe, and broke off the blowpipe. He reheated the glass and spun the punty round in the air so that, by the action of centrifugal force, the globular form opened up into a flat circular plate, which could be as large as 5 feet (1.5 metres) in diameter. The finished glass was thicker in the centre and thinner at the edges so window·glass made in this way is not of even thickness. In good-quality windows the central knob (the **bull's eye**), where the punty had been attached, was discarded as waste.

A = Collar Purlin
B = Crown Post
C = Collar Beam
D = Tie Beam

CROWN POST: a post standing on the centre of a tie beam in an open timber roof which supports a **collar purlin** and **collar beam**. Usually, braces or struts connect the crown post to the collar purlin and collar beam (see COLLAR BEAM, TIMBER TRUSSED ROOF).

CRYSTAL SET: an early type of receiver for wireless programmes (see RADIO). Many of these sets were home-made in the 1920s from instructions published in the popular wireless journals of the time. The receivers had a very limited range. They also needed frequent adjustment, there was considerable interference and, to get reasonable reception, it was necessary to have an exceptionally

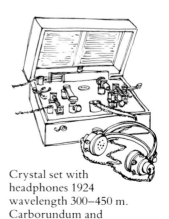

Crystal set with
headphones 1924
wavelength 300–450 m.
Carborundum and
galena crystal detectors
Copper cat's whisker

Carved oak open cupboard
Tudor period

Oak cupboard *c.* 1625

Polished steel curb suite
c. 1900

Brass curfew *c.* 1600

tall aerial which was unfortunately vulnerable to being struck by lightning.

The crystal diode was most often made of galena and a copper 'cat's whisker' was used to find the best location. Headphones were needed with the early sets but, by 1923, large horn-shaped loud-speakers became available.

CUPBOARD: originally, in the Middle Ages, a board (table) for the display of earthenware and plate. Even in Tudor times it was still a piece of furniture with open shelves, as in a buffet or court cupboard (see BUFFET, COURT CUPBOARD). On the other hand some late-15th-century cupboards, designed to hold food, were enclosed by doors (see AMBRY, LIVERY CUPBOARD).

From the 17th century onwards cupboards were in use for all kinds of storage, from food, plate and valuables to linen and clothes. The hanging ward-robe was a much later innovation (see WARDROBE) and many cupboards fitted with doors and con-taining shelves and pegs for clothes were called **presses** (see PRESS). Cupboards were often fine pieces of furniture, beautifully made in the style and wood fashionable in the period. Some were free-standing and of architectural design; others, like the **corner cupboard**, which was especially popular in the 18th century, were designed to fit into a special place such as a niche, a recess or the corner of a room. Many such cupboards (or **cabinets**) at this time were intended for the display of porcelain (see CHINA CABINET).

CURB (KERB) SUITE: a term used from the late 19th century to describe the matching fender and fire-irons of the domestic reception room hearth.

CURFEW: a metal cover with a handle on top which was placed over an open fire at night. Until the 19th century it was not easy to produce a flame to relight a fire. Also, in winter, the house would become too cold if the fire was allowed to go out completely. The custom at night was to draw the ashes over the embers to bank the fire down, and then to cover it with the curfew as a precaution against inadvertently setting the house on fire. In the morning the curfew was removed and fresh life was blown into the embers with the aid of a pair of bellows.

The word 'curfew' is an English corruption of the French *couvre-feu*. During the Middle Ages a bell was rung in the streets at a prescribed hour each evening to warn people to cover their fires. The term has survived in a military sense.

CURTAIL STEP: the lowest step (steps) of a stair in which the outer end is carried round in a scroll (see STAIRCASE).

CUSP: in Gothic tracery, the points formed by the meeting of the foils or small arches (see FOIL, GOTHIC ARCHITECTURE, TRACERY).

CUT GLASS: the decorating of glass objects by, first, marking out the form of the design with an incised line, and then grinding it by means of a metal wheel fed with abrasive.

Deep cutting, known as **faceting**, was developed in English glass-making in the 1730s, and the finest work was produced between about 1750 and 1800. The **lead crystal glass** process, initiated in the previous century (see LEAD GLASS), possessed an exceptional refractive quality which lent itself to deep cutting which further enhanced its brilliance (see GLASS).

CYLINDER GLASS: this method of making blown window glass (also known as **muff** or **broad glass**) was the most usual in Britain before the 18th century. The glass-maker gathered a lump of molten glass on to his blowpipe and blew it into a sphere. By swinging and twisting the pipe in the air he could blow the sphere into a sausage shape. The ends of the sausage were cut off and the glass cylinder was slit open. It was then cooled and flattened out in an annealing oven into a panel. These panels were not very large: medieval sizes were about 15 by 25 inches (38 by 63.5 cm) (see GLASS).

CYMA: a moulding, used especially in classical design, which comprises in section a concave and a convex curve. The **cyma recta** moulding, used particularly in cornices, has the concave curve at the top, then becomes convex; the **cyma reversa** has the convex curve uppermost.

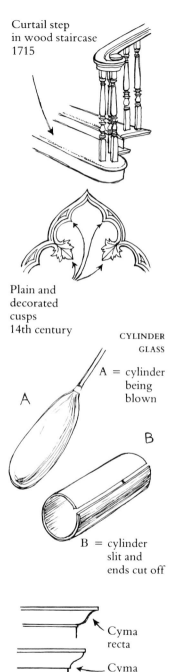

Curtail step in wood staircase 1715

Plain and decorated cusps 14th century

CYLINDER GLASS

A = cylinder being blown

A

B

B = cylinder slit and ends cut off

Cyma recta

Cyma reversa

DADO 1760

A = Dado
B = Dado Rail
C = Skirting or
    Plinth

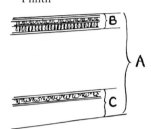

CLASSICAL
PEDESTAL

A = Cornice
B = Dado
C = Plinth

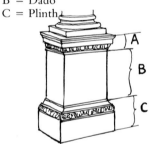

Japanned beechwood
day bed with
cane seat
c. 1730

DADO: in the decorative scheme of a room the dado is the lower part of a wall. There is a **plinth** or **skirting** at the bottom, and about 2½ feet (75 cm) above the floor is a moulded rail called a **dado rail** or a **chair rail** (see RAIL). In classical architecture the dado is the main part of a pedestal with cornice above and plinth or base below.

DAIS: the raised platform or the raised table at one end of a medieval great hall where the lord, his wife and family, and his principal guests, were seated to dine.

DAY BED: a typical piece of furniture of the Restoration period (see RESTORATION), designed for reclining (see also CHAISE LONGUE). The day bed was an extension of the carved wooden chairs of the time which had cane seats and backs. It had a long narrow cane seat; the wooden frame included a sloping back at one end, and there were six legs joined by richly carved stretchers (see STRETCHER). In the later 18th century the day bed gave place to the more comfortable reclining upholstered sofas and couches (see SOFA).

DECORATIVE PLASTIC LAMINATES: developed chiefly since 1945 as a tough, attractively patterned, easy-care finish for kitchen and bathroom surfaces.
     The best-known name in these veneers, which are applied to all kinds of core materials such as wood or particle board, is Formica laminate. This veneer, $\frac{1}{16}$ inch (1.5 mm) in thickness, consists of seven layers of paper impregnated with phenolic resin, on top of which is a patterned sheet of paper impregnated with melamine resin and a further overlay sheet of alpha cellulose paper similarly impregnated. The whole laminate 'sandwich' is bonded chemically under controlled heat and pressure into a single veneer.

DELFTWARE: a tin-glazed earthenware made in Holland (and later in England) from the early 16th to the end of the 18th century. Knowledge of the method of making this white opaque tin oxide glaze came to Holland from Italy (see MAJOLICA) and early Dutch ware was in imitation of Italian designs. By the mid-17th century the town of Delft had become the main centre of production and much of their ware was in blue and white designs based upon those of the popular imported Chinese porcelain. Also in the 17th century a delft type of ware was being made in England, first by immigrants from Holland, and then, by 1660, at manufactories established in Lambeth, Bristol and Liverpool; the decoration of this ware also owed much to oriental imports.

DENTILS: a form of classical ornament in the form of small rectangular blocks which are set in a row.

DIGESTER: a popular design of pressure cooker used in the 19th century. The appliance was invented as early as 1679 by the French physicist **Denis Papin**, principally for softening bones to make stock. He demonstrated its use successfully in 1681 to the Royal Society in London. The vessel had a tightly fitting lid and, to guard against an excessive rise in pressure, Papin had invented a safety valve. The 19th-century design was a cast-iron pot with a handle and, like Papin's, had a conical fitting lid and a safety valve.

DISCHARGING ARCH: see RELIEVING ARCH.

DOG GRATE: see BASKET GRATE.

DOG-LEGGED STAIR: a staircase in which there is no central well. The flights, which are joined by a landing, return parallel to one another with strings and handrails directed to one newel (see FLIGHT, NEWEL, STAIRCASE).

DOG TOOTH: a moulding ornament characteristic of the Early English (13th century) style of Gothic architecture (see GOTHIC ARCHITECTURE). A repeated decoration shaped as a formalized four-petal flower raised in the centre like a star.

DOLE CUPBOARD: see LIVERY CUPBOARD.

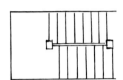
Dentil

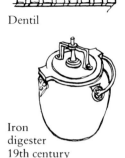
Iron digester 19th century

Plan and view of dog-legged stair c.1585

Dog tooth ornament 13th century

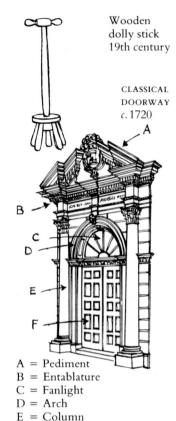

Wooden
dolly stick
19th century

CLASSICAL
DOORWAY
c. 1720

A = Pediment
B = Entablature
C = Fanlight
D = Arch
E = Column
F = Door Panel

PARTS OF A DOOR
AND ITS FRAME

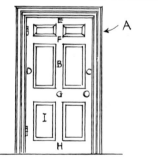

A = Architrave   G = Lock
B = Muntin   Rail
C = Shutting Stile H = Bot-
D = Hanging Stile   tom
E = Top Rail   Rail
F = Frieze Rail   I = Panel

DOLLY STICK: also known as a **clump dolly** and as a **peggy stick**, a traditional aid to washing clothes. The most common type resembled an upside-down wooden milking-stool with a long upright handle fitted to the seat centre; a cross-bar was usually attached to the handle to make it easier to use. The purpose of the dolly stick was to pound the washing up and down in the washtub, so forcing the soapy water through the material to loosen the dirt (see also POSSER).

DOOR, DOORWAY: the style reflected the architectural fashion of the day. Doorways might be arched or rectangular; the surrounding frame of mouldings is called the **architrave** (see ARCHITRAVE).

Medieval doorways were often arched, the shape of the arch varying according to the period (see GOTHIC ARCHITECTURE; also ARCH, EQUILATERAL ARCH, FOUR-CENTRED ARCH, LANCET, OGEE, POINTED ARCH), though the door was in many cases square-headed. The intermediate stone panel, the **tympanum** (see TYMPANUM), was then decoratively carved or painted. Medieval doors were of wood, vertically panelled and sometimes carved with Gothic tracery (see TRACERY).

The classical doorway was rectangular. The doorcase of more important examples comprised flanking columns or pilasters which supported an entablature and, sometimes, a pediment (see COLUMN, ENTABLATURE, PEDIMENT, PILASTER). In simpler designs cornices above the architrave were carried on consoles (see CONSOLE). In the 18th and early 19th centuries many doorways were enclosed in a round arch, the space above the door being filled by a painting, plaster decoration or a fanlight (see FANLIGHT). The classical door, usually of wood, single or double, was divided into square or rectangular panels. In the 17th century this division was often in two or three large panels. Towards the end of the century there were eight or ten panels but 18th-century doors were more commonly six-panelled. Panels were raised or sunk, the mouldings often carved decoratively.

By the mid-19th century the beautiful polished oak or mahogany panelled door had given way to a panelled type made of cheaper wood which was painted. In more recent times the plain plywood door mounted on a wood frame has become more usual (see DOOR FURNITURE, LINTEL, MUNTIN, PANEL-AND-FRAME CONSTRUCTION, RAIL, STILE, VENETIAN DOOR).

DOOR FURNITURE: the door handle, finger- and kicking-plates, and other metal or ceramic fittings.

DORMER: a window set vertically in a sloping roof with a separate roof over it. It is so-called because such windows generally illuminated sleeping quarters.

Ormolu door furniture by Robert Adam 1770

DOVETAIL: a method of joining boards in woodwork (when making a drawer, for instance) in which tongues shaped like the fans of dove's tails project from one board to fit precisely into correspondingly shaped slots in the other board.

DRAW TABLE: a table introduced about 1550 which had a double top. The lower part was in two leaves which could be pulled out on two runners, fixed in slots in the table frame, virtually doubling the extent of the table top. Known also as a **draw-out table** or **draw-leaf table**, such designs are still being made today.

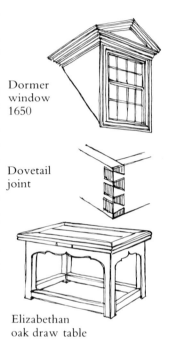

Dormer window 1650

Dovetail joint

DRESSER: from the Middle Ages a table in use in the dining-hall, which might incorporate shelves and/or cupboards, on which plate was displayed or food served.

It was in the 17th century that the dresser made its appearance as a kitchen item of furniture. At first it was only a flat board or table fixed to a wall, upon which food was 'dressed' or prepared. Soon shelves were fixed to the wall above the table top and, later in the century, the shelves, table top and some cupboards were united to form a single piece of furniture which often extended the full height of the room. By the 18th century the back was boarded and shelves (in the top part) were graded in depth to accommodate earthenware of varied sizes. Below the flat worktop were large cupboards to store linen. It was only in the 1920s that the kitchen cabinet was introduced to replace the dresser (see KITCHEN CABINET).

Elizabethan oak draw table

Victorian painted wood dresser

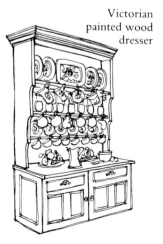

DRESSING-TABLE: the purpose-designed dressing-table was introduced as part of the bed-room furniture scheme in the later 17th century. Before this, small mirrors, boxes and toilet necessities were set out on a little table which was covered with a carpet or cloth. The Queen Anne dressing-table (see QUEEN ANNE) was generally small; on it was set a swing toilet glass on a box stand containing drawers.

Satinwood dressing-table
with painted and marquetry
decoration c. 1780–90

Mahogany dumb waiter
c. 1770

Dutch oven
to hang on fire-bars
19th century

As the 18th century advanced the dressing-table became a necessity instead of, as previously, a novelty. First there was the knee-hole design which had drawers and/or cupboards at the sides and which was convenient also as a place to write one's correspondence. An alternative type was the large chest or pedestal design which contained a long top drawer divided into numerous toilet compartments, also a mirror which could be raised when the drawer was open. Later dressing-tables intended for wealthy households became more elaborate. The tables were fine pieces of furniture fitted with hinged mirrors, drawers and toilet compartments.

Regency dressing-tables (see REGENCY) continued in the simply yet elegantly designed tradition of bedroom furniture, made from mahogany, rosewood or satinwood. They stood on tapering legs and were fitted with drawers and a toilet glass. The Victorian dressing-table was often, like the contemporary window and chimneypiece, draped with material. In the bedroom this was usually muslin and lace, decorated with flouncing and ribbons.

DRIPPING-TIN: the name given to the large rectangular metal tray placed under the meat roasting on a revolving spit in front of the open fire, to catch the fat known as dripping (see SPIT).

DUMB WAITER: an article of dining-room furniture introduced during the 18th century to dispense with the services of a waiter at table. The usual design comprised a central shaft standing on a tripod base to which circular trays (diminishing in size from lowest to top) were fixed at intervals. Often these trays were edged by a metal gallery to prevent dishes from sliding off. The dumb waiter was placed near to the host or hostess and carried dishes of food or bottles and glasses.

DUTCH OVEN: a metal box with a door which could be hung on the fire-bars or set in front of the open fire, and which contained a spit, turned by handle from outside the oven, for roasting small joints or fowl.

The term 'Dutch oven' is also applied to other types of cooking containers. In some areas and in parts of the USA the camp oven is so-called (see CAMP OVEN) and in England the hastener (see HASTENER) is sometimes so misnamed.

EARTH CLOSET: some form of earth closet consisting of a pail, with a seat fitted over it, into which earth could be sprinkled after use had long been in use for toilet needs. The mechanical earth closet, which was invented in 1860 by the **Rev. Henry Moule**, Vicar of Fordington in Dorset, was a welcome advance on the hand-sprinkling type and continued in use in country areas where no running water was available for water closets, until well into the 20th century. The Rev. Moule's closet was a wooden box containing a bucket; above, at the rear, was fitted a hopper, full of dry earth or ashes; when a handle was pulled, the hopper would shower an appropriate quantity into the bucket. In 1908 the price of this contrivance was £1.10s.0d. (£1.50). Portable earth closets were used in bedrooms.

EGG AND DART ORNAMENT: a classical form of decoration used to enrich a curved ovolo moulding (see CLASSICAL ARCHITECTURE). It consists of egg shapes alternating with darts. It is also known as **life and death** ornament. A similar decoration is called **egg and tongue**.

Egg and dart ornament

EGYPTIAN-STYLE CHAIR: Egyptian motifs were introduced into architectural, interior decorative and furniture design in 1798–9 at the time of Napoleon's Egyptian campaigns, and archaeological research in the early years of the 19th century stimulated this fairly short-lived Egyptian revival. Chairs in this style are characterized by scroll curving arms and backs, rounded X-frame front legs and decoration displaying the lotus leaf, scarabs and sphinxes.

ELECTRIC COOKING: the first electric cookers appeared in 1894. Most early cookers consisted of an oven, which was a metal box made of sheeting on a metal frame, heated inside by elements at top and bottom, and controlled by brass switches at the side. The heating elements were of wire coiled round cylindrical ceramic formers. The

Egyptian style of chair
*c.*1805

'Modernette' Belling
electric cooker
1919

Split-level electric cooker
with eye-level oven and
vitreous enamel finish
1927

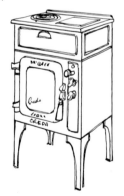

Creda electric cooker
with thermostatic control
and spiral-tube hob element
1933

other cooking appliances – grill, hotplate, kettle, frying pan – were all separate. They were placed on top of the oven, or on the floor, and were plugged separately into a row of switches in the wall above the oven.

The public did not take to these electric cookers, for many reasons. They were black, heavy, and difficult to clean; the elements were unreliable and kept burning out; they took a long time to heat up and so were costly to run. Most people already had gas cookers or solid fuel ranges. Only a proportion of homes were wired for electricity. People distrusted heat they could not see. Despite energetic advertising campaigns offering to rent ovens at seven shillings (35p) per quarter plus threepence halfpenny (1½p) per unit of electricity, sales were poor and rentals not much better.

Improvements came slowly. Elements lasted better after nickel-chrome alloy was adopted in 1906 for making resistance wire. **Mr C. R. Belling** began to make smaller cookers of light steel (the Modernette of 1919), fitted with a small oven, two burner hotplates, a grill and a plate-warmer. In the 1920s he brought out the first Baby Belling table model. By 1930 easy-clean vitreous enamel finish was replacing the black metal stove and, in 1933, Creda introduced automatic oven temperature control, with a thermometer fitted to the front of the oven door so that the cook could check it; before this she had had to keep opening the oven door to see how the cakes were doing. Finally, also in the 1930s, the fast-heating tubular-sheathed radiant rings were introduced to replace the old, slow-heating cast-iron plates with elements beneath.

By 1939 electric cookers were becoming more popular, used by about one-tenth of households, but 40 years later this had quadrupled as, due to technological advances, electric cooking had become cheaper, faster, more reliable and convenient. Among the advances were simmering heating rings, fast boiling rings, split rings, autotimers, fan-assisted ovens, two oven designs, combined grill and spit, and the ceramic hob (see CERAMIC HOB, ELECTRONIC CONTROL OF DOMESTIC APPLIANCES).

ELECTRIC HEATING: the earliest heaters, like cookers, were made by **Crompton & Company** in 1894. These were electric radiant panels in which the heating wires were embedded in enamel in a cast-iron plate. They were not a great success because, due to the differing expansion of the enamel and the iron during heating, they broke easily. They were followed by large sausage-shaped incandescent electric lamps used as heaters (see INCANDESCENT FILAMENT ELECTRIC LAMP); the Apollo of 1904 had four of these fitted into a cast-iron fire with a reflector behind. It gave out little heat.

By 1914 the efficiency of electric fires had been greatly improved. The use of nickel–chrome alloy for resistance wire, and Belling's element design, consisting of wire wound round a fire-clay former, made elements much more reliable. In the 1930s, by which time most households had been wired for electricity, the electric fire began to be popular.

The storage heater scheme was initiated in the 1930s but had only limited success. Re-introduced in the 1960s with much more efficient methods of storing the heat and the introduction of a fan to maintain the flow of air, it represented an economical method of space heating. The only problem was the large amount of room which the storage heater occupied, a problem which was later solved by the slim-line model (see also CENTRAL HEATING).

ELECTRIC IRON: a patent for an electric iron was issued in the USA as early as 1883, for a model which had to be separately heated on a stand and was not connected to the electric supply. In France, there was an alternative design, one which was heated by an electric arc passing between two carbon rods. By 1890 an iron had been developed which was connected by flexible cord to the electric supply.

In Britain, from 1891, Crompton & Company were making such electric irons which could be plugged into electric light sockets, but it was not until the late 1920s that sufficient numbers of homes were wired for electric current for such irons to be widely used. Early electric irons were very heavy and cumbersome; they had to be designed to store heat as the electric supply was unreliable. There was no thermostatic control until the late 1930s so the temperature of the iron still had to be gauged by guesswork, as was done for centuries, and it had to be switched on to heat and off to cool accordingly (see also STEAM-OR-DRY IRON).

ELECTRIC LIGHTING: as long ago as 600 BC the Greeks knew that if they rubbed a piece of amber it would attract lightweight materials; this

Two-bulb electric fire 1914

Bowl electric fire 1930

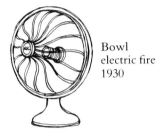

Belling electric fire early 1930s

Electric iron made of iron with wooden handle 1900

Edwardian central
electric-light fitting
made of brass with
silk shade

Art Nouveau central
electric-light fitting

Modern electric table-lamp

was due to static electricity. The Greek word for amber was *electron*, and from this **William Gilbert**, 16th-century physician and scientist, named such frictional attraction 'electric'.

The understanding of electricity and magnetism was immensely advanced by the experimental studies of **Michael Faraday** in the 1830s and, from this time onwards, western scientists endeavoured to comprehend and utilize the subject, but despite the experimentation in the possibilities of electrical illumination by the arc lamp, technology lagged behind and it was not until the generation of electricity was sufficiently advanced in the 1870s to provide a practical source of current that electricity could begin to be generally used as a source of illumination. Even then, as the arc lamp was unsuited to domestic illumination – it was too dazzling, too costly and needed constant adjustment – electric light in the home had to await the filament lamp, which was not satisfactorily effective until after 1878 (see INCANDESCENT FILAMENT ELECTRIC LAMP).

The fluorescent lamp, developed from the mercury vapour discharge lamp (used for street lighting) is now being fitted more frequently into the home, particularly for kitchen and bathroom illumination. Such lamps use less electricity and last much longer than the filament bulb.

ELECTRONIC CONTROL OF DOMESTIC APPLIANCES: the introduction of the use of electronics into the design of appliances used in the home is recent but such means of control is likely to increase. Modern technology has made possible these sophisticated devices which as yet are expensive; only when the superiority of, for example, a microprocessor-controlled sewing machine or toaster is generally established will market acceptance be achieved and increased production reduce the price (see TOASTER, WASHING-MACHINE).

Electronics is concerned with the design and action of devices which depend upon the conducting of electricity through a gas, a vacuum or a semiconductor. Many semiconductor devices have been developed since the Second World War, the transistor for example (see TRANSISTOR RADIO RECEIVER) and one of these is the **thyristor** which controls the development of electric power in electric motors and ovens more efficiently than by previous methods; it is incorporated in, for instance, microwave ovens (see MICROWAVE OVEN), food processors and mixers. Improved safety standards have also been made possible by the use of electronics in ignition systems and automatic flame monitoring controls in gas cookers.

The microprocessor, which is the central processing unit of a computer system realized on a tiny silicon chip, was introduced in California in 1971. Recently, it has been incorporated into several domestic appliances, notably toasters, washing-machines, gas and electric cookers and sewing-machines. It makes the action of such appliances more efficient and, therefore, more economical, also much easier to use.

Kenwood 'Chef' electronic food mixer 1978

ELECTROPLATING: in 1840 the brothers **George** and **Henry Elkington** received the first British patent for a silverplating process which they had based upon the laws of electrolysis enunciated by **Michael Faraday** a few years earlier. The Elkingtons passed an electric current from a battery through a solution of silver salt so that silver was deposited from the solution on to a copper article.

The electrolytic process is still in use. In addition to silver-plating, it is employed for coating steel with tin (for canning), also with metals such as nickel or chromium for decoration and protection.

Russell Hobbs electronic toaster 1981

ENCAUSTIC: refers to the ancient method of painting with wax colours fixed by burning; derived from the Greek word *egkaustikos*, meaning 'burn in'. Encaustic tiles, widely used in the Middle Ages and revived in Victorian Britain, were made of earthenware, into which coloured clays were pressed, making a design, before firing.

Singer 'Futura 2001' electronic sewing-machine 1981

ENGRAVED AND ETCHED GLASS: glass engraving by hand was practised as early as the late 16th century. The traditional 18th- and 19th-century method was to use a small copper wheel turning in a lathe, with an abrasive paste made from fine emery and linseed oil. Engraving was finer work than cutting so was more suitable for delicate glassware (see CUT GLASS). Today diamond-impregnated engraving wheels are used, powered by electric motors at a wide range of speeds.

Glass may also be etched using acid solutions to attack the surface of the material; areas not to be etched are covered with a wax resist. Another method is to obscure the translucent surface of the glass by sandblasting, so creating a given design.

Wheel-engraved glass finger bowl 1715–45

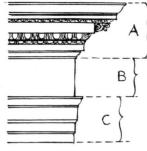

CLASSICAL ENTABLATURE

A = Cornice
B = Frieze
C = Architrave

Equilateral arch

'Etruscan' decoration by Robert Adam

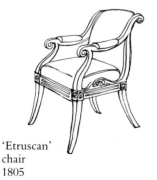

'Etruscan' chair 1805

Air containing an abrasive is blown under pressure at the part to be patterned.

ENTABLATURE: in classical architecture the upper part of an order which consists of horizontal mouldings. These are divided up into groups: the architrave is immediately above the capital, then comes the frieze, and above is the cornice (see ARCHITRAVE, CLASSICAL ARCHITECTURE, CLASSICAL ORDER, CORNICE, FRIEZE).

ENTASIS: in classical architecture the almost imperceptible convexity or outward curving along the outline of the column shaft – a subtle correction devised in ancient Greece to counteract the optical illusion which gives to a shaft bounded by straight lines the appearance of concavity (see CLASSICAL ARCHITECTURE, CLASSICAL ORDER, COLUMN).

In Elizabethan and Jacobean England (see JACOBEAN) the entasis was often exaggerated due to an incomplete understanding of the classical principles of Italian Renaissance architecture.

EQUILATERAL ARCH: a pointed arch in which the radius of each curve is equal to the span (see ARCH, GOTHIC ARCHITECTURE, POINTED ARCH).

ETRUSCAN: there was a fashion for the so-called 'Etruscan' decoration in the neo-classical designs of the 18th century (see NEO-CLASSICISM). The style was copied from murals and decoration found in the newly uncovered sites at Herculaneum (excavations began in 1738), and Pompeii (excavations began later, in 1763), also from Greek vases, and it was believed that the work was Etruscan, that is, belonging to the people who lived to the north of this area in Italy before the Roman period. It was, in fact, late Greek workmanship.

'Etruscan' design was popularized by leading architects (especially **Robert Adam**) and by cabinet-makers, artists and craftsmen. Complete Adam 'Etruscan' rooms survive, as at Osterley Park in Middlesex. **Josiah Wedgwood** named his new pottery manufactory, opened in 1769, 'Etruria'. There was an 'Etruscan' chair, characterized by curving legs and scrolled back and arms.

EWER: a jug or pitcher with a handle and a wide mouth and spout for easy pouring. Originally designed to hold water, the word derives from the

EXTRADOS: the outer curve of an arch defined by the line of the tops of the voussoirs (see ARCH, INTRADOS).

Medieval bronze ewer

FAIENCE: a tin-glazed majolica earthenware (see MAJOLICA) made in the Middle Ages in the Italian town of Faenza. In the 16th century potters from here settled in France where the ware was called *faïence*.

FANLIGHT: a round-headed window above a door divided into panes by decorative ironwork glazing bars, in the shape of a fan.

FARTHINGALE CHAIR: see BACK STOOL.

FESTOON: see SWAG.

FIBREGLASS: the commercial production of fine glass filaments dates from the 1930s. More recently the development of this branch of glass technology has greatly extended its domestic uses. There are two chief types of fibreglass: short fibres and continuous filaments. The short fibres are formed into a mat by the application of a binding agent for use in insulation.

The drawn continuous glass thread is used widely as a reinforcement material, especially of certain plastics, in order to produce an extremely tough, also load-bearing, material for construction purposes. A particular example is GRP (glass reinforced polyester) which was developed in the late 1950s. In the home it is utilized, for example, in making doors, roofing and building panels, piping, trays and lampshades. Fine, hair-thin, optical glass fibre is also being used in telecommunication. Such fibres are making possible the replacement of the heavy telephone cables, which transmitted the sound by radio waves, by slender cables, each of which can carry 100,000

Italian majolica
(faience) vase *c*.1480

Fanlight 1770

Sussex cast-iron
fire-back 1588

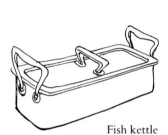

Fish kettle

Pewter flagon
18th century

two-way conversations, transmitting the sound on pulses of light produced by a laser. (See also PLASTICS.)

FIRE-BACK: a protective panel, usually of cast iron, placed in front of the wall and behind the open fire in a wall fireplace. Early medieval fire-backs were generally plain, but decorative designs, many made in the iron foundries of Kent and Sussex, were characteristic of the 16th and 17th centuries (see also BASKET GRATE).

FIRE-DOG: see ANDIRON.

FIRE-GRATE: a metal construction to contain the fuel of the domestic fire (see ANDIRON, BASKET GRATE, HOB GRATE).

FISH KETTLE: a lidded metal vessel, oblong or oval in shape, designed to cook a fish whole. It has a handle at each end and another placed centrally in the lid. The fish is laid inside, on a movable pierced inner bottom, to which may be attached two long handles, so that when cooked it may be lifted from the water without breaking it.

FLAGON: a large stoppered vessel with a handle, intended to contain wine or other liquid for drinking at table.

FLAT IRON: see SAD IRON.

FLIGHT: in a staircase, a continuous series of steps leading from one landing to another (see STAIRCASE).

FLOAT GLASS: a technological revolution in the making of window glass, a completely new process, which has replaced both sheet and plate glass methods (see PLATE GLASS, SHEET GLASS).

Float glass evolved from an idea which was put forward in 1952 by **Sir Alastair Pilkington**; seven years of research and development took place at Pilkingtons in St Helens, Lancashire, before this process was deemed commercially viable. In this method the raw materials are fed continuously into a regenerative tank furnace. The molten glass is then floated in a continuous band supported on a bath of molten tin in a chemically controlled atmosphere. During this float process the temperature is gradually lowered from 1500°C (2732°F) to 1000°C (1832°F) after which the surfaces become flat and parallel and the glass cools sufficiently for it to be removed without the surface being marked and without losing its fire finish. Over this temperature range the tin remains molten, yet is sufficiently dense to support the glass.

Float glass is perfectly flat so, unlike sheet glass, is free from distortion. Since its surface has not been marked it does not, like plate glass, require grinding and polishing. Its brilliance has not been dimmed by contact with any surface save that of the molten tin. The Pilkington float process has made the manufacture of flat glass cheaper and easier as well as creating a highly superior product.

Fluted column
Greek Doric Order
with flutes separated
by sharp arrises

FLOCK WALLPAPER: a decorative process invented in the early 17th century in France to imitate the more costly Genoese cut-velvet hangings. The design was printed on the paper with glue instead of colour and, while it was still sticky, finely chopped coloured silk or wool was blown on to the surface using a small pair of bellows, so making a velvety pattern. Much later, by the 1860s, the then popular Victorian flock wallpaper was made available in quantity as a by-product of the successful **shoddy** industry in which shredded wool rags were reprocessed into a poor-quality cloth.

Fluted Ionic column
with flutes separated
by filleted arrises

FLUORESCENT LAMP: see ELECTRIC LIGHTING.

FLUTE: vertical channelling in the shaft of a classical column which may meet in a sharp edge (an **arris**) or be divided by a narrow flat strip (a **fillet**). Fluting may be used on all classical orders except the Tuscan (see CLASSICAL ORDER) and the number of flutes per column was predetermined. For example, in the best examples of the Doric Order, the column usually had 20 flutes, in the other orders more, most often 24.

Fluting iron and board

FLUTING IRON: a 19th-century iron designed to make flutes in material. The equipment was usually in two parts: a fluter and a fluting board. The latter was made of wood or metal, its upper surface corrugated into sharp ridges. The cast-iron fluter or fluting iron (which had a wooden handle)

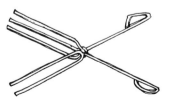

Iron fluting tongs

Quatrefoil window opening
*c.*1250

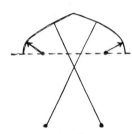

Four-centred arch

Carved oak four-poster bed
(curtains and bedclothes are
omitted) *c.*1525

Carved oak four-poster bed
(curtains and bedclothes are
omitted) late Elizabethan

was fashioned on the underside with ridges which exactly complemented and so fitted into those on the board. After washing, the material to be fluted was starched and, while still damp, was crimped by pressing the heated iron over the board. Also used were the earlier design of iron **fluting tongs**; these were scissor-like instruments resembling hair-curling tongs.

FOIL: the small arc repeated in Gothic tracery, each separated by cusps (see CUSP, TRACERY). The number of foils in a traceried arch is indicated by a prefix; the most usual are **trefoil** (3), **quatrefoil** (4), **cinquefoil** (5) and, for a large number, **multi-foil**.

FOLIATED: a decoration composed of leaves.

FOUR-CENTRED ARCH: a depressed pointed arch characteristic of the late 15th century (Perpendicular Gothic style) and early 16th (Tudor Gothic). A particularly flattened form seen especially in the years 1510–40 is also termed a **Tudor arch** (see GOTHIC ARCHITECTURE). As the name suggests, the four-centred arch is constructed on two pairs of arcs; the outer two are centred on the springing line, and the upper central pair have centres well below the springing line (see ARCH).

FOUR-POSTER BED: during the Middle Ages the bed was partially enclosed at night by side hangings which depended from rails under a canopy of material which was itself suspended from the ceiling by cords. In the early 16th century the four-post design evolved: a decoratively carved post at each corner of the bed and a headboard over it supported a framework for the hangings. By mid-century the suspended canopy was replaced by a decoratively panelled wooden tester which rested upon the posts (see TESTER).

These Elizabethan beds were large and expensive: much the most costly and important pieces of furniture in the home. The wooden bed frame was attached to the richly carved headboard and had two small posts at the foot, just within the canopy posts. The whole framework was heavy and solid and decorated all over with carving and/or inlay. Canopy posts were usually bulbous at this time (see BULB). The hangings were drawn at night to enclose the bed completely, so creating a rather airless 'room within a room' but at least excluding all draughts.

The four-poster bed continued in use until early Victorian times by which time it had been largely replaced by the half-tester design (see HALF-TESTER BED). The style of four-poster bed changed over the years, becoming less heavy as time passed, and less richly ornamented. By mid-17th century the canopy posts were most commonly in the form of classical columns which were mainly hidden when the curtains were drawn. Fashionable furniture styles were reflected in bedstead design: for example, **Chippendale** 18th-century beds included both Gothic and Chinese types. Regency beds were slenderer and more delicate in design; many had only half-testers.

FRENCH WINDOW: a tall window extending to floor level and opening outwards as a pair of doors.

FRET: an ornamental banding composed of a repeated pattern of straight horizontal and vertical lines. The best-known example is that of the **Greek key pattern** used in classical architectural decoration.

FRIEZE: the central section of the classical entablature between the cornice and the architrave (see ENTABLATURE). Many interior schemes are designed with a frieze and cornice only and, in some periods, notably Elizabethan and Jacobean interiors (see JACOBEAN), the deep plaster frieze is richly ornamented in high relief.

Mahogany four-poster bed
c. 1795

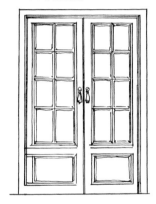

French window

Fret (Greek key pattern)

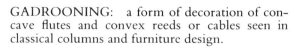

G

GADROONING: a form of decoration of concave flutes and convex reeds or cables seen in classical columns and furniture design.

GARDEROBE: originally a chamber or wardrobe (which could be locked) in which articles of dress or stores were kept; later extended to mean a

Gadrooning
early 17th century

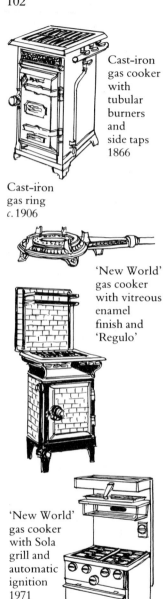

Cast-iron
gas cooker
with
tubular
burners
and
side taps
1866

Cast-iron
gas ring
c. 1906

'New World'
gas cooker
with vitreous
enamel
finish and
'Regulo'

'New World'
gas cooker
with Sola
grill and
automatic
ignition
1971

private room. 'Garderobe' was also a euphemism for a privy: in a castle or fortified house it would either be built into the thickness of the walls or made to project outwards from them so that it would drain into the moat.

GAS COOKING: when gas supplies became more widely available (see GAS LIGHTING) experiments were made into its use for cooking. Probably the earliest appliance which worked reasonably well was the prototype gas griller, made in 1824 at the Aetna Ironworks near Liverpool. This was a gun barrel, with holes pierced in it, bent round to form a circular gridiron. It was used horizontally for frying and boiling, the pan being placed on top; in order to roast it was turned vertically and the meat was hung in front of it.

A number of cookers were designed and publicized from the 1830s onwards but not until after 1850 was gas cooking taken up by any but a very few. People were nervous about using gas, believing that food cooked in this way might be harmed by the fumes. It was also expensive and thought to be dangerously explosive.

An important step forward resulted from the invention of the bunsen burner (generally attributed to **Robert Wilhelm von Bunsen**) introduced in 1855. In this device a specific quantity of air was introduced into the stream of gas before the point of ignition. The resulting flame was hotter and gave a safer, more efficient combustion. In the 1860s and 1870s a new generation of gas cookers appeared, fitted with the new atmospheric burner and further innovations. Among these were multi-burner hotplates, separate gas rings, more efficient ovens and more accessible taps.

Gas had still not become a serious competitor to solid fuel, partly because everyone possessed some type of solid-fuel cooking appliance, and chiefly because it was still too expensive. The breakthrough for gas came as a result of two incentives offered by the gas companies. During the 1870s cookers began to be offered for rental as well as for sale; then, in the 1890s, the pre-payment penny-in-the-slot machine system was·introduced which made gas cooking possible for nearly everyone.

Cooker design, however, changed only slowly between 1875 and 1920. Cookers were still made of cast iron which needed black-leading and the taps of brass or steel required constant polishing. Only after the First World War, when the ample supply of domestic servants abruptly dwindled, bringing about a firm demand from housewives for more labour-saving equipment, were the manufacturers stirred to action.

From the 1920s the black iron surfaces were gradually clad in white or light-coloured vitreous enamel finishes. At the same time better insulation improved oven design and, most notable of all, in 1923 **Radiation Ltd** (now TI New World Ltd) developed oven thermostatic control and introduced 'Regulo'. After the Second World War came the high-level grill, automatic burner ignition, lift-off oven doors, rotisseries and spits and, in 1965, auto-timer devices. More recently gas cookers are being designed to be built into kitchen unit schemes and make use of electronic control systems (see ELECTRONIC CONTROL OF DOMESTIC APPLIANCES).

Cast-iron gas fire with radiants of tufted asbestos 1885

GAS HEATING: the history of the development of the use of gas for space heating was similar to that of cooking (see GAS COOKING). Early designs of gas fire had appeared by the 1830s, the best of which were convector types in which tubes containing a current of air were heated by a gas flame applied to their exterior. These were costly to run, not very efficient and made the room smell because the combustion by-products were not satisfactorily disposed of.

As with cooker design, the invention of the bunsen burner provided an impetus to manufacture better models but it proved difficult to find a means of taking the next step forward which was to design a fire on the radiant principle: that is, one in which some material could be heated by the gas flame into incandescence. Many substances were experimented with – for example, wire, brick, pumice – but finally success was achieved with asbestos fixed in tufts into a fire-brick backing. In this the asbestos fibres became red hot and emanated a warm glow as the fire-brick was heated by the gas flame.

It was after 1880 before gas fibres became popular and, over the years, the design and material of the radiants has been steadily improved from the columnar ones introduced in 1905 to the later rectangular panels. Gas convector heaters have also improved greatly during the 20th century and in the post-1945 years gas central heating has become a most attractive proposition, especially since 1966 when a programme of conversion to North Sea natural gas was begun (see CENTRAL HEATING).

Gas fire with cubical radiants c. 1924

Radiant gas fire 1935

Portable gas fire 1950

104

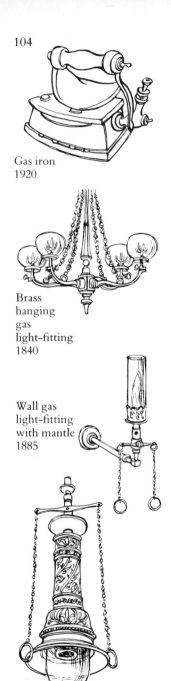

Gas iron
1920

Brass
hanging
gas
light-fitting
1840

Wall gas
light-fitting
with mantle
1885

Hanging gas lamp *c.* 1890

GAS IRON: irons fuelled by coal gas were introduced into England from the USA in the later 19th
century. These were fitted with flexible tubes
which connected to the gas supply. This type was
still in use up to 1939 and models designed to function with bottled gas were still being manufactured
in the late 1960s.

GAS LIGHTING: although simple experiments
had long been made to utilize gas made from
various substances for lighting purposes, it was
not until the late 18th century that the idea
was seriously considered. In 1784 **Professor
Minckelers** tried out a scheme aimed at lighting
with coal gas his lecture room at the University of
Louvain. In Paris in 1801 the French inventor and
engineer **Philippe Lebon** generated gas from
the distillation of wood and gave a public
demonstration of how it might be used for
illumination.

It was the contribution of **William Murdock**,
the Scottish mechanic employed by the engineer-
ing firm of Boulton & Watt, which initiated the
possible commercial development of gas lighting.
In 1792 Murdock successfully illuminated his
home at Redruth in Cornwall by coal gas and six
years later installed a lighting system at the
Birmingham Works of Boulton & Watt. Where
Murdock had led, others quickly followed –
Winzler, then **Clegg**, but it was the German
Frederic Albert Winsor who formed the
National Light and Heat Company (in 1812
granted a Royal Charter and renamed the Gas
Light and Coke Company) and, on George III's
birthday in 1807, gave the first public demonstra-
tion of street lighting when he illuminated part of
The Mall in London.

By 1816, 26 miles of gas mains had been laid in
London and gas lighting of the streets and many
public buildings was soon acclaimed a great success
but this form of illumination for the home was
much less popular. Until the later 19th century the
standard burners were still of the batswing or fish-
tail type; they flickered and smoked, emanating
sulphurous fumes which smelled offensive and
dirtied and damaged the interior furnishings. It
was not until the much later invention of the
incandescent mantle that these drawbacks were
eradicated (see GAS MANTLE).

GAS MANTLE: attempts had been made un-
successfully since 1840 to produce a suitable mantle

to replace the open gas burner. The invention of the bunsen burner in 1855 (see GAS COOKING) helped by giving a flame of higher temperature but it was the incandescent mantle produced in 1886 by **Carl Auer von Welsbach** (now generally known as the **Welsbach mantle**) which revolutionized gas lighting in the home. Welsbach devised a technique for soaking a spherical or cylindrical cotton net in a solution of rare earth oxides – 99% thorium oxide and 1% cerium oxide; he then burnt away the textile material leaving the earth oxides, in the form of the cotton net. This was the mantle, which became incandescent when burning with a gas flame.

The Welsbach mantle was manufactured from 1887. Improved versions followed, including the **inverted mantle** which directed the light downwards and so did away with the shadows previously caused by the fitting. Such gas mantles continued in use until replaced by electric lighting (see ELECTRIC LIGHTING).

GATE-LEG TABLE: a table in which one or more drop leaves may be supported upon a gate or gates which swing out for this purpose, so enlarging the surface area. The gate-leg design appeared in the early 17th century; in this, one of the table legs was divided vertically into two and framed to slender stretchers to form a gate. The next development was to make a more robust gate which had two legs (one of them being pivoted to the table frame), which were connected together at top and bottom by stretchers. In most designs the table frame was cut away to accommodate the gate when it was returned neatly to its folded position and the leaves were not in use.

GEORGIAN: a term which refers in England to the art and architecture prevailing during the reigns of the first four King Georges, that is, during the years 1714–1830. The term is sometimes extended to 1837 to cover the reign of William IV, bringing the period up to the accession of Queen Victoria. The domestic arts of this time, often described as 'the golden age', represented the climax of fine craftsmanship in all fields of work and media. The work was predominantly classical (see NEO-CLASSICISM, PALLADIAN, REGENCY, ROCOCO).

GESSO: the Italian equivalent for the Latin word *gypsum*, the mineral (hydrated calcium sulphate) from which plaster of Paris was made. Gypsum

Early gate-leg table *c.*1620

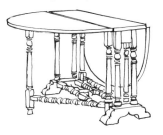

Oak gate-leg table *c.*1660

Mahogany gate-leg table *c.*1765

'New Rapid'
gas geyser
1884

Carved and
gilt pinewood
girandole
c.1755

Iron girdle

plaster had been prepared since the Middle Ages for use in sculpture and painting and, by the 16th century, it was being utilized for interior facing and the decoration of walls and ceilings (see PLASTER-WORK).

In the later 17th century, gesso, then a composition generally made from chalk and parchment size, was used as a base for decorative and gilded furniture. Especially fashionable between 1690 and 1730, the gesso was applied to the item of furniture in successive coats until it was thick enough for a decorative design to be carved or incised in it, after which it was gilded.

GEYSER: the gas geyser to provide hot water in the bathroom was invented in 1868 by **Benjamin Waddy Maughan**. He gave it this name from the Icelandic word *geysir*, which refers to a specific hot spring in that country and means 'gusher'.

A number of other designs of geyser were marketed in the remaining years of the 19th century but using them could be hazardous. If the instructions for lighting were not followed meticulously, the apparatus might explode. In early geysers there was no pilot jet and the water supply was often unreliable. Few geysers had attached flues and their use in the confined space of a small bathroom could also be dangerous. It was not until well into the 20th century that safety devices making it impossible for the main burner of the geyser to ignite until an adequate supply of water was flowing, and also an insistence upon adequate ventilation, became legally necessary.

GIRANDOLE: a decorative wall bracket, often with a mirror backing, incorporating fittings for candles, particularly seen in Rococo designs of the 18th century.

GIRDLE, GRIDDLE: a circular iron baking sheet suspended over the open fire by a metal half hoop. 'Girdle' is the more common word in the north of England, 'griddle' in the south (see also BAKESTONE, BRANDER).

GLASS: has been made since very early times. Glass objects, dating from about 2500 BC, have been found in Mesopotamia, and glass vessels were being produced there and in Egypt by 1500 BC. In Britain glass beads survive from the time of the Bronze Age but the making of glass vessels dates only from the Roman occupation of the country.

It was about this time also the making of glass was revolutionized by the invention of glass-blowing, believed to have come from Syria in the first century BC.

To make glass the raw materials – soda, lime and pure silica sand – have to be heated to a temperature high enough to fuse them together. The formed glass then needs to be cooled gradually in a controlled manner (that is, annealed) in order to avoid stress and cracking. Before the invention of glass-blowing the molten glass was poured into moulds but the use of the blowpipe (a hollow iron tube usually about 4 to 5 feet long, 1.2 to 1.5 metres) made a much greater variety of glass vessels possible as well as providing a means of mass production. In Britain blown glass was introduced by the Romans from glasshouses in the Middle East, Italy and Germany.

Early glass-making was very much a process of trial and error. The raw materials used differed slightly from one region to another and the purity of the sand was vitally important; even small traces of impurities would alter the colour, consistency and transparency of the glass. In a workshop blowing was usually carried out by a team of four or five craftsmen who enabled production to be continuous. The glassmaker would pick up a 'gob' of molten glass from the furnace on the end of his blowpipe, then blow it into a bubble, rotating it all the while to retain the spherical form. When the bubble had reached the desired size the glass-blower attached a solid iron rod (the punty) to the farther side, broke off the blow-pipe and, while the glass was still molten, shaped the vessel with the aid of shears, block and tools, returning it to the heat at intervals to maintain its partially fluid condition.

For different developments in making and decorating glass vessels see CRISTALLO, CUT GLASS, ENGRAVED AND ETCHED GLASS, LEAD GLASS, MOULDED GLASS. For the evolution of flat glass techniques see MIRRORS, WINDOW GLASS. See also FIBREGLASS.

GLAZE KETTLE: a metal double vessel used for keeping kitchen stock boiled down to a jelly: in the 19th century this jelly was termed glaze. The larger, outer vessel contained boiling water, the smaller one the glaze. In the lid of this vessel was a small hole into which a glaze brush could be inserted.

Bottle-maker's chair with two glass-blowing irons

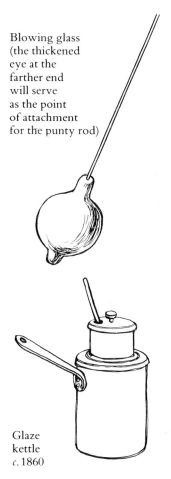

Blowing glass (the thickened eye at the farther end will serve as the point of attachment for the punty rod)

Glaze kettle c. 1860

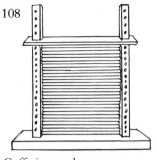

Goffering stack

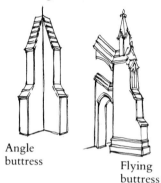

Angle buttress

Flying buttress

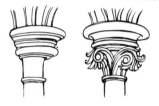

GOTHIC ARCHITECTURE

Early English moulded capital

Early English foliated capital

Early English lancet window

GOFFERING STACK, STACK PLEATER: a method of pleating or fluting material, which consisted of two wooden slotted posts, fixed about 12 inches apart (30 cm), into a horizontal board. The material to be goffered was damped and starched, then threaded in and out of about 25 wooden slats or spills. These were then slotted into the posts and secured by a wooden bar fixed on top. The complete stack was dried off in front of the fire (see also CRIMPING MACHINE, FLUTING IRON, GOFFERING TONGS).

GOFFERING TONGS: another method for making flutes in material. This scissor-like equipment resembled metal curling tongs and was similarly heated and used. Some designs were multi-pronged, so making more than one flute at a time (see FLUTING IRON).

GOTHIC ARCHITECTURE: the building style which evolved over a period of four hundred years during the Middle Ages, current in Britain and over most of Europe, and which was the subject of later revivals, notably in the 19th century. The term, coined by the 16th-century artist and historian Giorgio Vasari, was intended to convey contempt. Vasari was expressing the current thought of his (Renaissance) day, namely, that medieval architecture had advanced little beyond the age of the barbaric Goths who had helped to destroy the greatness of classical Rome.

Gothic architecture did not appear, fully developed, in the 12th century. It had evolved gradually from the earlier Romanesque (or Norman as it is often termed in Britain) type of building. The earliest structures in the new style were erected in the vicinity of Paris but the time was clearly ripe for a new approach, for transitional examples soon appeared elsewhere in France, and also in England. The chief characteristics of Gothic architecture, which is an arcuated form of construction, are the pointed arch (different from the Norman semi-circular one), the stone ribbed vaulted roof and its concomitant, the stabilizing flying buttress. Though the use of the pointed arch was not new in the 12th century (see ARCH, POINTED ARCH), it was its development which made possible the advance of Gothic architecture from the heavy solidity of its Norman origins to the characteristically pierced stone tracery and lace-work steeples of the mature work carried out in the later Middle Ages.

The transitional forms of Gothic design were

appearing in buildings of about 1150 and the first of the three great Gothic styles – the Lancet or Early English – was fully developed between 1200 and 1275. This type of work, sometimes described as the springtime of the style, was simple, fresh, finely proportioned yet sparingly decorated. The window openings were still fairly narrow, covered by lancet arches and arranged singly or in groups; vaults were of simple quadripartite design, column shafts were slender, single or clustered, and capitals plainly moulded or foliated; dog tooth was a characteristic ornament (see DOG TOOTH ORNAMENT, LANCET, STONE VAULTING).

The second stage, the high summer of Gothic architecture, is known by several names, all derived descriptively from its characteristic and complex window tracery – Decorated, Curvilinear, Geometric (see TRACERY). This phase of the work lasted for about 100 years from 1275 to 1375. By this time constructional knowledge permitted a much larger area of window to pierce the walls, buildings were taller and larger, abutment and vaulting more complex. Decoration in carved wood and stonework had become richer and this could be seen in doorway heads, capitals, bosses and corbels (see BALL FLOWER).

The final phase of Gothic architecture in Britain lasted a long time, changing only slowly, and was not abandoned until after the middle of the 16th century when Renaissance concepts finally filtered through from the Continent. Particularly in its later phase it was a style peculiar to England and one characterized by a restrained richness. Perpendicular Gothic architecture, as its name suggests, was an exercise in verticality (in churches evidenced in tall steeples and lofty vaults) but it was also a panelled style, panelled in stone or wood on walls and roofs, panelled in glass in the immense traceried windows; the pointed arch gradually gave way to the flattened four-centred Tudor style.

Gothic architecture was primarily an ecclesiastical expression; the Church was its chief patron and the largest, most costly buildings erected in the four hundred years from 1150 to 1550 were churches, abbeys and cathedrals. But domestic building, albeit less imposing and large-scale, followed the same architectural style and, especially during the 14th, 15th and 16th centuries, many important manor and town houses were erected, of which a considerable number survive in excellent condition (see BALL FLOWER, BOSS, CAPITAL, CORBEL, CUSP, DOG TOOTH ORNAMENT, EQUILATERAL ARCH,

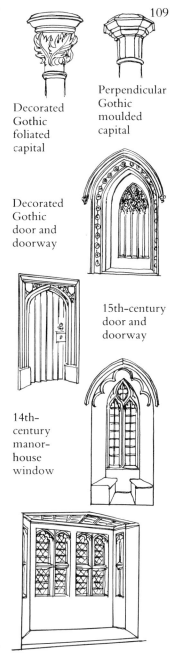

109

Decorated Gothic foliated capital

Perpendicular Gothic moulded capital

Decorated Gothic door and doorway

15th-century door and doorway

14th-century manor-house window

Perpendicular Gothic bay window

Gothic armchair
in.carved and
gilded beechwood
with embroidered
velvet covering
*c.*1825

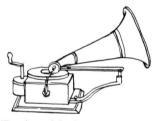

'Dog' model of
'His Master's Voice'
gramophone
1898

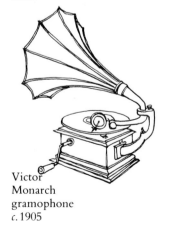

Victor
Monarch
gramophone
*c.*1905

FOLIATED, FOUR-CENTRED ARCH, LANCET, MULLION, OGEE, POINTED ARCH, STONE VAULTING, TRACERY, TRANSOM, WATER-LEAF DECORATION).

GOTHIC-STYLE CHAIR: during the Middle Ages chairs were rare articles of furniture; of the few chairs existing a number displayed features of later Gothic architectural design such as carved crockets, tracery and panelling. During the second half of the 18th century and the Regency period a romantic version of Gothic was adapted for chair forms by **Chippendale** and other furniture designers when ogee curves, pinnacles, crockets and cusped arches were incorporated. With the more serious and far-reaching Gothic Revival of the 19th century the Gothic style was adopted more widely for all kinds of seating furniture.

GRAMOPHONE: first devised, named and patented in 1887 by the American inventor **Emile Berliner** who demonstrated his machine in Philadelphia the following year. Berliner's gramophone played flat disc records first pressed in hard rubber. In 1898 the Gramophone Company was set up in London to market his instrument and the 'dog model' appeared which bore the famous pictorial trademark of 'His Master's Voice': the machine sold at 5 guineas (£5.25).

GRANDFATHER CHAIR: a late Victorian term for a wing chair (see WING CHAIR).

GRANDFATHER CLOCK: a colloquial name in use for the long-case clock since it was so called in H. C. Work's popular song of 1878 (see LONG-CASE CLOCK).

GRAPHOPHONE: an instrument designed in 1886 by **C. S. Tainter** and **C. A. Bell** (a cousin of Alexander Graham Bell, inventor of the telephone), which was an improved version of Edison's tinfoil phonograph of 1878. The graphophone employed a cylinder of cardboard coated with wax instead of tinfoil and had a flexibly mounted stylus; the recorded sound of this instrument was better than that of the early phonograph and this encouraged Edison to return to his equipment and improve it (see PHONOGRAPH).

GRAVITY SPIT: see MECHANICAL SPIT.

GREASEPAN: see CANDLE.

GREEK KEY PATTERN: see FRET.

GRIDIRON: a framework of iron bars, often fitted with a long handle, upon which food could be placed in order to grill it over or in front of the open fire. It was in use in Britain from Roman times.

GRIFFIN, GRIFFON, GRYPHON: a legendary beast depicted in classical decoration which has an eagle's head and wings and a lion's body and legs.

GRISAILLE: a style of painting in grey monochrome which represents low relief figures and detail. Particularly fashionable in the later 18th century.

GROTESQUE: a decorative painting or sculpture incorporating representations of human, mythical and animal forms interwoven in a fantasy with flowers and foliage. Renaissance artists adapted their designs from wall paintings and sculptural decoration found in the remains of ancient Roman buildings in Italy which had been disinterred by them: they gave them the name *grotteschi*, derived from *grotta*, 'cave' or 'grotto'.

GUILLOCHE: a classical moulding decoration consisting of repeated interlacing circles making an intertwined plait.

Medieval gridiron

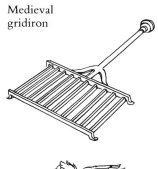

Griffin

Guilloche

Half-tester bed
*c.*1850

HALF-TESTER BED: a design in which the tester or canopy extends over only the head end of the bed. Particularly fashionable in Victorian times.

HAMMER BEAM: in a hammerbeam roof, the horizontal member supported by a curved brace carried by a corbel which, in turn, supports the **hammer post** and **principal rafter** above (see TIMBER TRUSSED ROOF).

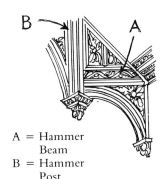

A = Hammer Beam
B = Hammer Post

Metal hastener with
brass bottle jack

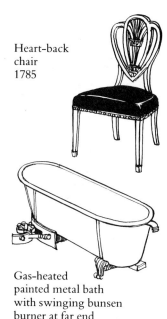

Heart-back
chair
1785

Gas-heated
painted metal bath
with swinging bunsen
burner at far end
1871

Hip
bath

HASTENER: a polished metal roasting screen which reflected heat from the fire and so 'hastened' the cooking of a joint, which was hung inside the curved screen, depended from the top, and turned by a **bottle jack** (see BOTTLE JACK). The open side of the screen was turned towards the fire and at the rear was a door which gave access for basting the joint.

HEART-BACK CHAIR: a neo-classical design of the later 18th century, the back of the chair being shaped like a heart.

HEATED BATH: during the 19th century before the gas geyser had been perfected (see GEYSER), the bath still had to be filled with hot water by hand. However, as many baths had taps which were attached to a cold-water supply, devices to heat the bathwater *in situ* became popular; for this purpose either charcoal or gas was used.

The usual charcoal heater was an enclosed design. Charcoal was put into the bottom of the heater and ignited. The equipment was fitted with two breathing tubes through which the air could circulate so that the fuel would burn well. When it was alight the charcoal heater was immersed in the cold bath water. The fuel continued to burn because the tops of the tubes extended above water level.

There were two chief types of gas heater. One was portable; it was connected to a gas lighting bracket and, like the charcoal heater, was placed in the bath water. The other, a more popular design, was fitted to the exterior of one end of the bath. A gas burner was swung out to be lighted, and then swung back so that the flames played directly on to the underside of the bath. Such devices were advertised to heat a bathful of water in six minutes. They also carried a warning to turn the gas off before entering the bath. It seems certain that no one would be so forgetful a second time.

HIGHBOY: see TALLBOY.

HIP BATH: a round or oval metal bath used over the centuries for bathing in the bedroom or in front of the kitchen fire when hot water was scarce and the bath had to be hand-filled with a jug. Such baths had high backs and were often fitted with soap rests. Many had hinged lids so the bath could be closed when not in use.

HOB GRATE: a design of open grate for burning coal, which came into use about mid-18th century. The fire-box was flanked by iron plates (which were often decoratively ornamented) and the grate was fitted into the fireplace instead of standing free as before (see BASKET GRATE). Kettles, pans and other utensils could be placed on the flat surfaces (hobs) on either side of the fire to keep hot.

HOOF FOOT: a termination representing a goat's hoof widely used on the early designs of cabriole leg (see CABRIOLE LEG).

HOPPER CLOSET: see WATER CLOSET.

HOUR GLASS: see SAND GLASS.

HOUSE OF EASEMENT: an euphemism for latrine or privy.

Hoof foot c.1710

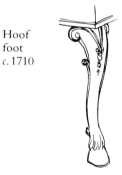

I

IMPOST: the block, pier, capital or bracket from which an arch springs (see ARCH).

INCANDESCENT FILAMENT ELECTRIC LAMP: many experiments to make a satisfactory domestic lamp of this type were carried out by researchers between 1847, when **W. E. Staite** demonstrated his short-lived lamp at a lecture in Sunderland, and the 1870s, when the first successful examples were made by Swan and by Edison. Electric illumination by means of arc lamps was in use in factories by the 1870s, once an adequate source of electric power had been established, but this method was unsuited to domestic lighting: the light was too dazzling, it was very costly and it needed constant adjustment.

The difficulties in producing a satisfactory incandescent filament lamp were three-fold: a sufficiently durable material had to be found from which to make the filament; it had to be possible to achieve a sufficiently high level of evacuating the air from the bulb which contained the filament; and

Impost c.1250

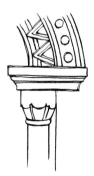

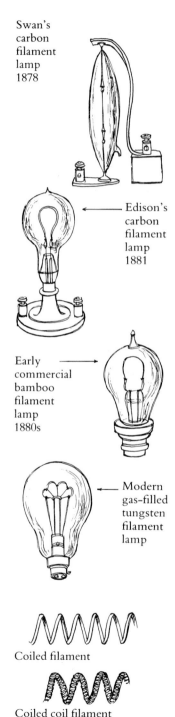

Swan's carbon filament lamp 1878

Edison's carbon filament lamp 1881

Early commercial bamboo filament lamp 1880s

Modern gas-filled tungsten filament lamp

Coiled filament

Coiled coil filament

a means had to be found adequately to seal the bulb at the point of entry of the wires which carried the electric current to the filament.

Many different materials were tried out for a suitable filament, among them bamboo, platinum, cotton thread and paper. Staite had used an alloy of platinum and iridium. The American inventor **Thomas Alva Edison** used all these materials; his first successful lamp had a filament of platinum alloy but better was his 1879 model which utilized carbonized paper. Meanwhile the Englishman **Joseph Wilson Swan**, who had as a young man attended Staite's demonstration, made his first effective carbon filament lamp in 1878 using cotton thread and he improved this two years later by treating the thread with sulphuric acid before carbonizing it.

By 1882 carbon filament incandescent lamps were being made in quantity, Edison lamps in the USA and Swan lamps in Britain; both were a great success. Very soon the two companies merged to become the Edison and Swan United Electric Company. Before long, the not very efficient carbon filaments were replaced by metal ones, osmium in 1902, then tantalum and, in 1906, tungsten. Further research led by **Langmuir** in the USA brought in 1913 the argon-filled coiled filament lamp and after this the even better coiled-coil filament. Since 1925 have come the frosted bulb and, later, the addition of a fuse to obviate possible bulb explosion as a filament burned out.

INLAY: a flush surface decoration made by cutting away the solid wood, stone or marble and inserting other materials such as different woods, ivory or metal. Inlay is recessed into a solid article and so differs from marquetry which is a veneer (see MARQUETRY). **Intarsio** is the Italian term for inlay.

INSTANTANEOUS LIGHT BOX: a method of producing a light introduced in the early years of the 19th century. This utilized the chemical or chlorate match (also known as an acid-dip match), the head of which was tipped with a mixture of chlorate of potash, sugar and gum arabic. In order to ignite the match it had to be dipped in vitriol (sulphuric acid). The instantaneous light box, which could be kept at one's bedside, contained a supply of tipped matches, a small bottle of vitriol, some candles and a holder. Using such a box when sleepy was a dangerous proceeding and the partially-mechanized box devised by **Henry Berry** in 1824 was a considerable advance. As long as the metal lid of this box remained closed the acid bottle stopper was kept in place. As the lid was opened a string on a pulley lifted the stopper which held one drop of vitriol. A turntable was then mechanically operated: this brought a chlorate-tipped match past the stopper, which ignited it, and carried it on to light a spirit lamp also provided in the box.

INTAGLIO: an engraved, incised design. The term derives from the Italian verb *intagliare*, 'to cut, incise or engrave'.

INTRADOS: the inner, under-line of the curve of an arch (see ARCH, EXTRADOS).

IRON AND STEEL: pure iron is a silvery-white metal which is one of the elements. It is rarely found naturally and is useful only when it is mixed with another substance, usually carbon. For centuries it has been of vital importance in the home, used structurally, decoratively and to make essential artefacts and fittings. It is generally to be found in ores where it is combined with other elements, most often oxygen, and these oxides are available in abundance in the world, particularly in Britain.

Iron is used in three main forms: wrought iron, cast iron and steel. Wrought iron is fairly pure and has been utilized since early times. The temperature of the ore is raised to red heat and the resulting spongy mass is hammered into shape. Cast iron came later. It is harder and more brittle, so cannot be shaped by hammering, but may be melted and poured into moulds. Steel is the most useful form but is a later development and of particular importance in modern life (see CAST IRON, STEEL).

IRONING: it was not until the 16th century in Europe that fabrics for household and personal linen were sufficiently fine to benefit from smoothing by the use of a heated iron and it was late in the century before metal irons were made which could perform this task (see TALLY IRON).

Before this the oriental pan iron was in use in the Far East and a Chinese painting showed one being used for ironing silk as early as the 8th century. Such irons were wood-handled and made of brass or bronze in the form of a small saucepan which contained burning coal or charcoal. Many such pan

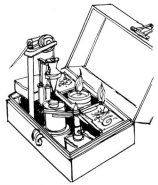

Berry's instantaneous light box, 1824

In the open box may be seen the stopper of the vitriol bottle held up by the pulley; and on the turntable the chlorate match which has been lighted and which has in turn lighted the spirit lamp.

Chinese pan iron with wooden handle

Mushroom
iron
19th
century

Box
iron
1750

Brass
and
mahogany
jardinière
c. 1880

irons survive in the West. An alternative method used early in Scandinavia was to employ unheated smoothing weights made of stone, glass or wood and rub them over the material.

In the later 16th century the Dutch were leaders in making heated irons of brass. In Britain such irons, generally made from iron by the local black-smith, were appearing by the early 17th century (see BOX IRON, SAD IRON). In the 19th century special-purpose irons were being made in different forms (see BALL IRON, FLUTING IRON, POLISHING IRON, SLEEVE IRON), and in the second half of the century the self-heating iron appeared. The gas iron was the first of these but before long various substances were being experimented with to fuel the iron; for instance, paraffin, naphtha, oil, methylated spirits and petrol (see GAS IRON, SPIRIT IRON, TILLEY IRON). The electric iron was intro-duced in the USA in the 1880s but in Britain its general use was delayed until the 1920s because comparatively few homes were wired for electricity before this (see ELECTRIC IRON, STEAM-AND-DRY IRON).

JACOBEAN: architecture and decoration of the time of James I of England, that is, 1603–25.

JAPANNING: a process carried out by furniture makers in England in imitation of Oriental lacquerwork. Both Chinese and Japanese lacquered furniture was imported into Europe during the 17th and 18th centuries. This became highly fashionable and, as demand exceeded supply, very expensive (see LACQUERED FURNITURE).

In japanning a coating of whiting and size was applied to the furniture, then several coats of coloured varnish. In the better-quality work relief patterns were built up with a paste made from gum arabic and whiting and the design was painted on in gilt and bright colours. Cheaper furniture was merely varnished.

JARDINIÈRE: an ornamental stand to hold a

potted plant. Particularly fashionable in the second half of the 19th century.

JASPERWARE: probably the best-known of all the wares produced by **Josiah Wedgwood** at his 'Etruria' manufactory and perfected in 1774. Jasperware was a fine stoneware of a porcelain nature. It was coloured with mineral oxides to produce the famous shades of blue (the most usual), lilac, sage green, yellow or black, and decorated with bas-relief classical figures in white. These were originally designed and modelled by the sculptor John Flaxman. Such ware is still marketed by Wedgwood.

JOINERY, JOINED FURNITURE: joinery evolved during the Middle Ages as the craft of the skilled woodworker who constructed furniture and parts of a house by joining together pieces of wood. His work was generally lighter and more ornamental than that of a carpenter (see also DOVE-TAIL, MORTISE, PANEL–AND–FRAME CONSTRUCTION, TENON).

JOISTS: the timbers laid horizontally which support the floorboards and to which the ceiling is attached.

Jasperware Wedgwood vase
(white relief sculpture
on a blue ground)
1786

Joined stool c. 1600

KETTLE TILTER: a mechanism which facilitated taking a hot kettle from over the open fire in order to pour from it. The tilter was an iron frame with a projecting handle which was so balanced that when the housewife pressed the tip of it, the kettle was tilted and would pour without needing to be lifted off its hanger. Different names were given to kettle tilters in different parts of the country: for example, idle-back, handymaid, lazy-back.

KEYSTONE: the largest, central block of the voussoirs of an arch (see ARCH).

KING (QUEEN) POST: see CROWN POST.

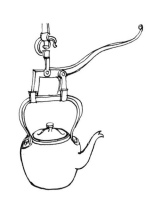

Kettle tilter

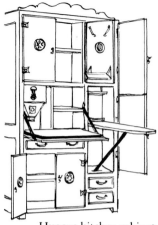

Hygena kitchen cabinet including flour sifter, pull-out worktop and ironing-board 1929

Early 19th-century iron cottage (open) kitchen range

Small closed kitchen range mid-Victorian

KITCHEN CABINET: a piece of furniture to provide storage and a working-top which, in England, replaced the kitchen dresser in the 1920s and 1930s (see DRESSER). The kitchen cabinet was introduced from America where it had been in use for some years. In 1925 the British firm **Hygena Cabinets Ltd** began to manufacture and market high-quality wood cabinets. These cabinets were fitted with enclosed cupboards and shelves to store food, utensils and cleaning equipment and included a pull-down worktop and a seat. The well-designed, easy-care kitchen cabinet was as characteristic of its time, when families had become smaller and servants rarer, as the open dresser had been of Victorian England.

KITCHEN RANGE: the first practical kitchen range was designed by **Thomas Robinson** in 1780. It was a roasting range based on the hob grate design, having an open coal fire with removable bars flanked on each side by metal hobs (see HOB GRATE), but under these were, on one side, an oven, and on the other, a water tank. The oven, which had an iron door, was lined with brick and fitted with shelves; the water tank was entirely of iron. Robinson's range represented a landmark in kitchen cooking facilities but it was very inefficient and in many ways unsatisfactory. The open-topped fire-grate smoked, and it burned coal extravagantly. The oven was only heated at one side so the food was partially burnt and partially under-cooked.

Robinson's prototype range was soon improved upon and in 1802 the enclosed kitchen range was patented by the Exeter ironfounder **George Bodley**. This range had an iron plate on top of the fire-grate which economized on coal and could be used for utensils to heat water and cook food. Flues built into the range helped to provide a more even supply of heat to the oven.

Despite the introduction of gas and electric cookers during the 19th century (see ELECTRIC COOKING, GAS COOKING), the iron and steel coal-burning kitchen range was in use in many parts of Britain until well into the 1920s. From 1802 onwards improvements were made to its efficiency and convenience but these came only slowly. Manufacturers produced many different models and strongly advocated the advantages of each individual design, but all were very hard work to clean, could make the kitchen insufferably hot in summer, and created a great deal of dirt from the open coal-burning grate.

There were two chief types of range, one being more enclosed than the other. The open type was more popular in the north of the country because it cooked the food and warmed the kitchen at the same time, so was more suited to a colder climate. The **cottage range** and the **Yorkshire range** were typical designs of this type. They were extravagant in the use of fuel and needed skill and experience on the part of the housewife in operating the dampers efficiently and so controlling both oven and fire heat. This design of range had an open fire-box with bars across, the upper ones of which could be swung down as needed to act as a trivet for pans and kettles. There was an oven at one side and a hot-water boiler or warm closet at the other. Though based on the Robinson type of 18th-century range, the models of the second half of the 19th century were a great improvement on the prototype; they were much more efficient and controllable.

Late-Victorian kitchen range

The closed range or **kitchener** was more to be seen in the south of England. It was based more on Bodley's type of enclosed fire-grate and was more economical in its use of fuel and more efficient to operate. The fire-box was fitted with boiling rings on top of its closed plate and a metal door enclosed the front fire-bars. Such a kitchener was designed to cook and to heat, but not to do both at once. When it was being used for cooking, the fire-box was completely enclosed. If the housewife desired to warm the kitchen, the door could be opened and the hot plate slid back.

Later 19th-century ranges were more complex. Many designs had two ovens, several hobs and a warming compartment for dishes. Heat was more carefully regulated and smoke was better controlled. Some models incorporated a back boiler to heat extra water.

Walnut knee-hole desk
c. 1715

KNEE-HOLE: a desk, bureau or chest with the centre section recessed to accommodate the sitter's knees. In some designs this section contains a cupboard at the rear of the recess.

KNEELING-CHAIR: see PRIE-DIEU.

KNIFE BOX: pairs of receptacles fitted to hold table silver were designed to stand on side tables and buffets from the late 17th century onwards. Elegant wood boxes, often inlaid and mounted with silver, were fashionable in the 18th century;

Painted satinwood neo-classical knife box
c. 1780

Kent's knife cleaner
and polisher
c. 1909

Uneck
knife
cleaner
c. 1890

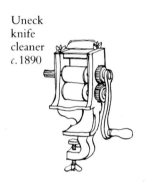

Knife sharpener
c. 1800

Gold and black
lacquered commode
c. 1755

the vase shape was characteristic of the neo-classical period (see NEO-CLASSICISM).

KNIFE CLEANER: the traditional method of keeping knives clean and bright before the advent of stainless steel (1930s) and the knife-cleaning machine (late 19th century) was by stropping the blades, using emery powder, on a knife board which was covered with leather or india rubber.

The rotary knife cleaner appeared in the 1870s and improved versions quickly followed which would clean up to 12 knives at once. Machines usually took the form of a circular wooden drum mounted on a cast-iron stand. Inside was an inner wheel fitted with leather leaves or felt pads alternating with bristles. The knives were put into holes in the periphery of the drum and, as a handle was turned, were cleaned and polished with the aid of an abrasive powder which had been poured into the inner wheel fitments. Unfortunately, this somewhat drastic method steadily reduced both length and thickness of knife blades.

From 1890 onwards machines became available which used different methods and were kinder to the knives. Typical was a design resembling a miniature mangle fitted with india-rubber rollers. It was clamped to a table; a handle could then be turned in order to move the rollers and so polish the knives.

KNIFE SHARPENER: various devices were introduced during the 19th century to sharpen knives. In the most common design the knife blade was drawn across a V of hardened steel segments.

LACQUERED FURNITURE: was imported into England from 1660. In this richly decorative process, which had originated in China, and then had been perfected in Japan, sap from a variety of sumac tree (also called a lacquer tree) was used. As the fashion for such ornamentation grew, and this species of tree was not grown in Europe, English furniture was sent to the Orient to be lacquered, then returned. By the early 18th century the

Dutch, the French and then the English had perfected a method of imitating oriental lacquer, a process which was logically described as 'japaning' (see JAPANNING).

LADDER-BACK CHAIR: a traditional rural design in which the high uprights of the back are joined by horizontal slats. Ladder-back chairs were made fashionable in the 18th century by **Thomas Chippendale** and other designers, and the pattern was subsequently repeatedly revived, notably in the **Ernest Gimson** chairs of the 1890s.

LADDER STAIR: a simple, wooden, ladder type of staircase constructed especially in medieval houses usually to connect the hall floor to the solar above. Such stairs had treads but no risers; some designs were built with a newel and handrail (see STAIRCASE).

LAMINATED FURNITURE: composed of several thin layers of wood bound together with adhesive and usually laid alternately across the grain to give greater strength (see PLYWOOD). A method developed especially by some Scandinavian designers in the 1930s, for example, Karl Bruno Mattsson of Sweden and Alvar Aalto of Finland, when laminated wood was bent into attractive and suitable shapes. With the availability of new bonding resins developed during the Second World War and modern techniques of bending and moulding the material by electrical heating means, laminated wood is now extensively employed for domestic needs where it is particularly suited to seating furniture.

Wood ladder staircase c.1400

LAMINATES: see DECORATIVE PLASTIC LAMINATES.

LAMP: a traditional means of lighting in Britain since Roman times where oil or spirit is burnt in a vessel by use of a wick (see ARGAND BURNER, CARCEL LAMP, OIL LAMP).

For lamps providing other forms of lighting, see ELECTRIC LIGHTING, GAS LIGHTING, INCANDESCENT FILAMENT ELECTRIC LAMP.

Lancet window 1230

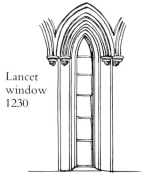

LANCET: the lancet arch is characteristic of the **Early English (Lancet)** stage of medieval architecture (see GOTHIC ARCHITECTURE). Such arches have sharply pointed heads as may be seen in arcading, doorways and windows of this date.

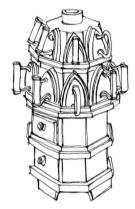

Lattice-back chair
c.1765

Iron laundry stove with sad irons

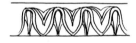

Leaf and dart ornament

Library chair
c.1725

Lancet windows, found singly or in groups of two, three or five, are tall and narrow. They are evidenced in both ecclesiastical and domestic building (see WINDOW).

LANTERN CLOCK: see CLOCK.

LARDER: see PANTRY.

LATTICE-BACK CHAIR: a chair back the design of which is made up from criss-crossed strips of wood or metal. Particularly to be seen in the 18th-century years of Chinese taste (see CHINOISERIE).

LAUNDRY STOVE: an iron kitchen stove on which were rests to hold sad irons, keeping them hot and ready for immediate use (see SAD IRON).

LAVATORY: originally a vessel or a place for washing; thus an apartment in which washing facilities were provided; much later such a room would include a water closet (see WATER CLOSET).

LEAD GLASS: a heavy glass of great brilliance which contains lead oxide. It was **George Ravenscroft** who, in the 1670s in England, attempted to produce a glass comparable with Venetian *cristallo* (see CRISTALLO). At first he added crushed flints but these caused a clouding of the glass (called crizzling) due to fine crazing so he then tried lead oxide. This lead crystal glass had a very high refractive index and so was exceptionally suited to cutting and polishing; it was also softer and less brittle than *cristallo*.

LEAF AND DART ORNAMENT: a classical form of decoration similar to egg and dart but where leaves replaced the ovoid form (see EGG AND DART ORNAMENT).

LIBRARY CHAIR: also known as a reading-chair, this design was introduced in the 18th century to be used in the library for reading and writing. The chair was of wood, generally upholstered and leather-covered. It was designed so that the reader could sit astride facing the back and rest his arms on the padded chair arms and back. Fitted with candle-holders, and trays to hold pens, etc., which swivelled out when needed, it had an adjustable board on which the book and writing-paper could be rested.

LIBRARY TABLE: in the 18th century especially, often a large flat-topped desk rather than a table, in pedestal design (see PEDESTAL DESK), containing drawers and decorated with classical motifs. Some library tables of rather later date were circular, fitted with drawers all round below the top.

Carved mahogany library table with brass mounts
*c.*1760

LIGHTS: the perpendicular divisions of a mullioned window, the space between the mullions (see MULLION). Lights are often subdivided into panes and when these small rectangular or diamond-shaped panes are set in lead strips, they are known as **leaded lights**.

LINCRUSTA: a particular type of heavily embossed wallpaper very fashionable in late-Victorian Britain and applied especially to dado surfaces (see DADO). Mr Walton, who first patented linoleum (see LINOLEUM), had by 1882 produced a thickening material made from oxidized oil and cork for embossing and finishing patterned wallpaper: he called his paper 'Lincrusta Walton'. As anyone who has tried to remove lincrusta from the walls of a Victorian house will testify, it is an almost indestructible material (especially when covered with subsequent layers of paint) of infinite wearing quality.

Linenfold panelling
*c.*1515

LINENFOLD PANELLING: carved decoration in wood panelling characteristic of the Tudor period (*c.*1490–1550) which represents, in each panel, a piece of material folded vertically.

LINOLEUM: the first satisfactorily easy-care floor covering which could be washed or polished. The Englishman **Frederick Walton** set up a factory in 1864 in Staines to make the first linoleum. This manufacture had a burlap base which was coated with a substance made from linseed oil, gum and resin to which coloured pigments were added. At first linoleum was of plain colour but soon a variety of patterns were being produced.

Linoleum continued to be manufactured up until about 1950 by which time it was increasingly being replaced by modern synthetic floor covering materials such as vinyl (see PLASTICS).

Stone lintel, wooden door

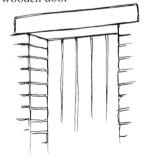

LINTEL: a horizontal stone slab or timber beam spanning an opening – for example, a door or window – and supporting the wall above it.

Carved oak
livery cupboard
c. 1500

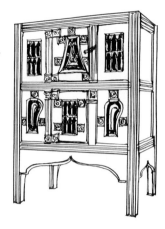

Mahogany
long-case
clock
c. 1775

LIVERY CUPBOARD: from the French *livrer*, 'to deliver up'. In the Middle Ages a cupboard which contained 'liveries', that is, the daily allowance of food and provisions to be dispensed to servants and retainers. Similar was a **dole cupboard** containing food to be doled out or distributed but, in this case, as a charity. In large medieval houses and castles such a dole cupboard stood in the great hall or the kitchen in order to provide food for travellers and the needy. The cupboards were of oak, simple in design, a decoratively carved feature being made of the necessity to include air holes for ventilation (see AMBRY).

LONG-CASE CLOCK: as the lantern (wall) clock was gradually improved and perfected to become a 30-hour, and later an 8-day, timepiece, so it became more difficult to hang the clock on the wall due to the heavier weights and, before long, the pendulum also (see CLOCK). To accommodate these and to enclose the movement and dial face, in order to protect them from dust, the wooden long case clock evolved. From about 1660 designs comprised a glass-fronted hood, a body which enclosed the weights and pendulum, and a base for the piece of furniture to stand upon. These clocks (see GRANDFATHER CLOCK) became important items of furniture and, according to period, the cases were often beautifully decorated with veneers, marquetry, japanning or carving (see JAPANNING, MARQUETRY, VENEER).

LONG GALLERY: an innovation in the design of Tudor houses, in general, from about 1560, and a customary feature for about a century (though a few examples are to be found which date from the 1670s as in, for instance, **Sudbury Hall** in Derbyshire). The purpose of the gallery was to provide an extensive, warmed and pleasant area indoors where children could play, ladies sew, chat or make music, and where people danced or played card games.

In an Elizabethan or Jacobean house the gallery was situated on the first or second floor and occupied the whole of one long elevation of the building. It was a long, narrow chamber, typically about 100 to 170 feet in length (30 to 50 metres) and 17 to 20 feet in width (5 to 6 metres). Windows were set along one long side and on both short sides, with fireplaces and doors along the other long side (see **5**, p. 21).

LOUNGE BATH: a full-length bath where the bather can recline in the water (see BATH).

LOUVRE: a structure on the roof of a medieval hall or kitchen to provide ventilation and allow smoke from a central hearth to escape. Some louvres were merely a simple arrangement of overlapping boards or slats with air vents; more elaborate designs were in the form of turrets or lanterns.

LOWBOY: from about 1620, a chest on stand, developing later into a chest or table with drawers.

LUCIFER: an early type of non-safety match so-named in 1831; the ancient name, meaning 'light-bringer', was used both for the morning star and for Satan, the fallen angel. The match was a flat stick of wood, the head of which had been dipped in a substance consisting of chlorate of potash and sulphide of antimony made into a paste with the addition of gum arabic and water. In order to obtain a flame the head had to be nipped in a fold of sandpaper. This type of match was invented in 1827 by **John Walker**, a pharmacist, who called it a **friction light**.

LUNETTE: a semicircular opening, window or panel generally to be found above a door.

LYE: an alkaline solution used for making soap at home before the days of inexpensive, easily available domestic soap for purchase (19th century). Lye was generally made at home by using a lye dropper. This was a wooden box with holes made in the bottom. A layer of brushwood was laid inside on this base and the box was filled up with wood ash. Water was then poured over the ashes and the resulting solution dripped through the box base into a tub which had been set under it. The process was repeated until the solution was strong enough. The lye was then boiled for many hours together with rendered-down animal fat from the kitchen in order to produce an odoriferous soft soap. Flower perfumes were added to make it pleasanter for toilet use.

LYRE-BACK CHAIR: an elegant design of the 18th-century neo-classical period (see NEO-CLASSICISM), where the back was carved in the shape of a lyre, the strings being of metal.

Painted iron lounge bath mid-Victorian

Kitchen louvre (Glastonbury Abbey) c. 1320

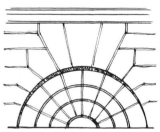

Lunette (Blenheim Palace) c. 1700

Lyre-back armchair c. 1775

Majolica
jug
*c.*1515

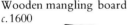

Wooden mangling board
*c.*1600

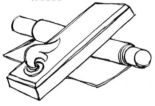

Mannerism:
flanking pilasters
(Bramshill House)
Jacobean

MAJOLICA: a tin-glazed earthenware. The addition of tin oxide renders a glaze white and opaque, so obscuring the colour of the clay. Knowledge of this tin-glazing was introduced into Spain by Moorish invaders and such ware was imported into Italy from Majorca (hence 'majolica') as early as the 13th century. Manufacture of this type of pottery (under the Italian name *maiolica*) was perfected in Italy during the 15th and 16th centuries, the opaque glaze providing an excellent ground to receive the gaily coloured painted decoration (see DELFTWARE, FAIENCE).

MANGLING BOARD: a method of pressing clothes before irons became available. The idea stemmed from Scandinavia and the Baltic region, the word deriving from the Middle High German *mangelen.* The mangling board was of wood, about 24 inches long and 3 or 4 inches wide (60 cm by 8 to 10 cm) and had a handle on top at one end. Still damp, the garments were rolled round a cylinder which was placed on a table top. The mangling board was pressed on to the roller, propelling it backwards and forwards across the table until the clothes were suitably flat. Surprisingly the method was very successful, so much so that it continued to be used in northern Europe until well into the 19th century; it was even exported by colonists to North America and South Africa.

MANNERISM: a term used specifically in relation to classical architecture where it may refer to a rigid form of academic classicism but is most commonly applied to structures whose architect has used classical forms and motifs in a manner different from that traditionally accepted. There are two principal examples of this type of interpretation: firstly, in England, the Elizabethan and Jacobean (see JACOBEAN) Renaissance domestic buildings where the orders, being imperfectly understood, were employed decoratively and incorrectly rather than structurally; and, secondly, in 16th-century Italy, the work of the great architects, notably **Michelangelo**, **Romano** and **Vasari**, who intentionally broke some classical rules in order to create a new and different effect (see CLASSICAL ARCHITECTURE, CLASSICAL ORDER).

MANTELPIECE: used as a synonym for chimneypiece (see CHIMNEYPIECE) but may also refer only to the mantelshelf or the fireplace framing.

MARQUETRY: a technique in the making of fine furniture which developed from veneering (see VENEER) and was particularly fashionable from the 1660s until the early 18th century. There was also a considerable 19th-century revival. In marquetry different coloured woods are cut into shapes to make patterns. There were three principal designs in vogue in England: seaweed, floral, arabesque. In all of these instances the design was drawn out on paper. Copies were made and these were pasted on to layers of veneer. The marquetry cutter then cut all of these layers simultaneously to the design shown. The patterns were fitted together and married into the ground veneer and the whole marquetry panel was then affixed to the carcase of the piece of furniture. More elaborate designs were obtained by introducing other materials into the marquetry veneer; these included ivory, mother-of-pearl, brass and pewter (see INLAY, PARQUETRY).

MECHANICAL SPIT: from the late 16th century various mechanical means were devised to turn a roasting spit in front of the kitchen fire (see BASKET SPIT, BOTTLE JACK, SMOKE JACK, SPIT, TURN-SPIT). These were known as **mechanical jacks**, the word 'jack' being generally applied to a contrivance which replaced human or animal labour. The mechanism functioned as a system of weights and gears. A weight was suspended by a cord which was wound by a handle round a cylinder. The power was transmitted via cog wheels to another cylinder and, by way of a pulley, to the spit. The grooved wheel at one end of this was turned as the weight descended under gravity. Such contrivances went by various names: gravity spits, clockwork spits, weight-driven spits.

MICROPROCESSOR CONTROL: see ELECTRONIC CONTROL OF DOMESTIC APPLIANCES

Table decorated with floral marquetry
c.1680

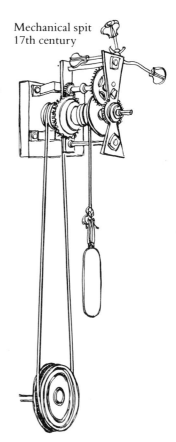

Mechanical spit
17th century

Philips' microwave 5000 with defrost feature 1981

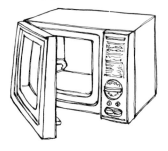

Carved and gilt pinewood mirror frame 1725

Rococo mirror with candleholders *c.* 1760

MICROWAVE OVEN: this is a different method of cooking from the traditional one where heat is directed at the food from an external source using wood, coal, gas or electricity. Microwave cooking makes use of very short radio waves, as short as 5 inches (12 cm) in length. These very high-frequency radio waves penetrate easily to the centre of the food and there raise its temperature. (In all forms of cooking the effect of heat is to raise the temperature of the food and so increase the agitation of its molecules.) Microwave cooking is very fast: five minutes for a jacket potato. Food may be defrosted equally fast: less than half an hour for a medium-sized chicken. There is thus a great saving in electricity and it is the food which is heated rather than the oven, the interior of which is easily kept clean.

It was during the Second World War that electronic devices were developed in Britain and America to generate these very short radio waves for use in radar. Soon afterwards, in the USA, the microwave cooker was manufactured, a way of cooking which was introduced into Britain in 1959.

MINSTRELS' GALLERY: in most medieval great halls there was a gallery from which people could look down upon the activities below and which, in many cases, gave access to smaller chambers at this level. The usual place for this gallery was over the screens passage at the opposite end of the hall from the dais (see DAIS, SCREENS PASSAGE). This was because the gallery was often used by performers and minstrels entertaining the diners, and the best view of them was from the dais where the lord of the manor, his family and guests were seated.

MIRRORS: wall mirrors were an important constituent in interior decorative schemes of the principal rooms of a house, especially during the later 17th and the 18th centuries. This was partly because of the attractiveness of their painted, carved or inlaid frames but also, importantly, because of their reflective contribution to the inadequate level of artificial illumination at the time (see CANDLE). Many mirror frames incorporated clusters of candleholders.

After the introduction of the making of plate glass in England in the early 17th century (see PLATE GLASS) larger mirrors of high quality were produced in the second half of the century at the **Duke** of **Buckingham**'s manufactory at **Vauxhall**. Before this, mirror glasses had been small and of poorer reflective quality.

The experimental discoveries by **Baron Justus von Liebig**, the German chemist, in 1835 of a new chemical method of depositing metallic silver upon glass led to a greatly improved process of silvering, incorporating a shellac coating and a backing of red lead. Before this the method of giving reflective properties to the glass was a lengthy one of coating with tinfoil amalgamated with mercury (see CHEVAL GLASS, PIER GLASS, TOILET GLASS).

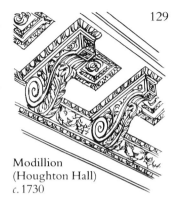

Modillion
(Houghton Hall)
*c.*1730

MODERATOR LAMP: see OIL LAMP.

MODILLION: in classical architecture one of a series of curved, decorative brackets supporting the upper mouldings of the cornice of the Corinthian and Composite Orders (see CLASSICAL ORDER).

MODULE: a unit of measurement by means of which the proportions of a building (or sections of it) may be measured. In classical architecture the diameter of a column at the base of its shaft was such a measure. Le Corbusier evolved a system derived from the proportions of the human figure. In the years since the Second World War a system of modular design has become accepted in modern building in which separate building parts have been standardized to an overall three-dimensional unit of measurement. This ensures the accurate fitting of all parts – bricks, doors, furniture, etc. – no matter where or by whom manufactured. In Britain the Modular Society was founded in 1953 to promote such a system of uniformity. The members come from all concerned with building: architects, craftsmen, clients.

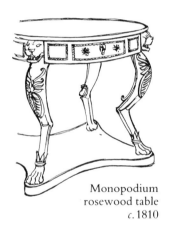

Monopodium
rosewood table
*c.*1810

MONOPODIUM: in furniture design a classical form which was especially fashionable in the later 18th and early 19th centuries when a table (or other piece) was supported by forms consisting of an animal's head and body terminating in a single leg and foot.

MORTISE (MORTICE):

1. In a joint the mortise is the cavity cut into one member to receive the tenon of the intersecting member (see PANEL-AND-FRAME CONSTRUCTION, TENON).

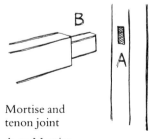

Mortise and
tenon joint

A = Mortise
B = Tenon

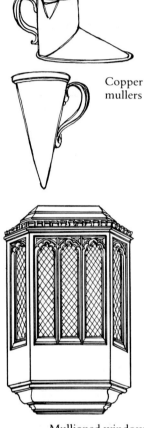

Copper
mullers

Mullioned window
c. 1530

Music
centre
1977

2.   In a lock the mortise type is fitted into a recess in the edge of the door, so cannot be removed without breaking the door.

MOSAIC: a decorative surface for walls and floors made by inlaying small cubes (in Latin, *tesserae*) of coloured stone, glass and marble. This hard-wearing surface was widely employed by the Romans and has been revived in later ages.

MOULDED GLASS: making a glass artefact by pouring the molten material into a mould has been carried out since early times (see GLASS). By the early 19th century such moulds were hinged and could be opened and closed quickly and so speed up production. Decoratively embossed, moulded glass articles were being manufactured by 1800. In the later years of the century machines were turning out bottles and containers of glass and, during the 20th century, such mechanization was gradually perfected and automated.

MUFF GLASS: see CYLINDER GLASS.

MULLER: a special warming device made of copper or iron in the shape of a slipper or a cone and with a handle attached. In cold weather ale or wine could be mulled in this. The liquid was mixed with sugar and spices, then heated over the fire. The slipper shape was most favoured as it could be stood in the hearth to keep warm.

MULLION: the moulded vertical member of wood or stone dividing the lights of a window (see LIGHTS).

MUNTIN: a vertical piece of timber in a framed door, panel or item of furniture. In a door it is usually the central upright which is so-called, the external ones being designated **stiles** (see DOOR).

MUSIC CENTRE: modern audio stereo equipment which combines in one instrument the means of playing recorded discs and recording and playing magnetic tape cassettes, and a radio.

N

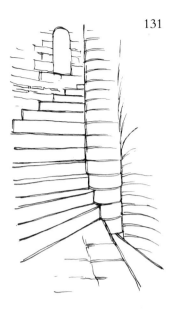

NEO-CLASSICISM: the fashionable style of architecture and decoration during the years 1760–90. Though still classical in theme, the work of these years was less rigidly based upon the model of ancient Greece and Rome promoted by the various textbooks published in European countries. From about 1750 there arose a desire by aristocratic patrons, architects and artists alike to travel and study 'on the spot'. This *in situ* research was carried out not only in northern Italy and Rome as hitherto, but also in southern Italy where new sites at Herculaneum, Pompeii and Paestum were opened up, and further afield in Greece, Dalmatia and the Middle East.

Stone newel staircase
12th-century castle

From this research and from new publications produced by such 'on the spot' study (**Robert Wood**'s *The Ruins of Palmyra*, or **Stuart** and **Revett**'s *Antiquities of Athens*, for instance), architects and craftsmen gained a richer, deeper understanding of antique classical building. From this they evolved their own designs, still eclectic yet no longer derivative copies but an interpretation more original and imaginative. The leading exponents of this in Britain were **Robert Adam** and **Sir William Chambers**.

NEWEL: the main posts at the angles of a staircase to which the string and handrail were fitted. In a **newel staircase** the post is a central pillar round which the steps of a spiral stair wind (see STAIRCASE).

NIGHT COMMODE, NIGHT STAND: see COMMODE.

NON-FERROUS METALS: those which do not contain iron (see IRON AND STEEL). A knowledge of working these metals dates from very early times, even antedating the mining of ores. Metals such as gold and copper were found on the surface of the earth's crust and only when supplies proved inadequate was mining of such ores undertaken.

Carved wood newels
(Ham House) 1638

Copper, tin and lead were all widely used in the home. Copper was mostly utilized as an alloy (see BRASS, BRONZE). Tin was also important as an alloy (see PEWTER) but even more so for plating other metals; this became an essential industry in the 19th century with the growth of the manufacture of cans for preserving food. Lead has long been of great importance in the building industry, notably for roofing and piping, where it was poured into moulds or, on boards, into sheets.

Gold- and silver-working were ancient crafts. These metals have for centuries been used to make artefacts of beauty as well as utility for the home. As time passed and these metals became more costly, new methods of deposition and plating were evolved in order to economize in the material (see ELECTROPLATING, MIRRORS, SHEFFIELD PLATE). During the 19th and 20th centuries many new metals have been discovered and produced and a wide range of uses have evolved for them in industries such as mining, oil drilling, electrical equipment, communications, radio and television. Such metals include platinum, nickel, cobalt, tungsten, uranium, molybdenum, cadmium, manganese. Aluminium is of particular application in the domestic field (see ALUMINIUM).

NON-STICK COATING: see PLASTICS.

Oculus in Baroque style
c. 1705

OCULUS: a round or oval window. A **bull's eye window**, in England also known as *oeil-de-bœuf*, is such a feature in which, generally, the glazing bars radiate from a circular centre.

OGEE: a form seen in window tracery and arches which is shaped in an 'S' double curve, one part convex, the other concave.

OILCLOTH: a fabric treated with oil and gum to make it water resistant. By 1803 an oiled canvas (often gaily patterned) was on the market and was widely used to cover table and dresser tops; it was waterproof and could easily be wiped over. A heavier version was available as a floor covering.

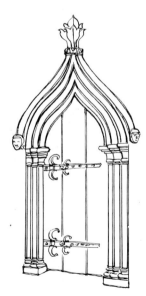

14th-century doorway with ogee-arched head

OIL LAMP: a very simple version consisting of a shallow bowl or shell in which a fibrous, burning wick floated in oil was in use from early times. Roman lamps designed to burn olive oil were of pottery or bronze. They were oval or circular, shallow, and moulded in two halves joined together so that the lamp was almost enclosed. There was a handle at one side and, at the other, a spout from which protruded a twisted flax wick. Some designs had several such apertures with their wicks burning simultaneously in order to give a higher level of illumination.

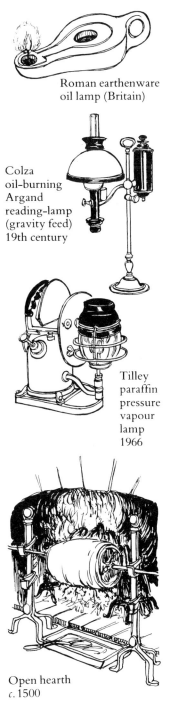

Roman earthenware oil lamp (Britain)

Colza oil-burning Argand reading-lamp (gravity feed) 19th century

For centuries after the departure of the Romans such simple oil lamps were an important means of providing artificial lighting at home. Some were of earthenware, many of iron or bronze. They were made to hang on the wall, to stand on a piece of furniture or to be carried in the hand. Animal and vegetable fats were burned: olive oil or rape seed oil (colza) derived from kale. By the late 18th century whale oil was in use, and in the 1860s, when paraffin became available, this gradually replaced other fuels.

The Argand burner was a great advance (see ARGAND BURNER). Further improvements followed this, notably the Carcel lamp of 1800 (see CARCEL LAMP) and the **Moderator Lamp** of 1836, patented by another Frenchman, which was similar but less expensive.

Modern oil lamps give a brighter light than earlier designs because the fuel is vaporized before it reaches the flame, by means of heat and pressure, and so wastes less energy. In a **Tilley Pressure Vapour Lamp**, for instance, methylated spirit-soaked pads are clipped to the centre tube and set alight. The control valve is opened and the fuel pumped up from the reservoir. Heat from the burning pads vaporizes the paraffin in the tube and the mantle ignites.

Tilley paraffin pressure vapour lamp 1966

OPEN HEARTH: for centuries cooking was done on the open hearth: that is, food was roasted in front of an open fire or was boiled and simmered in cauldrons supported over it (see ANDIRON, CHIMNEY-CRANE, FIRE-BACK, GRIDIRON, HASTENER, POSSET DOG, SPIT).

At first the fire burned on a stone or brick hearth set in the centre of the room, the smoke escaping through the roof above (see LOUVRE). During the Middle Ages the hearth was transferred to a wall fireplace with a chimney built into the wall and the smoke was directed upwards through chimney stacks above. As coal gradually replaced wood as a

Open hearth
c. 1500

Open well
staircase
with carved
panel balustrade
(Dunster Castle)
1681

fuel, various forms of grate were evolved to contain the fuel and to provide more efficient combustion (see BASKET GRATE, FIRE-GRATE, HOB GRATE) and more labour-saving methods were also developed to roast and grill the food (see BOTTLE JACK, MECHANICAL SPIT, SMOKE JACK, TOASTER, TRIVET).

It was not until the 19th century that the enclosed forms of kitchen range were sufficiently advanced in design to begin to replace the open hearth method of cooking (see KITCHEN RANGE) and this latter way survived in rural areas until well into the 20th century.

OPEN WELL STAIRCASE: one built so that the flights ascend the walls of a square well leaving an open space in the centre between the outer strings and newels (see STAIRCASE). In England the open well stair evolved from the Elizabethan dog-legged design (see DOG-LEGGED STAIR) and can be seen in the great houses of the Jacobean period of the early 17th century (see JACOBEAN), for example, at **Hatfield House**, Hertfordshire.

Oriel
window
(Bramshill
House)
c. 1610

ORIEL WINDOW: a projecting window, often very large, which is curved or poly-sided. Such a window, unlike a bay window (see BAY WINDOW), is situated on an upper floor and does not reach the ground but is carried on a corbel or bracket.

ORMOLU: a gilded bronze or brass employed extensively in decoration and mounts for furniture especially in the 18th century. The word derives from the French *or moulu*, literally 'ground-up gold', though the French themselves refer to ormolu as *bronze doré*. Neo-classical architects, notably Robert Adam, used ormolu more widely as an interior decorative material on, for instance white marble chimneypieces (at **Syon House**, Middlesex, for example) and for all forms of door furniture.

Ormolu now refers to an alloy of copper, zinc and tin which possesses the colouring of gold.

OTTOMAN: a generously upholstered and cushioned sofa or chair for sitting and reclining but usually having no back or arms: so-named in the later 18th century after the Turkish Empire of the time.

Mid-Victorian
buttoned ottoman

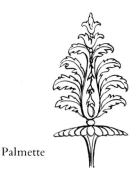

Palmette

PALLADIAN: a style of classical architecture named after the 16th-century Italian architect **Andrea Palladio**, whose buildings in the Veneto displayed a Renaissance interpretation of the symmetry and splendour of ancient Roman building. **Inigo Jones** introduced Palladianism into England in the early 17th century and this style of work was revived a century later to flourish in the country-house design of the years 1720–60 by such architects as William Kent and Colen Campbell. These houses are symmetrical and impressive, if austere, on the exterior but palatially and colourfully Roman within.

PALMETTE: a fan-shaped classical ornament resembling a palm leaf, also similar to honeysuckle (see ANTHEMION).

PAN CLOSET: see WATER CLOSET.

PANEL-AND-FRAME CONSTRUCTION: this type of construction was introduced into England during the 15th century from Flanders and was a great advance upon the earlier method of boarded wood covering which was fastened by nails or wood pegs. This method continued in use in rural districts until the 18th century but tended to warp as it was rigidly pinned.

In panel-and-frame construction the thin sheets of wood (the panels) were tapered on all four sides and fitted into narrow grooves in a framework of thicker vertical strips (stiles) and horizontal strips (rails) (see DOOR, MUNTIN, RAIL, STILE) and fastened by oak pegs. Such panelled construction was used to line walls, and to make doors and pieces of furniture such as chests, chairs, settles and buffets (see DOVETAIL, LINENFOLD PANELLING).

PANTRY (LARDER): a storeroom for food. Large houses from the Middle Ages onwards would possess more than one pantry to contain different types of food, for example, one for bread and another in which meat and game could be hung

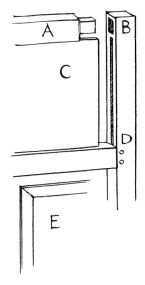

PANEL-AND-FRAME CONSTRUCTION

A = Rail with Tenon
B = Stile with Mortise
C = Panel
D = Wood Pegs
E = Back of Panel (with tapered edges)

Papier mâché tea table
decorated with gilding
and mother–of–pearl
*c.*1840–50

Papier mâché writing-cabinet
*c.*1850

Valor
paraffin
stove
*c.*1940

prior to cooking; there was also a butler's pantry to contain plate and a housemaid's pantry for cleaning materials. In the Victorian era the pantry was important even in smaller homes. It was usually a walk-in room in the basement with a stone floor and shelves of marble or stone to keep the food cool.

PAPIER MÂCHÉ: a material used to make furniture of prepared paper pulp, pressed and baked to produce a very hard substance. The process is an ancient one, originating in the Orient, but its European use stemmed, as its name suggests, from France, whence it was introduced into England in the 1670s.

A fine–quality papier mâché was produced in the 18th century from a method patented in 1772 by **Henry Clay** of Birmingham. In this process the sheets of paper were soaked in a mixture made up from resin, flour and glue, then were applied sheet by sheet to a moulded core, after which they were baked, sanded smooth and finally decorated and japanned.

Papier mâché furniture was especially fashionable in the early Victorian period up to the 1850s. The Clay method was still used; there was also a different process whereby the pulped paper was pressed between dies and then received many coats of varnish to produce a very hard material which could be turned, planed or filed. The article of furniture was then painted, gilded and, often, inlaid with mother-of-pearl and given a final coat of varnish.

PARAFFIN HEATING STOVES: such stoves began to be made from the 1860s when paraffin became available. They were particularly useful for many decades in rural areas where homes had no gas or electricity laid on. The 19th-century models were not very efficient and smelled unpleasant. The **Valor Oil Stove** of the 1920s was a marked improvement; in this the paraffin was contained in a removable brass vessel on which stood the wick holder. This became the traditional design of heater.

PARCEL GILT: partly gilded, as in silverware where only the interior surface of a cup or bowl has been treated.

PARQUETRY: a geometrical form of marquetry where the panel was composed of oyster veneer pieces of woods such as holly, box, laburnum or walnut arranged in geometrical patterns (see MARQUETRY, VENEER).

PARTICLE BOARD: a wood product made from chips and shreds of wood bonded under pressure with synthetic resin. **Chipboard** is a variety of this.

Patera *c.*1770

PATERA: an oval or circular decorative motif used in classical architecture and particularly in the neo-classical years of 1760–90 (see NEO-CLASSICISM).

PEDESTAL DESK: a flat-topped desk in which the top is supported upon a bank of drawers at each side (see LIBRARY TABLE).

PEDESTAL LAVATORY: see WATER CLOSET.

Pedestal table *c.*1830

PEDESTAL TABLE: one in which the top (usually round or oval) is carried on a single central pillar which often terminates in spreading or tripod feet.

PEDIMENT: the triangular feature in classical architecture which resembles the Gothic gable. It can be seen supported on classical entablatures or merely cornices over porticoes, doors and windows. In Renaissance and later classical building, pediments are sometimes **segmental** instead of triangular, and they may also be **open** or **broken**. These terms tend to be used indiscriminately to refer to a triangle which is incomplete at the apex or to a cornice which is not complete in the centre, as when its line is interrupted by a lunette window (see LUNETTE). In general, an open pediment more accurately describes the former design and a broken pediment the latter. A **scrolled pediment** is an open segmental design where the segments have scrolled terminations.

Open pediment

Broken pediment

Scrolled pediment

PELMET: a valance or structural fitting designed to conceal the curtain rails or pole above a window.

PEMBROKE TABLE: a small table fashionable from the 1770s. It had side flaps which, when open, were supported from beneath by brackets to give a rectangular or oval top. The table had four slender, tapering legs and a drawer in one

Pembroke table *c.*1790

Pendant
ceiling
decoration
1600

Edison Home
Phonograph
1896

Phosphorus
box
c. 1800

Carved
mahogany
pie-crust
table
c. 1760

side. Both **George Hepplewhite** and **Thomas Sheraton** designed such tables, generally of mahogany or satinwood with veneered or painted decoration.

PENDANT DECORATION: ornamentation which includes a drop or a drooping form, to be seen, for example, in the elongated boss terminations of medieval open timber roofs and Elizabethan and Jacobean plaster ceilings (see BOSS, PLASTERWORK).

PEWTER: an alloy of tin and lead which was used extensively to make domestic vessels and plate from the early Middle Ages onwards. High-quality pewter contained a greater proportion of tin as well as small quantities of copper and brass; from the early 17th century antimony or bismuth was also added.

PHONOGRAPH: a mechanism to record and reproduce sound, precursor of the gramophone, invented by the American **Thomas Alva Edison** in 1877. Edison's first 'talking machine', which he soon christened a phonograph, was a tinfoil-covered brass drum. On one side of this he fitted a recorder with mouthpiece, diaphragm and stylus, and on the other a reproducing apparatus. His first recording of 'Mary Had a Little Lamb' is only just distinguishable. It was the 1890s before reliable phonographs were manufactured commercially for home use and these soon became very popular. They had clockwork motors. There was a large horn for sound amplification, and the 'record' was a wax cylinder which played for two minutes.

PHOSPHORUS BOX: first made in 1786 in Paris, where it was called *le briquet phosphorique*, this box, which contained equipment to make a flame, was soon available in Britain. In it were a supply of sulphur-tipped matches, a bottle coated internally with phosphorus, and a cork. To obtain a light the match tips were inserted into the bottle to collect some phosphorus and were then rubbed on the cork; this friction generated enough heat to ignite the match.

PIANO NOBILE: an Italian Renaissance term meaning, literally, 'noble floor'. It was taken up generally in Europe (including Britain) to refer in such classical houses to the principal floor which was the first.★

★In American usage, the second.

PIECRUST EDGE: a descriptive term for the scalloped raised edge of a round-topped table fashionable in the mid-18th century (see p. 138).

PIER, PIER GLASS, PIER TABLE: a **pier** is a solid, single support and a **pier wall** the solid wall between two windows. A **pier glass** is, therefore, a mirror hanging on the wall between two windows; a **pier table** is similarly placed, often, especially in the 17th and 18th centuries, being set beneath a pier glass.

PILASTER: in classical architecture a column of rectangular form with low projection and engaged with a wall. Pilasters conform to the column design of their respective orders (see CLASSICAL ORDER, COLUMN).

PILLAR AND CLAW: the support of a tripod table terminating in three claw-and-ball feet (see TRIPOD TABLE) (see illustration, p. 140).

PIPKIN: an earthenware version of a skillet (see SKILLET) (see illustration, p. 140).

PLASTERBOARD: began to be used in quantity after the First World War as a replacement for lath and plaster ceiling surfaces due to a temporary shortage of plasterers. The plaster panels of this date were composed of a layer of gypsum plaster sandwiched between sheets of strong paper. As plasterers returned to work after demobilisation, so the use of plasterboard declined. When, once again, there arose a shortage of craftsmen after the Second World War, it reappeared. This time the shortage was more acute and the higher cost of labour made lath and plaster ceilings prohibitively expensive. Also the plasterboard product had been greatly improved, so until the advent of plastic products (see PLASTICS), it became the usual ceiling covering. The panels could be applied directly to brick and concrete surfaces and, with a backing of aluminium foil, provided good thermal insulation.

PLASTERWORK: during the 16th century the wood-boarded, beamed ceilings which had succeeded the open timber roofs of the earlier Middle Ages (see TIMBER TRUSSED ROOF) were themselves being replaced by decorative plaster ceilings. Elizabethan ceilings were decorated all over with ribbed designs, many of which were in pendant form (see PENDANT DECORATION); from the 1590s

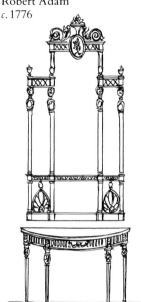

Pier glass and pier table   139
(Culzean Castle)
Robert Adam
c. 1776

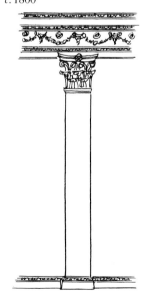

Pilaster
James Wyatt
c. 1800

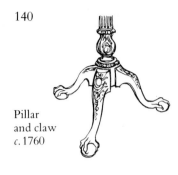

Pillar
and claw
c. 1760

Pipkin
c. 1600

Plaster ceiling roundel
1612

Rococo
plaster
wall
decoration
c. 1750

these tended more and more towards richly orna-mented strapwork patterns (see STRAPWORK), a fashion which lasted into the 1630s.

Since the Middle Ages the ordinary plaster used for interior work had been made from lime, sand and mortar with the addition of a variety of sub-stances to help bind the mixture and avoid crack-ing, for example, animal hair, dung and blood. (Gypsum plaster, that is, plaster of Paris, had been available but was very costly; see GESSO.) The ordinary plaster was not fine or malleable enough to be used for the ornamental ceilings, and Eliza-bethan craftsmen, who were designing their ceil-ings in Renaissance manner derived from pattern books from Europe, adopted the European form of plaster also. Italian craftsmen had for some time experimented with and perfected a type of plaster which had been used by the Romans. It was malleable, very fine and set extremely hard: they called it *stucco duro*. It contained lime and gypsum and, in addition, powdered marble. Craftsmen in 16th- and 17th-century England used stucco and, by trial and error, adapted it to their own prefer-ence by adding a variety of substances to the mix: ale, eggs, milk, beeswax.

Although the style of plaster decoration changed markedly over the centuries and, from the later 17th century, was used on the walls also, plaster remained the normal interior finish until com-paratively modern times. In all periods it was commonly coloured and gilded. In the 18th cen-tury, in particular, the very elaborate designs demanded a fine stucco and many patents for new, improved materials were granted: **Robert Adam** is especially noted for the importance he accorded to using the best stucco for his elegant neo-classical ceiling patterns. (For the trends in style, see illus-trations and text in the Introduction.) With factory production available in the 19th century, architects and builders tended to purchase their decorative motifs and mouldings by the yard and attach them to their ceilings and friezes. Walls were then usually wallpaper-covered (see PLASTERBOARD).

PLASTICS: it is difficult to think of any material which has changed life in the home as greatly as plastic; no room in the house has been unaffected by its myriad uses.

Plastics are not just a 20th-century phenomenon. The first plastics were derived from a number of natural substances – paper, wood, cotton fibre, for example – dissolved in certain acids. The first plastic was **Parkesine**, named after its originator **Alexander Parkes** and shown at the Great Exhibition of 1862. It was followed by **celluloid** and **casein** and, in 1907 in the USA, the first synthetic plastic, **Bakelite**. This was a trade name for a phenol resin patented by **Dr Baekeland**. It was a hard, shiny, dark brown or green material which became familiar in every home of the 1920s and 1930s. It was used for casing wireless sets and clocks, and for making stamped-out cigarette cases and ash trays, as well as a variety of other household articles.

All plastics are polymers: that is, their structure is like a chain of large molecules each of which is formed from smaller ones. The word 'plastic' comes from the Greek *plastikos*, 'something which may be moulded or shaped'. 'Polymer' also has a Greek source: *polus*, 'many', and *meros*, 'part'. This applies whether the polymer is a natural one as in Parkesine or synthetic as in Bakelite. Modern plastics are synthetic. They are made by a process of polymerization in which the small molecules are combined artificially into chains of longer ones. So, many of the long names of present-day plastics, prefixed by 'poly', tell us from which type of molecule they have been polymerized: for example, **polyvinylchloride (PVC)** from vinyl and chloride molecules. Nowadays most plastics are made from chemicals derived from oil or coal.

Though much of the early work on modern plastics was done in the 1930s, it is only since the Second World War that plastics have been produced in quantity. In manufacture, the material is heated to soften it, made into the desired shape, then cooled to harden. Many different methods are used for shaping: extrusion, spinning, spraying, rolling, injection, compression.

There are a considerable number of different plastics which are made into a tremendous variety of articles, furniture, furnishings and finishes. They possess different characteristics suited for specific purposes. Those in most common use are polyethylene (polythene), polystyrene, polyvinylchloride, polypropylene and polyester.

There are two chief types of **polyethylene**; the thinner version used in sheets to wrap and protect, and the heavier one made into bowls, buckets and dustbins. **Polystyrene** also comes in different versions. Probably the best-known are the two packaging materials, the clear transparent one made into food containers and the expanded one which is a lightweight foam product. **PVC (poly-**

Hand mirror, handle and backing of celluloid

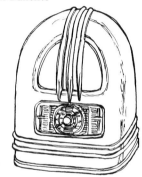

Wireless receiver case of Bakelite

Perspex cake-stand

Polystyrene cups and saucers

Vegetable rack made of polypropylene

Polypropylene moulded table

Chair shell of moulded polypropylene and non-woven nylon fabric

vinylchloride) in its different forms has a great variety of uses. In its rigid form (often just called vinyl) it is useful for all kinds of articles from piping for plumbing needs to gramophone discs, while the more flexible types are made into floor tiles, wallpaper and furnishing fabrics.

Polypropylene is a rigid thermoplastic which, due to its great resistance to liquids and solvents, is extensively manufactured into kitchenware. A great deal of unbreakable stainproof furniture is also made from it and this is especially useful in kitchens, bathrooms and nurseries. **Polyester** is widely employed as a furnishing fabric but, strengthened with fibreglass, is suitable for structural needs as well, for such fittings as water tanks. A most helpful cooking aid is **polytetrafluorethylene**, usually abbreviated to **PTFE**, which, because of its resistance to sunlight and moisture and its inertia to a wide range of chemicals, is used to give a non-stick coating to the insides of cookware.

PLATE GLASS: **Sir Robert Mansell** introduced the manufacture of plate glass in England in about 1620. This was made by the same method as **cylinder glass** (see CYLINDER GLASS) but to a greater thickness and of as pure materials as possible. It was then ground, using sand, to remove all unevenness and afterwards was polished, using rouge, in order to obtain a lustrous finish. Because of these factors plate glass was a luxury product, reserved for coach windows and mirrors. Indeed the name 'plate glass' seems to have derived from the latter as they were called 'looking-glass plates' (see MIRRORS).

The French evolved a more rapid system of making plate glass by casting and this was taken up in England in the 1770s. A new factory was built at St Helens in Lancashire and the huge casting hall there produced its first glass in 1776. In this process the molten glass was run directly on to a flat table where it was rolled out. Both sides of the glass lost their transparency due to contact with the table and roller so a long grinding and polishing process still had to be undertaken to restore the lustre.

During the 19th century more factories were built to supply the demand for large panes of window glass and mirrors from the increasing number of well-to-do house owners as well as factories and department stores. The casting method continued in use until 1923 after which plate glass was made by a continuous process called

rolled plate glass. In this the molten glass flowed down an inclined plane between two water-cooled rollers. Despite improvements in systems of grinding, polishing and annealing, plate glass continued to be expensive and it was only the introduction of the Pilkington **float glass process** which obviated the need for these time-consuming operations (see FLOAT GLASS).

PLINTH: in classical architecture the lowest member of the base of a pedestal or column. Also the projecting base or skirting of a wall (see DADO).

PLUG CLOSET: see WATER CLOSET.

PLYWOOD: a patent for plywood was taken out as early as 1840 and it was used during the 19th century as a substitute for solid wood. Made of an uneven number of thin sheets of wood glued together, the grain of each sheet being placed to run at right angles to the previous one, plywood has been greatly improved during the 20th century, partly due to the development of knife-cutting machines which can cut round a log to produce a continuous sheet, and partly, after 1945, to the introduction of synthetic resins for bonding purposes. Modern plywood is immensely strong and very lightweight. It can be bent into curved shapes so that one piece will form the back and seat of a chair or the sides and bottom of a drawer (see LAMINATED FURNITURE).

PODIUM: a continuous base or plinth.

POINTED ARCH: one of the chief characteristics of medieval architecture in northern Europe, including Britain (see GOTHIC ARCHITECTURE). The classical arch and the Norman (Romanesque) arch were both round structures (see SEMICIRCULAR ARCH). The pointed arch was not a new invention when it was adopted for the Early English stage of Gothic architecture; it had long been used in the Middle East and, by the 12th century, was also being constructed in Christian building in areas subject to North African influence, such as Spain and Sicily.

The pointed arch was adopted in early Gothic architecture because its greater flexibility in construction became the key to building structures suitable for the time. It was very difficult to roof the interiors of churches and monastic structures with stone using the semicircular arch, and the

143

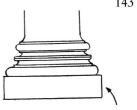

Plinth

Moulded plywood chair with metal legs, 1940

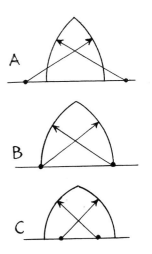

POINTED ARCH

A = Lancet
B = Equilateral
C = Obtuse

Mahogany pole screen with needlework panel *c.*1760

Polishing iron with convex sole 19th century

Chelsea soft-paste porcelain teapot *c.*1770

existing timber roof coverings were periodically devastated by fire. The difficulty in vaulting a church using only round arches stemmed from the fact that nave, choir and their aisles often had different heights and widths. Also vaulting is constructed in bays on columns or piers and the semicircular arch lends itself to a square bay. In a ribbed vault (see STONE VAULTING) the diagonals crossing the square were longer than the ribs connecting each side of the bay. It was therefore impossible for all the ribs to be of semicircular section. Either the vault had to be domical or the diagonal ribs segmental (see SEGMENTAL ARCH); alternatively the side arches had to be squeezed (see STILTED ARCH).

Because of these problems, few Norman buildings were stone vaulted. Empirically it was discovered that the pointed arch, which could be tall and narrow (lancet, see LANCET), medium (equilateral, see EQUILATERAL ARCH) or wide (obtuse), was ideally suited to vaulting at varied spans and heights. The French term for this arch, *arc brisé*, the 'broken arch', clearly illustrates its convenience.

POLE SCREEN: a fire-screen supported on a central pole and stand. Of particular importance in 18th- and 19th-century homes when the banner could be rectangular or circular, and with a stitchwork or painted design.

POLISHING IRON: an iron of the later 19th century which had a convex sole in order to provide increased pressure. It was used to glaze starched garments.

PORCELAIN: a hard, translucent ceramic material. The true, hard-paste porcelain was made in China as early as the 9th century AD (see CHINA) and for centuries was a prized import in Europe. It was called *porcellana* in 13th-century Italy because of its translucent resemblance to the sea shell of that name: in France this then became *porcelaine*.

This type of porcelain is made from a compound of kaolin, ball clay, felspar and silica: it is fired at a high temperature (1400°C or 2552°F). There were many attempts in the late 17th century to make such porcelain, and in 1710 the German chemist **Johann Böttger** of the **Meissen** manufactory near Dresden was successful. Böttger added ground alabaster or marble to the local white clay. French scientists from the State Manufactory at **Sèvres** near Paris achieved success in 1768, and in England

William Cookworthy experimented with Devon and Cornish clays.

Also in the 18th century a parallel line of research in England succeeded in producing an artificial or soft-paste porcelain. This contained powdered glass instead of felspar and was fired at a lower temperature (1100°C or 2012°F). Experiments with this soft-paste version had been carried out in 16th-century Florence and later in France. The English version was first made at **Stratford-le-Bow** in the 1740s and soon improved soft-paste porcelain was being manufactured at **Chelsea**, where bone-ash was added to the mix to make it harder and more translucent.

POSSER: also known as a **posset** or **vacuum clothes washer**, this was an aid to washing clothes. It consisted of a long wooden pole fitted at one end with a metal cone with holes in it. The posser was used to pound the washing up and down in the washtub, so driving the soapy water through the fabric to loosen the dirt (see DOLLY STICK).

POSSET DOG: a type of andiron fitted at the top with a cup-shaped container which was intended to hold a mug or bowl of a hot drink and keep it warm by the heat of the fire (see ANDIRON).

POTTERY: a generic name for all kinds of ware made from fired clay, but more specifically 'pottery' usually refers to softer, more porous wares which are fired at lower temperatures, then often painted and glazed. The term **'earthenware'** is generally used indiscriminately with 'pottery' but may also specify white or buff-coloured ware (see CERAMICS). For harder, more translucent ware fired at higher temperatures, see CHINA, PORCELAIN, STONEWARE.

PRESS: a term with more than one connotation. In articles of furniture the chief of these are:

1. **Clothes or linen press**
   A heavy wooden structure in use since Roman times to press washed household, table and personal linen, the size varying according to requirements. Larger presses were made with their own stands, smaller ones stood on a table; most designs incorporated drawers to contain the finished linen. A wooden turnscrew con-

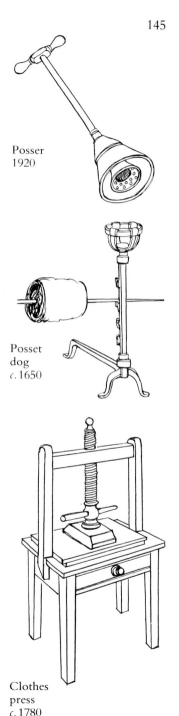

Posser
1920

Posset
dog
c.1650

Clothes
press
c.1780

Oak press cupboard *c.* 1640

trolled the pressure of two heavy smooth boards between which the linen was pressed.

2. Press cupboard
A dining-room cupboard used for containing linen and plate for serving at meals from the later 16th century onwards. The lower part had shelves enclosed by cupboard doors, the upper a recessed cupboard often splayed to allow shelf space for plate.

PRIE-DIEU: a kneeling- or praying-chair to be found in medieval homes and recurring in later periods, especially in the Gothic Revival years of the 19th century. Many examples survive from this time; they are upholstered low chairs with high T-shaped backs providing support for the arms while praying.

PRINCE OF WALES' FEATHERS: a motif composed of three ostrich plumes used in late-18th-century furniture, notably the backs of chairs designed by **George Hepplewhite**.

PUTTO: an Italian word for a sculptured or painted representation of a young child widely adopted to describe the babies depicted in Baroque architecture (see BAROQUE). In domestic design sculptured *putti* often form part of the pedimental groups over important doors and windows.

Prie-dieu chair *c.* 1850

Prince of Wales' feathers

Q

QUATREFOIL: see FOIL.

QUEEN ANNE: strictly, the furniture and interior decorative styles of the reign of Queen Anne, 1702–14, but design rarely changes in close accord with the accession and death of a monarch and the term is more generally used to cover the years from the late 17th century until about 1720.

Putti, James Gibbs, 1720

QUEEN'S WARE: the famous cream-coloured earthenware produced by the first **Josiah Wedgwood** and still available today. In 1762 Wedgwood presented a breakfast service in this ware to Queen Charlotte and with her patronage named it after her.

QUERN: simple equipment used in the home for centuries to grind grain for flour to make bread. From Roman times there were two chief types: the **saddle quern** which consisted of a large, slightly concave stone upon which the grain was placed, a smaller stone being rubbed across it by hand; and the later **rotary quern**, a handmill operated with a circular motion, which consisted of a hollow upper stone with a wooden handle, which fitted over a lower cone-shaped stone. When grain was poured in through a hole in the top of the upper stone, the handle was turned to grind the grain.

Queen's ware Wedgwood tureen 18th century

Saddle quern

Rotary quern

RADIO: during the First World War radio telephony was utilized militarily for sending messages from individual to individual but it was not until after 1918 that the possibilities of the medium for entertainment began to be realized. Britain was one of the pioneer countries and in 1920 set up a transmitter at Chelmsford to broadcast short daily programmes of news and music. Two years later, under the call sign 2LO, a business enterprise called the British Broadcasting Company began to transmit programmes from the Strand in London.

   After this expansion was rapid. The public took to wireless (it was not generally called radio until after 1945) with enthusiasm. The making and receiving of entertainment and news in the home had changed for ever. By 1927, when the British Broadcasting Corporation received its Royal Charter, the Post Office had issued over two million licences for sets which received programmes from a new high-powered transmitter at Daventry (see CRYSTAL SET).

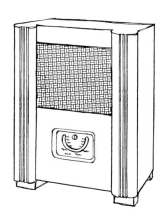

Murphy console 5-valve radio receiver 1934

Radiogram
1932

Refrigerating, wooden
steel-lined, insulated cabinet
1925

Electric refrigerator,
compressor and cooler on top
of cabinet, 1932

The years 1927–39 represented the 'golden age' of wireless; by 1939 licence-holders totalled nine million. During the Second World War it was the wireless which was of the greatest importance in keeping the British people informed in their own homes about what was happening at home and overseas; it provided a vivid auditory link between members of families separated over great distances by war (see also RADIOGRAM, TRANSISTOR RADIO RECEIVER, VHF RADIO RECEIVER).

RADIOGRAM: by the 1930s the popularity of both the wireless and the gramophone (see GRAMO-PHONE, RADIO) led to the manufacture of a combined instrument. Wireless receiving sets of the time contained valves and so were quite large pieces of equipment housed in a cabinet. The radiogram, which included both radio receiver and a turntable to play discs, was a free-standing piece of furniture, often quite expensively manufactured in quality woodwork and given pride of place in the living-room. Sophisticated improvements included automatic record-changing – a great advantage when, at 78 r.p.m., a recording of a symphony took up many discs. The radiogram was the progenitor of the music centre (see MUSIC CENTRE).

RAIL: a horizontal piece of timber in a panelled door (see DOOR), wall panelling or dado (see DADO, PANEL–AND–FRAME CONSTRUCTION).

REFRIGERATION: it had been understood since early times that fresh food would keep longer if the temperature could be lowered, so all natural means of cooling were employed. Ice-cellars were used by the Chinese as long ago as 1000 BC. The ancient Greeks and Romans put their food in earthenware dishes which stood in cold water; in northern Italy under the Roman Empire ice and snow were used to cool drinks and preserve food.

   In Britain from the Middle Ages onwards at large houses storage places were built to keep ice. This was collected in winter from rivers and lakes and stored underground. Many of these ice-houses, tunnelled into the ground and built over with brick, may be seen today in the grounds of such houses. By the mid-19th century, with an unprecedented growth in population and thus greatly increased demand, ice was imported from America and from Norway. Soon many kitchens possessed an ice-box. This was a wooden cabinet lined with metal or slate and insulated between the wood and the lining with one of a variety of substances: charcoal, asbestos, felt, cork, etc. Fresh ice was delivered daily. It was kept in the top of the cabinet while the food was stored below.

During the 19th century many efforts were made to lower the air temperature artificially which in later years were successful, both scientifically, in laboratory research, and empirically, in shipping fresh food long distances (e.g. lamb from Australasia to Europe). It was not, however, until the early 20th century that it became possible to manufacture a household refrigerator. The stimulus for such equipment came from America where the population was wealthier, and the climate more extreme. Early models appeared in 1913 and 1914.

With a more temperate climate Britain was later in the field. Several models were imported in the early 1920s; then in 1927 Electrolux set up a plant in Luton to make the model designed at their parent plant in Sweden. It was not until after 1945 that the 'fridge' really 'took off' in Britain and it was 1969 before 56% of the population had use of one. Also in the 1960s the idea of the separate home freezer achieving an even lower temperature than the 'fridge' became popular. Later, improvements were made to refrigerator design: better insulation, automatic defrosting, etc.

Modern combination fridge-freezer Hotpoint 1982

REGENCY: literally, the years of the Regency of George, Prince of Wales (later George IV), 1811–20; but in architecture, interior decoration and furniture, usually refers to a longer period when a specific classical style was paramount, that is, from the late 1780s until about 1830.

RELIEVING ARCH: one constructed above a load-bearing arch or lintel to relieve the load.

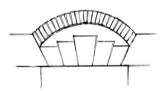

Brick relieving arch over stone lintel opening

RENAISSANCE: literally a rebirth and, in this case, a new flowering of the classical arts and architecture. The movement began as a turning away from the more rigid concepts of hierarchical medieval Christianity towards Humanism and sought means of expressing, first in literature, later in the visual arts, the world of ancient Rome.

The Renaissance began in 14th- and 15th-century Italy and gradually spread westwards. English interest in the movement was aroused in the 1520s and 1530s; it was delayed by insularity and by Henry VIII's break with the Roman Catholic Church. The decorative arts and archi-

The Queen's House, Greenwich 1616–35

Architect: Inigo Jones

Carved
mahogany
ribband-
back
chair
c. 1755

19th-century roasting range
Royal Pavilion, Brighton

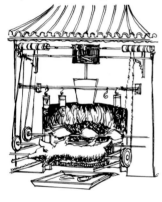

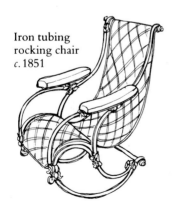

Iron tubing
rocking chair
c. 1851

tecture of England in the second half of the 16th century under Elizabeth I took on a Renaissance aspect but it was one based not on Italian sources, but on Flemish, German and French interpretations, and so was second- or third-hand. The results were not genuinely classical but were specifically English, full of vitality and interest if not truly Italianate.

The first buildings erected in Britain on true Italian Renaissance lines were those of **Inigo Jones** in the years 1620–50: the Banqueting Hall in Whitehall, and the Queen's House at Greenwich. He set the pattern for **May**, **Pratt**, and then **Sir Christopher Wren**, in a complete English flowering of the style.

RESTORATION: the return of the monarchy under Charles II in 1660; in decoration and furniture, more broadly, the years 1660–80.

RIBBAND-BACK: Rococo design of chair particularly associated with **Chippendale** mahogany chairs of the mid-18th century where the splat was carved to represent intertwined ribbons (see ROCOCO, SPLAT).

ROASTING RANGE: a very large open fire of the 18th and 19th centuries with an elaborate arrangement of roasting spits generally turned by means of a smoke jack (see SMOKE JACK, SPIT). Such ranges used great quantities of fuel so were only suitable for the kitchens of great houses and palaces, clubs and halls. A fine, well-known example is that in the Regency kitchen at the Royal Pavilion, Brighton.

ROCKING CHAIR: a traditional country chair with a curved base attached to the chair feet to enable it to be rocked backwards and forwards. Especially popular in Victorian England when many designs were made with bentwood frames; later in the century iron piping often replaced the wood (see BENTWOOD FURNITURE).

ROCOCO: from the French *rocaille coquille*, 'rockwork and shell'. A decorative art form fashionable in England from about 1740 to 1760 between the Palladian and neo-classical phases (see NEO-CLASSICISM, PALLADIAN). Rococo motifs were lively, delicate and curving (a late phase of Baroque, see BAROQUE); they included 'C' and 'S' scrolls, shells, flowers, ribbons and birds.

This decoration was found in stucco wall ornamentation, doorway and window heads, furniture and, especially, mirror frames and chimneypieces.

RUSHLIGHT: an inexpensive means of artificial lighting made at home, since Roman times, in dwellings where candles were too costly. Rushes were gathered, soaked, peeled, then dried in the sun. After this they were repeatedly dipped in melted animal fat from the greasepan (see CANDLE).

Good long rushlights, held in a metal holder, would burn for nearly an hour and needed no snuffing or trimming. In his *Natural History of Selbourne* (1775), Gilbert White says one pound (450 grammes) of dry rushes would provide a poor country family with 800 hours of artificial light.

Rushlight in iron holder

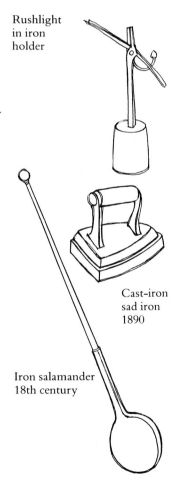

SAD IRON: a solid iron usually made entirely of cast iron; also known as a **smoothing** or **flat iron**. The term 'sad' is thought to derive from the medieval use of the word to mean solid or heavy. Sad irons were made in many sizes from quite small to very large; they were especially in use during the 19th century when a succession of irons was needed, some keeping hot on the kitchen range or laundry stove while one was in operation (see IRONING, KITCHEN RANGE, LAUNDRY STOVE). An iron or brass trivet was kept on the table or in the hearth on which to rest the hot iron while the garment fabric was being rearranged (see TRIVET).

Cast-iron sad iron 1890

SALAMANDER: a traditional means of browning food in use since medieval times. This was a long-handled implement attached to a slab of iron which was made red hot in the fire, then was held over the dish which required browning. The salamander remained in use until gas and electric grills made it obsolete.

Iron salamander 18th century

SALOON: in the 18th century the most important reception room in a large house.

SALT BOX: before the days of refrigeration (see REFRIGERATION) large quantities of salt were re-

Wooden
salt box

quired in the home for the preservation of fresh food so that it would keep as long as possible. Salt was taxed so it was a valuable commodity. It was stored in a box or jar near the hearth in order to keep it dry. Boxes were of wood with leather hinges to avoid rust. Often a cavity, closed with a door and called a **salt cupboard**, was made in the wall of the fireplace so that the heat of the fire would ensure dryness.

SAND GLASS: see CLOCK.

SASH WINDOW: a sash is a wooden frame for holding the window glazing which is made to slide up and down in vertical grooves. In these, sashes are controlled by cords and counterbalanced by weights. A **sash window** is a double hung sash; the cords are **sash lines**.

The sash window made its appearance in England from about 1685 and gradually replaced the casement design (see CASEMENT WINDOW). Early sashes had no weights so had to be wedged to keep them open. Panes became larger as time passed and wooden glazing bars slenderer; 18th-century designs are renowned for their fine proportions. With the greater area of glass available, Victorian sash windows often had no glazing bars but were made in two large panes.

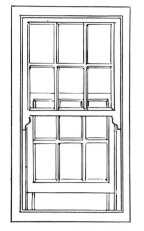

Sash window

SCAGLIOLA: a composition of gypsum, glue, isinglass and colouring made to imitate marble. This cheaper substance was very durable and took a high polish. It was known to the Romans but in England was especially utilized in 18th-century work where it may be seen in floor coverings (as, for example, in the richly coloured anteroom floor at Syon House, Middlesex), column veneers and decorative inlay in chimneypieces and table tops.

SCONCE: a metal wall-fitting comprising an ornamental back plate and a holder for one or more candles. Beautiful sconces, often in silver, were characteristic of 17th- and 18th-century light-fittings.

SCREENS PASSAGE: a passageway separated from the medieval great hall by a decorative wooden screen, above which was the gallery (see MINSTRELS' GALLERY), reached by a ladder or staircase. In many houses the front entrance gave ingress to the passage and the screen prevented draughts from this opening, as well as from the

Silver
wall
sconce
1755

doorways which led off the passage to the buttery, pantry, kitchen, etc., from reaching the hall. It also provided a covered way through which food could be brought into the hall (see **1**, p. 9).

SCROLL FOOT: a scroll termination in furniture design.

Scroll foot
*c.*1760

SCUFFLE OVEN: a common name for the simple brick ovens used over the centuries which were heated by burning wood on the oven floor, then raking it out and inserting the food to be baked. The ashes were 'scuffled' out on to the hearth floor.

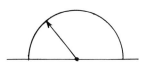

Segmental arch

SCULLERY: traditionally the smaller room adjoining the kitchen where the washing-up and many household chores were dealt with. In the 19th and earlier 20th centuries the scullery equipment would include a sink, a copper for boiling clothes, a plate rack, and vegetable containers.

SEGMENTAL ARCH: a round arch whose centre is below the springing line (see ARCH).

Semi-circular arch

SEMICIRCULAR ARCH: a round arch widely used in classical and Norman (Romanesque) architecture, where the centre is on the springing line so giving a rise and radius of equal dimensions (see ARCH).

SETTEE: an upholstered seat for two or more persons with back and arms, its design over the years closely related to that of chairs.

SETTLE: an older form of seating for more than one person, made entirely of wood.

Walnut settee
*c.*1720

SEWING-MACHINE: although the double-pointed needle with a central eye was patented as early as 1755, and the earliest sewing-machine in 1790 and although a number of machines were made in the following half century, notably in France and the USA, the real beginning of a means of sewing mechanically at home derived from **Isaac Merrit Singer**'s machine of 1851. Singer countered many of the drawbacks of earlier models and, though he and several others before long improved on his first one, it represented an important milestone.
The sewing-machine could not have come at a better time for in the 1850s the crinoline skirts were

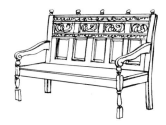

Carved oak settle
*c.*1645

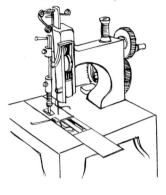

One of the first Singer sewing-machines, operated by treadle mechanism, 1851

approaching their apogee in popularity and sewing by hand the immense yardage of material together with its decorative trimming of flounces and ruffles presented an interminable task. It was of no less help in sewing the yards of flouncing, net and velvet which constituted the furnishing materials of the average Victorian home.

Since then all kinds of improvements have appeared: positive take-up (1872), reversible feed (1919), the electric machine (1889), zig-zag sewing (1947) and, now, microprocessor control.

SHAVING-TABLE: a small cabinet on legs, found in a gentleman's bedroom of the 18th and 19th centuries, which was fitted with drawers and a top which slid open to reveal a bowl, receptacles for shaving equipment and a mirror. The table was of a convenient height for the gentleman to be seated whilst shaving.

Singer family sewing-machine hand-operated, 1865

SHEET GLASS: an improved method of making cylinder glass (see CYLINDER GLASS), developed in Europe during the 18th century. Full-scale manufacture in Britain was delayed until the 1830s by the effects of a complex system of tax and excise duties on window glass but, by that time, sheet glass was being made in greater quantity than crown glass (see CROWN GLASS) for fenestration needs. Probably the best-known instance of its use was in supplying the 900,000 square feet of glass required for the Crystal Palace built to house the Great Exhibition in 1851.

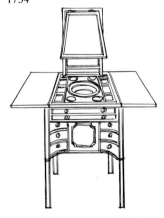

Chippendale shaving-table 1754

SHEFFIELD PLATE: a process of soldering a thin sheet of silver to a thicker one of copper, first discovered by **Thomas Bolsover**, a Sheffield cutler in 1742: he used it to coat buttons. A few years later **Joseph Hancock** realized the commercial possibilities of the method to supply householders who could not afford solid silver but who were attracted by the idea of replacing their more homely pewterware with silverplate. During the 1750s Hancock used the process to plate all kinds of ware from candlesticks to teapots.

Sheffield became the centre of production and the name adopted was **Old Sheffield Plate** though other manufacturers (for example, **Matthew Boulton** in Birmingham) were producing it elsewhere. Later in the 18th century pieces were silvered on both sides and plated wire was utilized to handle decorative surfaces. Powered machinery was designed to speed up the processes which made the ware much cheaper than the solid silver designs from which the plated articles derived. In the 1840s Sheffield Plate was gradually replaced by electroplating methods (see ELECTROPLATING).

SHIELD-BACK: a pattern of chair characteristic of the neo-classical period (see NEO-CLASSICISM), with a carved or upholstered back in the shape of a shield. Seen particularly in the designs of **Robert Adam** and **George Hepplewhite**.

SHOWER BATH: an apparatus of the second half of the 19th century consisting of a lounge or hip bath fitted with shower curtains and a tank shower unit above, carried on metal legs. A hand-pump operated the shower (see HIP BATH, LOUNGE BATH).

SIDEBOARD, SIDEBOARD TABLE, SIDE TABLE: the side table was in use from the early years of the 17th century, its design following fashion during the succeeding two centuries. Of various sizes, it was set against a wall and used especially in the dining-room as needed to hold silver or plate.

It was **Robert Adam** who initiated the idea of a sideboard table to fit between matching pedestal cupboards on each of which was mounted an urn. Adam's designs of the 1760s and 1770s were neo-classical, elegant in mahogany or satinwood, the restrained decoration in veneer or inlay, painting, gilt or metal mounts (see NEO-CLASSICISM).

In the Adam sideboard set, one of the pedestals was generally used as a plate warmer, the other as a cellaret (see CELLARET). The urns on top were metal-lined, one containing iced water for drinking, the other hot water for washing the silver (the great number of courses eaten at a meal made it necessary to do this in the dining-room). The table top was often fitted with a gallery at the back for supporting plates, and a knife box (see KNIFE BOX).

In the later 1780s **George Hepplewhite** and others combined Adam's three pieces into one item of furniture: a sideboard. Side pedestal cupboards flanked a central drawer. By the 19th century the sideboard had become a large piece of furniture and, in Victorian times, a heavily decorated one comprising a variety of cupboards, drawers, shelves and, often, incorporating a mirror(s).

SILL (CILL): the horizontal slab of timber or

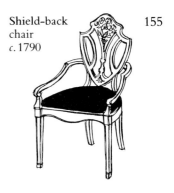

Shield-back chair
c. 1790

Shower bath
c. 1860

Adam sideboard
1775

Mahogany sideboard
c. 1795

Metal
skillet

Sleeve
iron

Slipper
bath

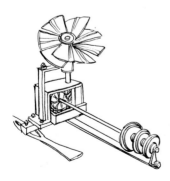

Smoke jack

stone set into the base of a window or doorway opening, and projecting outwards from the face of the wall in order to throw off rain-water.

SITZ BATH: a 19th-century shallow sitting bath in which the water only came up to the waist of the bather so that clothes could be retained on the top half of the body.

SKILLET: a cooking vessel which was the ancestor of the saucepan. Made of iron or brass it had a rounded bottom and a long handle, and stood on three legs.

SLEEVE IRON: a 19th-century long-handled iron designed to press the fabric of the complex sleeve designs of this time.

SLIPPER ALE WARMER: see MULLER.

SLIPPER BATH: also known as a **boot bath** because it was made of pieces of sheet metal joined together in the shape of a boot. When a bather sat in such a bath, only the head and shoulders were visible. It was a traditional design in use for many years as it was suited to family bathing in front of the fire, both warmth and modesty being retained. The bath was filled from the top opening and drained out from the toe.

SLIPWARE: an old, traditional method of decorating pottery by use of slip – clay mixed with water to produce a creamy liquid which can be painted or trailed across the surface of the ware to make simple patterns. Slip may be of the same colour as the pot or may be mixed with other shades (see CERAMICS).

SMOKE JACK: a method of turning a roasting spit powered by the control of the hot air rising up the chimney from the open fire; it was introduced into Britain from the Continent in the second half of the 18th century. At the point where the chimney narrowed to ascend the shaft, a vane was fixed horizontally so that the rising hot air caused it to revolve. This vane was connected to the power shaft by a system of gears and thence to chains which could turn simultaneously a set of spit wheels (see MECHANICAL SPIT, ROASTING RANGE, SPIT).

SNUFFERS: metal candle snuffers were in use

from medieval times and were generally kept near or were fitted to candlesticks and holders. There were two chief types: one shaped like an inverted funnel which was inserted over a lighted candle and extinguished the flame by cutting off the oxygen supply; the other, which trimmed the wick as well as extinguishing the flame, shaped like a pair of scissors with a box attached.

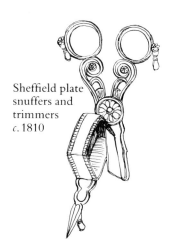

Sheffield plate snuffers and trimmers *c.*1810

SOFA: by the later 18th century the word was practically interchangeable with settee (see SETTEE) but, in general, sofas, which had developed from the Stuart day bed (see DAY BED), were made more for reclining than sitting. Many Regency and early Victorian sofas (see REGENCY) were of couch form, upholstered, with a low roll-over back and short curved legs; a roll cushion was placed at one or both ends.

SOFA TABLE: a larger version of the Pembroke table, from which it had developed (see PEMBROKE TABLE). The sofa table was very much a Regency and early Victorian design (see REGENCY). The top extended up to 5 or 6 feet (1.5 to 1.8 metres) in length when the flaps were up; these were supported on trestle ends connected by a stretcher or by brackets from a central pedestal with outward curving feet.

Regency sofa *c.*1820

SOLAR: a private room situated on the upper floor of a house which was intended, from the early Middle Ages, for the owner and his family to retire to, away from the noise and smoke in the hall below (see **2**, p. 11).

Regency sofa table *c.*1810

SOLAR CONTROL GLASS: window glass of this type is available in modern building to reduce excessive heat in the room from the sun and to protect furnishings from fading. There are two chief types of this tinted glass: in one a sun-reflecting coating is added to the glass surface in manufacture; the other is laminated and contains a treated inter-layer.

SPANDREL: the triangular-shaped area between the arch of a doorway, window or fireplace opening and the horizontal and vertical mouldings which surround it. Such an area may also occur in a staircase between the outer string and the floor and in a stone vaulted roof covering. Spandrels in stone and wood are usually decorated all over with carved ornament (see STAIRCASE, STONE VAULTING).

Carved wood spandrel 15th century

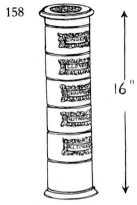

16"

Wooden spice cabinet
each compartment slotted
into the one below

SPICE CABINET: spices were important in past centuries to flavour food which had to be kept over long periods in imperfect conditions. They were imported and costly so were kept in locked boxes and cabinets, the key being held by the mistress of the house. Spices were stored whole, and ground only when needed.

SPIRIT IRON: one of the early forms of self-heating iron (see GAS IRON), which was manufactured from the 1850s and became in general use by the 1890s. Not unlike the charcoal-burning iron in appearance (see BOX IRON), the spirit iron had a row of air holes along both sides and at the back was fitted a tank for the methylated spirits fuel. From this a pipe led to the burner, the flow being controlled by a valve.

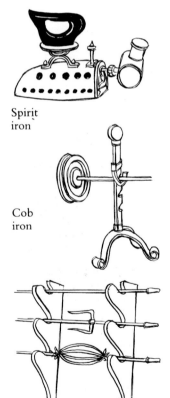

Spirit
iron

Cob
iron

Spit rack

SPIT: one of the earliest means devised by man of cooking meat, fowl and fish was by spearing it with a rod, supporting this on forked posts, then turning it in front of a fire. Roasting whole animals in this way took a long time and a steady, continuous rotation was essential for even cooking. At first the spit was a sharpened wooden stake but by Roman times it was made of iron. It was supported on iron posts and turned by hand. To make this easier the non-sharpened end was made into a handle.

During the Middle Ages improvements were made to this equipment. The iron supports were fitted with rests at intervals so that the level of a spit could be altered at will and several could be operated simultaneously, roasting large animals at the same time as fowl or fish. By the 15th century these spit rests were ratcheted and called **cob-irons** or **cobbards**. Reserve spits were kept in a wooden spit rack attached to the outward face of the chimneybreast, above the hearth. The open hearth spit continued in use until the development of the 19th-century kitchen range replaced its function (see BOTTLE JACK, KITCHEN RANGE, ROASTING RANGE).

As time passed, varied means of turning the spit were evolved (see MECHANICAL SPIT, SMOKE JACK, TURNSPIT). Apart from these traditional and well-tried methods, some more unusual means of motive power were experimented with. During the 18th and 19th centuries a few great houses employed water power (at Chatsworth, Derbyshire, for example) and in 1845 a patent was taken out for an electrically powered spit utilizing two magnets but, by this time, the days of the roasting spit (apart from rotisserie fittings in modern gas and electrical cookers) were almost over (see BASKET SPIT, HASTENER).

SPLAT: the vertical member in the centre of a chair back, its decoration often being an indicator of style and period.

SPRINGING: the point at which an arch or vaulting shaft rises (or springs) from its support. The **springing course** is the horizontal course of blocks from which the arch springs; the **springer** is the lowest block of the arch (see ARCH).

Decoratively carved walnut splat *c.*1710

STAIRCASE: during the Middle Ages many staircases were of the newel or spiral type, generally built into turrets or the thickness of stone-walled structures (see NEWEL). Alternatively there were stone stairs up the exterior of buildings or wood ladders inside, leading from one floor to another (see LADDER STAIR). By the 15th century straight, single-flight (see FLIGHT) staircases of wood were constructed inside the house.

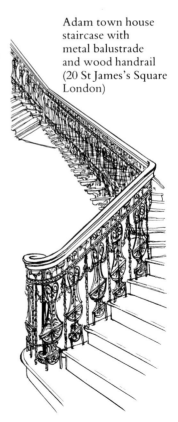

Adam town house staircase with metal balustrade and wood handrail (20 St James's Square London)

These types of simple stair continued to be built during the 16th century though, in Elizabethan times, with the construction of the larger great houses of the time, the **dog-legged** design was being introduced, followed early in the 17th century by the **open well staircase** (see DOG-LEGGED STAIR, OPEN WELL STAIRCASE). These 17th-century staircases were on the grand scale. They were made entirely of wood, usually oak, and were constructed with heavy, decoratively carved balusters, string and newels. The ornamental panel balustrades, carved elaborately in scrolls and foliage, were characteristic of the second half of the century (see BALUSTER, BALUSTRADE) (see **6**, p. 23).

18th-century and Regency staircases (see REGENCY) varied greatly in design and, in many instances, were very beautiful. All of a high level of craftsmanship, some were entirely of wood, generally mahogany, others had stone or marble steps, mahogany handrails and turned balusters (see TURNING) or wrought-iron balusters or balustrades. Some designs were in flights, others on a circular or elliptical plan, the steps cantilevered, one end built into the wall. Gothic Revival influences could be seen in many mid- and late-Victorian staircases where both wood and cast iron

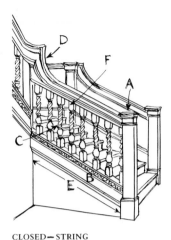

CLOSED – STRING
STAIRCASE c. 1680

A = Newel
B = String
C = Baluster
D = Handrail
E = Riser
F = Balustrade
G = Tread
H = Rise
I = Nosing

OPEN – STRING
STAIRCASE c. 1715

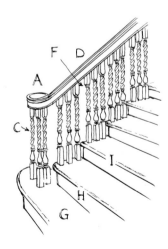

were widely used. In contrast to these elaborate staircases, and characteristic of the mid–20th-century idea of open-plan living at home, were the excessively plain stairs which had treads but no risers; such staircases often reverted to the spiral type with central newel. (See **10**, p. 33.)

The flights of most staircases are constructed with a balustrade, a string, steps and newels (see BALUSTER, BALUSTRADE, FLIGHT, NEWEL). The **rise** of a flight is its total height from bottom to top. Each step is composed of a **tread**, the horizontal surface; a **riser**, the vertical front part; the **nosing**, the rounded front edge of the tread projecting beyond the riser; and the **soffit**, the under-surface of the stair. The **string** is the inclined baulk of timber which supports the steps (see SPANDREL). A **closed-string stair** is one where the balusters, of equal length, stand on the sloping string. An **open-string stair** is one where the balusters stand directly upon the treads, two or three per tread, so that their height varies according to their position along the string (see CURTAIL STEP).

STEAM-OR-DRY IRON: while in use, emits jets of steam to dampen dry fabrics as needed: a 1950s innovation.

STEEL: contains more carbon than wrought iron but less than cast iron (see CAST IRON, IRON AND STEEL). Before the 19th century only very limited quantities of steel were made. From the 17th century the **cementation process** was utilized in which wrought-iron bars were sealed with charcoal in containers, then heated to a high temperature for a long time so that the iron would absorb some of the carbon from the charcoal. The **crucible method** was introduced into England in the 1740s by an instrument-maker, **Benjamin Huntsman**. This produced a better-quality steel with more uniform carbon content. It was similar to that made in and imported from India since Roman times. Huntsman re-melted cut-up pieces of cemented steel in closed crucibles.

It was **Henry Bessemer** in England who solved the then great problem of steel-making which was how could the impurities and excess carbon be removed more cheaply and quickly from the molten cast iron. In 1856 he designed his **converter**, a vessel in which a stream of air could be blown through the molten metal and so raise the temperature and save fuel. The converter was then tilted to pour the steel into ingots.

An alternative method was evolved in the 1860s in Germany by the **Siemens** brothers where a still higher temperature was achieved by converting the solid fuel (coal) into gas. This led to the **open-hearth** way of steel-making which, by 1900, had become the principal one and remained so until after 1945. It was then gradually superseded by the **oxygen lance process** in which pure oxygen is injected into the molten steel in the converter with a water-cooled lance. This and the **electric furnace system** are the chief modern methods of steel production.

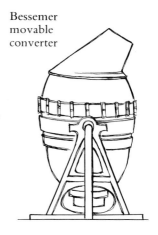

Bessemer movable converter

Steel is in great demand in the 20th century. In the modern domestic market, sheet steel is vital for the manufacture of home equipment such as cookers, refrigerators, kitchen units and washing-machines. A wide variety of **alloy steels** is also available wherein small quantities of other elements such as nickel, chromium, tungsten, etc., are added during manufacture to give the material special qualities, such as tensile strength, heat-resistance or a stainless finish. Two such domestic needs are the steel construction skeletons of tall blocks of flats, and stainless steel cutlery.

STILE: vertical members in wood-panelled construction (see DOOR, PANEL-AND-FRAME CONSTRUCTION).

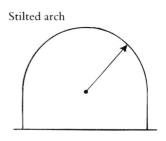

Stilted arch

STILTED ARCH: a round arch where the centre is above the springing line (see ARCH).

STONE VAULTING: an arched roofing made of stone over an interior. Such vaults were an essential characteristic of Gothic architecture in the Middle Ages and in the 19th-century revivals of the style but, due to the cost of construction and the large spaces requiring to be spanned, were more usual in ecclesiastical building (see GOTHIC ARCHITECTURE). In domestic architecture, however, certain interiors in large and important houses and castles were also vaulted, particularly chapels, undercrofts and entrance areas.

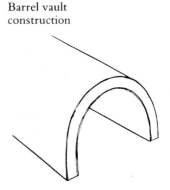

Barrel vault construction

Over the four hundred years in which Gothic architecture was the current style, the increased knowledge gained by experience enabled builders to construct even wider, higher and more complex vaults. The Romans and, later, the Normans had used the simplest style of vault, the **barrel** or cylindrical form. This is like a tunnel, semicircular

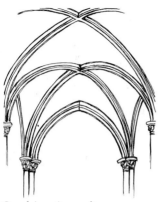

Quadripartite vault

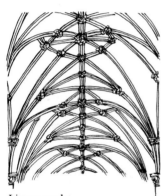

Lierne vault

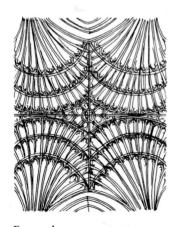

Fan vault

in section, supported on side walls. It is danger-ously unsuited to wide spans due to the immense thrust it maintains upon the walls.

With the development of pointed arch construction in the early Middle Ages (see POINTED ARCH), the **ribbed vault** evolved. During the building of such roofing a framework of stone ribs was supported upon wood centering; when the spaces between had been filled with stone panels it became self-supporting. Such a structure was much lighter and more flexible than a barrel vault.

The initial ribbed vaults were of **quadripartite** design, that is, the area was crossed by diagonal ribs making four compartments (see BOSS). During the early 14th century more complex patterns were constructed introducing intermediate ribs called **tiercerons**, which extended from the vault springing to the ridge rib (see SPRINGING) and, soon after this, the **lierne vault** was developed in which extra ribs (liernes) were introduced, crossing from rib to rib and making elaborate patterns.

In the last phase of Gothic architecture in the 15th century the **fan vault** appeared. It had evolved from the wish to build a vault which could accommodate ribs of different curvature as they sprang from the capital (see CAPITAL). The radiating ribs of a fan vault are of equal length and are bounded with a rib in the shape of a semi-circle. The whole group of ribs is in the form of an inverted concave cone. Lierne ribs cross the radiating ribs so producing a panelled surface.

STONEWARE: a harder, more durable ceramic material than earthenware, fired at a higher temperature (1300°C, 2372°F), and made from a purer clay, containing more silica and some felspar. It was manufactured as early as the 16th century in the German Rhineland, so it became known as **Cologne ware**.

First made in England in 1671 by **John Dwight** at the **Fulham Pottery** in London, before long it was being manufactured in Staffordshire and called 'stoneware'. It was salt-glazed, the salt being thrown into the kiln while firing was in progress.

It was in the 18th century that a number of improvements were introduced into the manufacture of stoneware, by then a staple Staffordshire product which was not expensive so could be used in many homes. A finer, light-coloured stoneware was made from about 1710, using a white-burning West Country clay mixed with grit and sand. By

1720 calcined flint was being added and this produced a still whiter ware and one which could be fired at a still higher temperature and so make a harder product.

In 1750 **Enoch Booth** introduced double firing: the pottery was first fired to the earthenware stage; then it was decorated and glazed, and fired once more. This method gradually eliminated salt-glazing and was more reliable. In 1762 the great potter **Josiah Wedgwood** produced his improved stoneware (Queen's Ware) which achieved immense popularity (see CERAMICS, CHINA, QUEEN'S WARE).

Slab-ended oak stool *c.* 1515

STOOL: until almost 1600 the usual seating accommodation consisted of stools, benches and settles (see CHAIR, SETTLE) and the term 'stool' was in general use to describe a seat for one person.

Turned oak joint stool *c.* 1660

The stool, a seat with no back or arms, was of ancient origin, used widely in the classical world and earlier. During the Middle Ages there were several designs, notably the folding **X-frame stool** with soft leather or cloth seat, the uncomfortable **triangular stool** with three legs connected by stretchers and a rush seat (see STRETCHER), and the wooden **slab-ended stool** with flat seat, carved side supports, and apron front and back. By the end of the 16th century the four-legged **joint** (joined) **stool** was replacing the medieval designs (see JOINERY). Its slightly splayed, turned legs were joined by an under-frame and ground-level stretchers.

From the 17th century onwards, despite the increase in the availability of chairs (see BACK STOOL, CHAIR), the stool continued in general use, its style reflecting that of other seating furniture of the time. **Upholstered stools** were soon introduced, also designs with carved stretchers and cabriole legs (see CABRIOLE LEG); and, in Regency times (see REGENCY), the X-frame pattern returned to fashion. There were also special-purpose stools such as the Victorian adjustable **piano stool**.

Mahogany X-frame stool *c.* 1800

STRAPWORK: a Renaissance surface decoration of Flemish origin composed of ornamented interlacing broad bands or straps, to be seen especially in Elizabethan and Jacobean England on ceilings, friezes, wood panelling and furniture (see JACOBEAN, RENAISSANCE) (see illustration overleaf, p. 164).

Gilded wood upholstered stool, *c.* 1775

Strapwork ceiling decoration
c. 1600

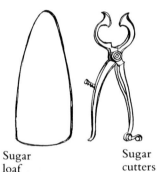

Sugar
loaf

Sugar
cutters

Sugar
grippers

Swag c. 1730

Festoon, 1795

STRETCHER: a plain or decoratively carved horizontal bar connecting the legs of a piece of furniture.

STUCCO: see PLASTERWORK.

SUGAR LOAF: until comparatively modern times sugar was purchased in a loaf: that is, in a solid conical shape weighing up to 14 pounds (6.3 kg) and measuring 1 to 3 feet (0.3 to 0.9 metre) in height. At the refinery the liquid sugar was poured into moulds to produce these 'loaves'. At home they were stored in cord cradles hanging from the kitchen ceiling. For cooking purposes the sugar was pounded into crystalline powder. For the table it had to be cut up into lumps and, for this purpose, **sugar grippers** were designed to hold the loaf and **sugar cutters** to chop it up. The cutters could be held in the hand like a pair of scissors; for larger quantities, a bigger cutter was available, mounted on a wooden block.

SWAG: an ornamental motif composed of draped fabric suspended from two points and hanging in a curve between: similar to a festoon, which is a floral decoration.

TABLE: during the Middle Ages and into the 16th century dining-tables were of trestle type, that is, heavy boards set up temporarily at meal-times on trestle feet. More settled social conditions in Tudor England were reflected by the use of the solid, joined table, its top permanently fixed to the under-framing and its legs connected by stretchers (see STRETCHER). In Elizabethan England these legs were of bulb form (see BULB). Very large heavy tables were still in use in the great hall, but with the establishment of the private family dining-chamber, smaller tables became more suitable, notably the draw table and the side table (see DRAW TABLE, SIDE TABLE). In the early 17th century came the gate-leg table (see GATE-LEG TABLE) which had evolved from the earlier designs with folding tops and pivoted supports; this was a useful design which has never gone out of fashion.

From 1650 onwards an increasingly wide range of tables became available: for cards, for sewing, for tea, for writing, for serving food. The style of legs, stretchers and tops as well as the wood and the decorative medium used followed the fashion of the other furniture of its day (see CARD TABLE, CABRIOLE LEG, CLAW-AND-BALL FOOT, CONSOLE TABLE, DRESSING-TABLE, GESSO, LIBRARY TABLE, MARQUETRY, PAPIER MÂCHÉ, PEDESTAL TABLE, PEMBROKE TABLE, PIECRUST EDGE, PIER TABLE, SCAGLIOLA, SHAVING-TABLE, SOFA TABLE, TOILET TABLE, TRIPOD TABLE, TURNING, VENEER, WORK TABLE).

TALLBOY: a chest-on-chest introduced about 1710; a style transported to the American Colonies where the chest was carried on a stand with drawers and was called a **highboy**.

TALLY IRON: the name is an English corruption of 'Italian' since the iron originated in Italy in the 16th century to heat and press the convolutions of the starched ruff. The iron, which is of metal, continued in use until the early 20th century for finishing frilled edges to garments. It consisted of one or more cigar-shaped barrels into which iron **poking** or **setting sticks** which had been heated in the fire, were inserted. The damp starched material was pressed around the hot barrels by the thumbs until dry.

TAMBOUR: in **furniture**, the flexible shutter of a roll-top desk or cupboard front running in grooves and made from thin strips of wood glued to a canvas backing; in **embroidery**, a circular frame of one wooden hoop fitting within another, holding taut between them material to be embroidered.

TAPESTRY: a handwoven patterned fabric widely used in pictorial form as wall hangings, and also to cover beds, tables and seating furniture from the Middle Ages onwards.

By the later 14th century wealthier households were importing large tapestries to hang on their walls. These tapestries were in great demand for their decorative colourful quality, and also because they made the large stone apartments much warmer. They were highly valued and were

Walnut veneered tallboy 165
c.1735

Tally iron

Secretaire with tambour front
c.1800

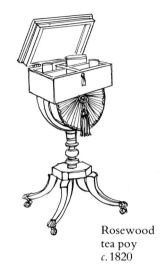

Rosewood
tea poy
c. 1820

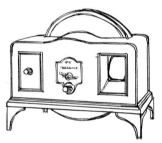

Baird televisor, 1930

Super emitron
electronic television
camera tube first used
at Lord Mayor's Show of 1937

carried around the country in great chests as the family travelled.

At first, tapestries were imported from Arras or Paris but by the 15th century centres of production had been set up in Norwich and London. In 1619 a factory was established by Sir Francis Crane, with royal patronage, at Mortlake. The tapestries made here (until production ceased during the Civil War) were costly but famous for their quality.

TEA POY: a small table containing tea-making equipment, fashionable during the 19th century.

TELEVISION: the broadcasting through space by electrical means of visual images which are then received and displayed on a screen in the family living-room is an apparent miracle now accepted as an essential part of life. Technology was not sufficiently advanced to make television broadcasting possible before the 1920s but attempts to send line-drawn pictures by means of an electric-telegraphy method began before 1850. Then in 1873 **Willoughby Smith** in Britain made the first study of photoconductivity and discovered the light-sensitive properties of selenium which becomes a better conductor of electricity when it is exposed to light. This led to research by scientists in several countries to try to utilize this discovery for the transmission of pictures by means of scanning an image in order to break it down into a sequence of tiny pictorial elements.

Before the First World War two different methods of scanning were experimented with, one mechanical, the other electrical. The best mechanical scanner first devised was by the German **Paul Nipkow** in 1884. This was a disc with holes arranged spirally near its edge. When it was rotated a beam of light was directed through the holes at the scene to be transmitted. A battery-operated photoconductive (selenium) cell was used to transmit the scene in the form of electrical impulses. It was this method which was adopted after the War by the Scotsman **John Logie Baird** and in 1925 he devised a transmitter which he demonstrated at the Royal Institution the following year. The improvements which he then made to his receiving and transmitting equipment encouraged the BBC to begin an experimental service of 5½ hours a week transmission from the Baird Television Company in 1929. Baird's system was still being used by the BBC in 1937 but was then abandoned because, despite the incorporation of more light-sensitive cells and other improvements, the mechanical scanning method gave pictures which were too poorly defined.

It was the electrical method of scanning which proved the most successful one and it was the Russian scientist **Boris Rosing** who suggested as early as 1907 that the cathode ray tube, work on which had been initiated by **Sir William Crookes** in England in 1879, and which had been perfected in Germany by **Karl Braun** in 1897, might be used to reproduce a picture in the receiver. The idea was soon taken up by the English scientist **Alan Campbell-Swinton** who proposed using the tube for both transmitting and receiving.

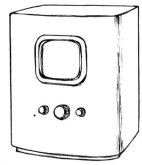

Ekco television receiver 1938

After the First World War it was the Russian emigré electronics engineer **Vladimir Zworykin**, earlier a pupil of Rosing in St Petersburg, who achieved the important breakthrough in electrical scanning. In America in 1923 he invented the iconoscope; this became the first practical transmitting device to televise studio and outdoor scenes at a high standard of definition. In 1929 he produced the first satisfactory tube for television reception. Since then the technology of television has advanced steadily and greatly by the stages of the emitron electronic television camera (Britain), the orthicon in 1939 (an American advance on the iconoscope), the 1949 vidicon photoconductive tube (also American) and the Dutch plumbicon of the 1960s, a tube particularly suited to colour broadcasting.

Philips portable television receiver with built-in radio, cassette recorder and digital alarm clock 1979

The BBC began transmission of the first regular public television service in the world in 1936 from Alexandra Palace. After closure, for security reasons, during the Second World War, the service recommenced in 1946. By 1955 there were 4,500,000 licence-holders and both commercial television and colour television began to be transmitted. The launching of artificial earth satellites from 1965 has led to world-wide live transmission of high-definition television (see also VIDEO-RECORDING, VIEWDATA TRANSMISSION).

TENON: the projection fashioned on a piece of wood (or other material) to fit into the cavity of a mortise and tenon joint (see MORTISE, PANEL-AND-FRAME CONSTRUCTION).

TENT BED: a 19th-century design, less costly than the more elaborate four-post tester bedstead,

Tent style of bed (also known as a crown or Polonaise design) iron frame c. 1855

Paraffin-burning tilley iron
*c.*1940

Cruck construction

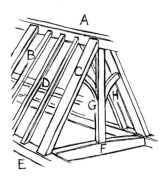

TIMBER TRUSSED ROOF

A = Ridge-piece
B = Rafter
C = Principal Rafter
D = Purlin
E = Wall Plate
F = Tie Beam
G = King Post
H = Brace

in which a metal frame supported the canopy curtains. So-called because when these were drawn the bed resembled a tent (see FOUR-POSTER BED, TESTER).

TERRACOTTA: a fired earthenware material introduced from Italy in the 16th century for moulded decorative work on buildings. Terracotta is harder and less porous than brick and its mix includes grog, that is, previously fired earthenware ground to a powder. The word derives from the Latin *terra cocta*, 'cooked earth'.

TESTER: canopy of wood or material over a bedstead (see FOUR-POSTER BED, HALF-TESTER).

TILLEY IRON: a self-heating iron fuelled by petrol or paraffin used mainly during the years 1920–40.

TIMBER TRUSSED ROOF: until the late 16th century such open timber roofs covered the large apartments of both churches and houses: the trussed roof was the equivalent in wood to the vault of stone (see STONE VAULTING, TRUSS). The earliest type of construction was by use of **crucks**. In this type of building the interior was divided into bays, each bay being about 12 to 16 feet wide (3.5 to 4.75 metres). The crucks, which marked the bays, were immense tree trunks bent over and shaped to meet at the top in a gable where they supported a ridge pole running horizontally along the apex of the roof. Smaller timbers helped to hold up the roofing of thatch or wood shingles.

Cruck structures were common in Saxon and Norman England and the method continued in use for smaller homes until the late Middle Ages. But the interiors lacked headroom as walls and roof were of one curved form, and gradually a more advanced roof structure evolved for the main rooms of larger homes, such as the great hall and solar (see SOLAR). There was a considerable variety of designs and, as the centuries passed, these became more elaborate (see **1**, p. 9; **2**, p. 11).

In general, the medieval roof was gabled at each end, with a fairly steep pitch. A long beam, the **ridge** (ridge piece), extended horizontally along it from one end of the hall to the other, and further beams, called **purlins**, were set at intervals parallel to it, down the pitch from apex to wall, where a timber called a **wall plate** was laid along the top of the wall. It was secured by stone corbels. At right angles to these timbers were laid the rafters set at the bottom on to the wall plate and at the top into the ridge. At intervals, marking the bays, were heavier timbers called **principal rafters**; between were slenderer **common rafters**.

One of the simplest structures utilized a **tie beam**. This was a massive beam thrown across the apartment at wall-plate level to counteract the outward thrust of the roof on the walls. It was pinned to the wall plates and often curved slightly upwards in the centre. On this tie beam was usually set a vertical post or posts to strengthen the structure. The **king post** design had one central post rising from tie beam to ridge. **Queen posts** were in pairs and supported the principal rafters. **Collar beams** were like tie beams but set higher up in the roof above wall-plate level. There were many structures of collar-beam type as in, for example, **crown post roofs (see** COLLAR BEAM, CROWN POST). Straight **struts** and curved **arch braces** were introduced as needed for reinforcement (see ARCH BRACE). **Coupled roofs** were constructed without tie or collar beams. They gave better visibility and enhanced the lofty appearance of the roof.

The later, more complex phase was represented by the **hammerbeam roof** which evolved at the end of the 14th century (see HAMMER BEAM). The **hammer beams** were like abbreviated tie beams; extended at wall-plate level, they were supported from corbels by means of arch-braced wall posts, and both corbels and the beam ends were often decoratively carved into figures or animals. The shorter hammer beams gave better visibility than the tie beams and reduced lateral pressure. The vertical **hammer posts** rose from the inner end of the hammer beams to a collar beam above, which joined the purlins. The whole roof was gilded and painted and often decoratively carved. In a **double-hammerbeam roof** there were two sets of hammer beams and posts, one above the other. The whole system of timbers (the **truss**) was tenoned and pinned to provide a stable structure to resist all thrusts.

TINDER BOX, TINDER PISTOL: from Roman times in Britain the traditional way to start a fire was by means of flint, steel and tinder, and for centuries the **tinder box** continued to be the staple means of creating a light. It was a metal or wooden box kept ready and containing a steel, dry 'tinder' of cotton or linen rags, and a hard stone flint. It was

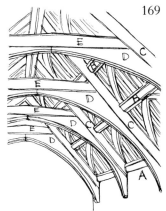

COLLAR BEAM ROOF

A = Wall Plate
B = Purlin
C = Principal Rafters
D = Arch Brace
E = Collar Beam

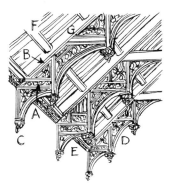

DOUBLE HAMMERBEAM ROOF
A = Hammer Beam
B = Hammer Post
C = Corbel
D = Arch Brace
E = Wall Plate
F = Purlin
G = Principal Rafter

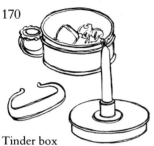

Tinder box
containing flint and tinder,
and shaped steel;
fitted with
lid with candle

Tinder pistol *c.* 1820

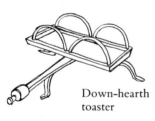

Down-hearth
toaster

Standing
toaster

not easy to make a spark to ignite the tinder; the sharpened flint (later known as a **strike-a-light**) had to strike the steel hard enough to pare a minute fragment from it, so making it very hot. As this fragment fell in the tinder, it smouldered and had to be coaxed into flame. Small wonder that once a fire had been lit, it was carefully kept burning (see CURFEW).

In later centuries tinder boxes were equipped with a candle and snuffer in the lid and a supply of home-produced sulphur matches.

In the 17th century the **tinder pistol** was produced, based on the flint-lock pistol. In this a small charge of gunpowder was ignited when triggered and this lit the tinder. 18th-century designs usually made the spark by means of flint and steel. However, these pistols and the various distinctly dangerous, chemical methods of making a flame which were devised in the late 18th and early 19th centuries, were not inexpensive and, for most people, the tinder box continued to be the only valid way until matches became readily available and reasonably cheap in the second half of the 19th century.

TOASTER: from medieval times a variety of designs of toasting-equipment evolved for use with the open fire. These were intended for toasting bread and slices of meat or cheese. Apart from the traditional hand-held **toasting-fork**, there was the **standing toaster** set in front of the fire which had adjustable attachments to raise or lower the prongs as required. Some toasters were designed to clip on to the fire-bars. The small **down-hearth toaster** was set on the floor of the hearth; this was a flat metal platform on short legs which was fitted with hoops at the sides to hold the slices of food. It also had a long handle so that it could be turned at different angles to the fire without burning the operator. Such toasting equipment continued in use until well into the 20th century when replaced by oven grills and the electric toaster.

The 1920 **electric toaster** had three heating elements made of sheets of mica wound with wire. It was not earthed electrically. A slice of bread was held in place by spring-loading and had to be turned by hand in order to toast its other side. By 1923 a more advanced design would turn the slices for you. Nowadays the bread is toasted on both sides at once and pops up when ready (see ELECTRONIC CONTROL OF DOMESTIC APPLIANCES).

TOILET GLASS, SET, TABLE: the word 'toilet' was originally used to refer to the often rich and elaborate cloth which covered the **toilet table** (see DRESSING-TABLE). By the later 17th century the word came to be used to describe the articles upon the table which made up the **toilet set**: perfume bottles, cosmetic boxes and bowls, combs. There was also a matching **toilet glass** supported on a strut or hung on a stand.

TORCHÈRE: a tall ornamental candlestand.

TRACERY: the design of the carved stone mouldings extending upwards from the mullions in a Gothic window head (see GOTHIC ARCHI-TECTURE, MULLION, POINTED ARCH).

Tracery appeared early in the development of Gothic architecture. The need evolved from the idea of grouping two or more lights under one arch head (see LIGHTS, LANCET). This created a space above, the spandrel (see SPANDREL), which presented an awkward feature of design. To resolve this problem the space was carved into foiled circular shapes (see FOIL). These were pierced, so creating the earliest form of tracery: **plate tracery**, in which stone-infilling occupied a larger area than the window glass.

After the mid 13th century **bar tracery** began to develop from the plate form. In this type of work the stonework was narrower, in 'bars', and the area of glass much greater. The window area also became larger and the head was encompassed by an equilateral rather than lancet arch (see EQUILATERAL ARCH). The window was divided by several mullions giving three, five, seven or even nine lights and the tracery design became still more complex. At first the pattern was geometrical, based on circles, trefoils and quatrefoils (**geometric tracery**); then, in the 14th century, there were introduced flowing, flame-like shapes based on the ogee form (see OGEE), called **curvilinear tracery**. A variation on this was **reticulated tracery** where the design was made up solely of circles which formed ogee shapes at top and bottom, so creating a net design. There was also **intersecting tracery** in which the mullions extended in curves to the head of the arch crossing one another *en route*.

The last phase of tracery design came in Perpendicular Gothic work in which window design followed the pattern of panelling seen then in wall and vault treatment. Windows were so

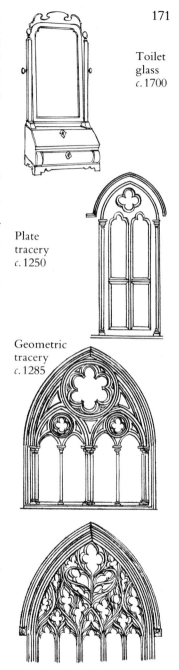

Toilet glass c. 1700

Plate tracery c. 1250

Geometric tracery c. 1285

Curvilinear tracery c. 1350

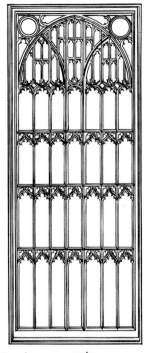

Panel tracery, 1510

divided by mullions and transoms (see TRANSOM) to create **rectilinear** or **panel tracery**. The proportion of the window was also often wider than before, its head enclosed by the flatter, four-centred arch (see FOUR-CENTRED ARCH).

TRAFALGAR CHAIR: a design of the Regency period (see REGENCY) named after the naval battle of 1805. It was generally characterized by a rope moulding on the top rail, anchor and dolphin motifs, curved (sabre) front legs and a cane seat and back panel.

TRANSISTOR RADIO RECEIVER: the invention and development of the transistor in the Bell Telephone Laboratories in the USA during the years 1948–51 led to a revolution in the design of radio receivers. A transistor is a tiny electronic amplifying device made from a semiconductor material such as silicon. Its use gradually replaced the much larger thermionic valve and made possible the miniaturization of receivers. The first transistor receivers were introduced into Britain in 1956. They soon became popular as they were portable, efficient and, as they operated at a low voltage, were suited to battery powering. Transistors in modern integrated circuits can make the receiver even smaller.

Trafalgar chair
c. 1815

TRANSOM: the horizontal bar(s) dividing a window into lights (see LIGHTS, MULLION).

TREFOIL: see FOIL.

TRIPOD TABLE: a design with three legs, most commonly turning outwards from a central pedestal.

TRIVET: a traditional three-legged pot stand used over the centuries in conjunction with the open fire or kitchen range. Trivets were made of metal, usually iron, steel or brass, and many had wooden handles. They were manufactured in a wide variety of sizes and designs. Some, for keeping food hot, were small, only 5 or 6 inches high (12 to 15 cm). Others might be 3 or 4 feet tall (0.9 to 1.2 metres) and incorporate a toasting device (see TOASTER). A 'cat' trivet was made with six spokes extending from a central ball, three above

Tripod table
c. 1750

and three below; it was so-called as it could be used either way up so 'always fell on its feet'.

TRUSS: a self-supporting framework of wood or iron constructed to cover a space or form a bracket (see TIMBER TRUSSED ROOF).

TUBULAR METAL FURNITURE: hollow metal tubing of japanned iron or of brass was used in furniture-making in Britain as early as the 1830s and in the second half of the century manufacture of rocking chairs (see ROCKING CHAIR) and bed-steads using these materials was widespread. In the early 1920s Continental designers were experimenting with bent tubular steel for various types of furniture, notably chairs and tables (see CHAIR); later, such steel was chromium plated. Alternatively aluminium was used because of its light weight.

TUDOR ARCH: see FOUR-CENTRED ARCH.

TUDOR FLOWER: a formalized foliar ornament of diamond shape used especially for parapets and cresting during the years from 1480–1540.

TUFTED CARPET: a carpet with a long, shag pile based on the weave of a candlewick bedspread; an idea originating in the USA. By 1950 machines to make such carpets had been developed and in Britain it is since the decade 1950–60 that such hard-wearing, easy-care carpets have become popular. In most manufactures the tufts are attached by an adhesive and the carpet is backed by polyurethane foam.

TUNBRIDGE WARE: a decorative wood ware made from the 17th to the early 20th century in the area of Tunbridge Wells in Kent. In the 17th and 18th centuries many kinds of decorative means were used – marquetry, painting, japanning (see JAPANNING, MARQUETRY) – but from about 1800 onwards the ware was mainly ornamented with cube forms of different coloured hard woods. The mosaic pattern was made by glueing together lengths of cube-sectioned different woods, then sawing these into thin sheets and applying them as a veneer. Examples of Tunbridge ware are usually small pieces of furniture or decorative articles as these are most suited to this process.

Brass 'cat' trivet

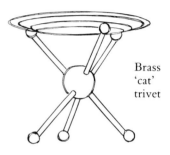

Tubular steel armchair 1929

Tudor flower ornament
c. 1500

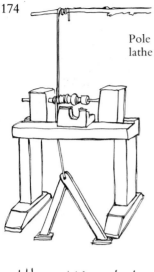

Pole
lathe

TURNING: the shaping of the legs and stretchers (see STRETCHER) of pieces of furniture by use of a lathe. During the late 16th and the 17th centuries turning was the characteristic form of such decoration. It was carried out by means of a simple, foot-operated pole lathe. A driving cord was attached to the free end of the pole and the foot pedal, passing round the work in between. By controlling this cord the turner kept the piece of wood turning round so that he could shape it with his chisel as it spun.

In the later 16th century **baluster turning** was fashionable; this was a columnar form which could be varied to a vase, straight or tapered shape. Early-17th-century work was often **bobbin turned**, the series of balls and discs representing spools or bobbins. After about 1660 an improved design of lathe made **spiral turning** a possibility. Popularly known as **barley-sugar twist**, this form was produced by a device which enabled an oblique cut to be made, so turning spirals which were then finished by hand.

Turning returned to fashion towards the end of the 18th century and reappeared at intervals during the 19th. With the onset of mechanization in the second half of that century, it gradually became possible to carry out various forms of turning by machine and so imitate more cheaply furniture designs of the past.

Baluster   Bobbin   Spiral
turning   turning   turning
c.1540   c.1630   c.1690

TURNSPIT: the operator, human or animal, who turned the roasting spit (see MECHANICAL SPIT, SPIT).

In large medieval kitchens the spit was usually turned by a boy. He was responsible for seeing that the meat was fully and evenly cooked (the phrase 'done to a turn' had a precise meaning). He was protected from the heat of the fire by a screen of wetted woven straw or of metal.

In smaller homes spits were still turned by hand long after the Middle Ages but in larger kitchens the **dog turnspit** began to replace the boy during the 16th century. Short-legged dogs were bred to work in pairs, taking it in turns to pad round and round in the wooden dog wheel. The dog had to keep moving or he would lose his balance. These dog treadmills were about 2½ feet (0.75 metres) in diameter. They were made of wood and were fastened to the wall above and to one side of the fireplace. The treadmill was connected to the pulley of the spit wheel by an endless chain.

The types of dog bred for this task varied in

Boy turnspit
15th century

different parts of the country. One used in Abergavenny (South Wales) is displayed (stuffed) in the local museum. Of a now extinct breed, it was short-legged, long-bodied and had a coat of long golden hair. Dogs continued to be used as turnspits until well into the 19th century especially in rural areas.

TYMPANUM: the space between the sloping and horizontal cornices of a classical pediment (see CLASSICAL ARCHITECTURE, PEDIMENT). Also the space between the lintel of a doorway and the arch above it.

Dog turnspit

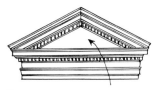

Doorway tympanum

UPHOLSTERY: in England upholstered furniture appeared soon after 1600; before this cushions were used to soften hard seats while bedsteads possessed a wood-board or rope-mesh foundation upon which were piled one or two feather beds. 17th-century upholstered chair seats comprised simply the cushion encased in the covering material and were padded with feathers, wool, horsehair, down or rags.

Springs were available in the 18th century but they were used for carriages not furniture. In 1826 **Samuel Pratt** patented a spiral spring intended to make a swinging seat to be used on board ship as an aid to relieve seasickness. Soon he appreciated its possibilities for furniture and the spiral spring began to be incorporated into chair and sofa design. Such seating furniture became very large and bulky because of having to accommodate the springs inside a great thickness of horsehair and feather stuffing. The French *confortable* easy chair was typical. Soon such furniture was over-decorated with fringing, tassels, embroidery and antimacassars. In 1865 the woven wire mattress for beds, supported on spiral springs, was patented and became very popular by 1880.

In more modern times new materials have replaced the sprung and stuffed upholstery with a simpler, more comfortable, cheaper and more

Deep-buttoned stuffed upholstered armchair
*c.*1880

Spring wire mattress
*c.*1870

Booth's electrically
operated Trolley vac
1906

Harvey
two-person
bellows-
operated
vacuum
cleaner
1910

Star hand-
pump operated
vacuum cleaner
1911

hygienic upholstered form. This is based upon plastic foam material, used for cushions and seat backs (see PLASTICS), which is supported on rubber webbing or cable springing. In mattresses many combinations, firm or soft according to taste, are available, which combine sprung, padded and suspension systems.

VACUUM SUCTION CLEANER: during the second half of the 19th century there were many attempts to design a machine to blow away or suck up dirt and several such, not very efficient, types of apparatus were made. The construction engineer **Hubert Cecil Booth** produced the first successful machine in 1901; this was a powered suction cleaner.

Mr Booth's interest in the matter had been aroused the previous year when he was invited to attend a demonstration at St Pancras Station of a new machine to clean railway carriages. This blew the dirt from one end of the carriage to the other by means of compressed air. Booth did not think that this was a good way of cleaning and believed that sucking was better than blowing. In a now well-known domestic experiment he placed a piece of damp fabric over the arm of his easy chair and sucked it. The resulting black ring on the cloth proved the point to his satisfaction.

He patented (and named) his vacuum suction cleaner in 1901 and formed the Vacuum Cleaner Company to manufacture the machines (now Goblin BVC Ltd). But, although his machine worked very well and was in demand, it suffered the handicap of all machines then being designed to relieve drudgery in the home: lack of a small electric motor to power it (see REFRIGERATOR, WASHING-MACHINE). Large electric motors had been available since the early 1880s but it was not until the Yugoslav-born American inventor of the prototype AC motor, **Nikola Tesla**, designed the first small 1/6th h.p. motor to drive a Westinghouse fan in 1889 that the means of utilizing electricity to power household appliances became a possibility. Even so, it was the early 1900s before motors were manufactured for such appliances.

The first Booth vacuum cleaner was 4½ feet long (1.3 metres). It was powered by a petrol-driven engine and transported through the streets on a horse-drawn van. A team of operators accompanied it to clean, for a fee, carpets, curtains and upholstery in your house. Although a great boon to those who had their houses cleaned in this way, the process was too costly for all but a few.

Attempts were made to produce a more convenient method but the alternatives remained: either a large, expensive, heavy machine, or a smaller one needing two persons to operate it. Of the former alternative Booth's produced the Trolley Vac powered by an electric motor and drawn round the house on a trolley but it was still very expensive (35 guineas in 1906) and far too heavy to take upstairs. Of the latter alternative many designs were produced in the USA and Britain. Nearly all worked by means of one person powering a bellows by hand or foot and another operating the suction device on the end of a long handle. Only one type of inexpensive, lightweight device was one-person-operated; this resembled an overgrown bicycle pump. It was hard work and not very efficient.

The first person to succeed in marrying a small electric motor to a convenient suction cleaner was **J. Murray Spangler** of Ohio who devised in 1907 a prototype which worked. It consisted of a sweeper inside a tin canister, and a dustbag supported on a long handle. Spangler lacked the financial means to capitalize on his invention and sold the rights to a firm of saddlers who developed it and manufactured in 1908 the first one-person-operated, electrically powered, domestic vacuum cleaner. This firm was **W. H. Hoover**. The machine was an instant and complete success and was followed by many others developed by different companies. Today there are two chief types of design: the upright (like the original Hoover model) and the cylinder (a type pioneered in the 1920s by firms such as Goblin and Electrolux). In the 1980s electronic control has been introduced to both designs (see ELECTRONIC CONTROL OF DOMESTIC APPLIANCES).

VALANCE: a long, narrow piece of drapery attached lengthwise to hang in short folds as, for

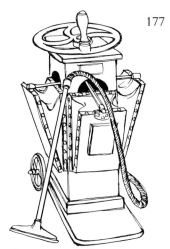

Two-person bellows vacuum cleaner operated by turning the wheel
c. 1912

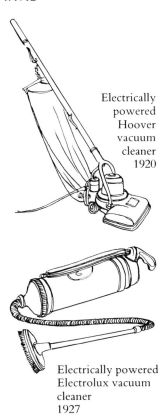

Electrically powered Hoover vacuum cleaner 1920

Electrically powered Electrolux vacuum cleaner 1927

Walnut veneered
dressing-table
*c.*1725–30

Mahogany veneered
bookcase
mid-18th-century

example, over a curtain fitting or from a bed tester.

VALVE CLOSET: see WATER CLOSET.

VAULTING: see STONE VAULTING.

VENEER: a cabinet-making technique where thin sheets of decorative high-quality woods were glued to the flush surface of a carcase which was made from cheaper wood (see CARCASE), so displaying the figure of the veneer. (It was during the 19th century that some poor-quality workmanship gave rise to the word 'veneer' becoming synonymous with a shoddy article which was thinly veiled by something finer.)

The art of veneering is very old; it was practised in ancient Egypt and by the Romans. The idea of decorating furniture with patterns of ornamental woods and other materials was revived during the Renaissance with Italian inlaid work (see INLAY) and later further developed in France and the Low Countries. In the later 17th century foreign craftsmen (for example, the Huguenots) came to England and introduced the techniques of marquetry (see MARQUETRY) and veneering to English furniture-makers who became specialists in these arts (cabinet-makers).

By the early years of the 18th century the technique had advanced so that it was possible to saw fine woods, such as walnut, maple, yew, kingwood and laburnum, to a thickness of 1/16 inch (1.5 mm) and successfully glue fairly large sections of these to the carcase. The style of veneering then changed from the decorative **marquetry** patterns to ones which displayed the figure of the grain of a single wood. Many different designs could be obtained by using successive sections of the same figure (for veneers sawn from one log repeated its pattern), either matched, reversed or opposed on, for example, a table top or drawer front. Particular cuts were also taken to give specific figures. For instance, transverse cuts from small branches produced **oyster veneers**, and trunk malformations **burl (burr) veneers**. Furniture surfaces were also often bordered with bands in which the veneer was applied with the grain running across the border width.

In England the summit of artistic achievement in veneering was during the late 18th century in the work of such designers as **Hepplewhite** and **Sheraton**. During the 19th and 20th centuries techniques of cutting and applying the veneers were improved. In modern veneering it is possible to cut much thinner sheets by rotary mechanical saws and knives and a variety of specific adhesives are available, as well as equipment for drying and applying pressure.

VENETIAN DOOR, WINDOW: a **Venetian window** is a tripartite design with the central section arched and taller than the two flat-topped flanking lights. Also known as a **Palladian window** or **Serliana** because it was first illustrated in Serlio's *Architettura* published in 1537 (later to be translated into English); this, deriving from Palladio, was a characteristic of English Palladian architecture. A **Venetian door** is similar, the central doorway being arched and flanked by lower flat-topped windows.

Venetian window, 1776

VHF RADIO RECEIVER: VHF (Very High Frequency) transmission, using these very short wavelengths, was begun by the BBC in 1955. The shorter the wavelength the greater is the frequency of the electromagnetic oscillations. Such transmission gives a notable freedom from background interference and a higher quality of sound received (see RADIO).

VIDEO-RECORDING: a modern development which is a visual extension of the magnetic tape audio-cassette. A video-cassette recorder makes it possible to record a television programme in your home during your absence, to be viewed later.

Sony video recorder, 1981

VIEWDATA TRANSMISSION: information systems which broadcast data on demand from a teletext organisation on the domestic television screen or are linked by the telephone system network (Telecom) to an adapted television set to provide a more comprehensive information service from computer banks.

Vitruvian scroll

VITRUVIAN SCROLL: a classical border decoration depicting a continuous wave or scroll. Also known as **running dog**.

VOLUTE: a spiral scroll which is the predominant feature of the capital of the Ionic Order in classical architecture. Smaller volutes are part of the Corinthian and Composite capitals (see CAPITAL, CLASSICAL ORDER).

Ionic volute

VOUSSOIR: see ARCH.

Wafering
iron

Wooden baby-walking
cage on castors

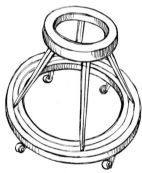

WAFERING IRON: ancestor of the waffle iron, an implement used from the Middle Ages onwards to cook sweet patterned biscuits. Made of iron or steel it comprised two hinged blades, the inner surfaces of which were cut into decorative patterns (these would be pressed into the biscuits). The blades were fitted with long handles and operated like a pair of tongs. The prepared biscuit batter was poured on to the ready-greased blades, then the iron was held over the fire to cook.

WAINSCOTING: wood panelling to cover part or all of the interior walls of a building (see PANEL–AND–FRAME CONSTRUCTION). Wainscot was a medieval term for a high-quality oak imported from Russia, Germany and Holland. The word is thought to derive from 'wain', an early English form of wagon. The imported timber was also used for the making of wagons.

WALKING-CAGE: a traditional piece of equipment for helping a baby to practise walking in safety. The design varied over the years but was usually made of wood and wheels were attached to the legs. The baby was held firmly yet comfortably by the central wooden circlet and straps.

WALL HANGINGS: from the early Middle Ages some type of fabric was used to cover interior walls, partly for warmth and partly for decoration and colour; these draperies were often of home-produced wool, embroidered or painted. By the 14th century, in wealthier homes, such hangings were of richer, imported materials: silk, velvet, brocade. Alternatively, imported tapestries were hung (see TAPESTRY).

Towards the end of the 15th century, as wood panelling became a fashionable wall covering (see PANEL–AND–FRAME CONSTRUCTION), hangings were used less. Another alternative wall covering in the 16th and 17th centuries was embossed and gilded leather.

The most usual wall decoration during the 18th century was by stucco (see PLASTERWORK) since, by this time, rooms were less draughty and better heated, but in bedrooms, hangings of silk or velvet were usual, extending down as far as the dado rail (see DADO). This range of coverings, varying from room to room, of stucco, panelling and fabric hangings continued in fashion until wallpaper became less expensive and available in quantity (see WALLPAPER).

WALLPAPER: the idea of using paper to cover the walls stemmed from the need to produce a cheaper substitute for the very expensive leather and tapestry coverings used by wealthy households. By the early 16th century designs were being printed on small squares of paper by means of wood blocks. The earliest example found in England, at Christ's College, Cambridge, is dated 1509. This was printed only in black and white. Soon colour was being introduced, using several blocks to give a complete pattern. Wallpaper was first made in long strips in France in the 1760s. The individual sheets, each 12 × 16 inches (30 × 40 cm) were pasted together. Flock wallpapers were also being made (see FLOCK WALLPAPER).

Wallpaper began to be a fashionable wall covering during the 17th century when small sheets of printed papers were imported from China. These were costly but in considerable demand as a foil to the then modish Oriental porcelain and furniture (see PORCELAIN, LACQUERED FURNITURE). In the 18th century, English imitations of these Chinese papers began to be manufactured and **John B. Jackson** set up his manufactory in Battersea to produce printed papers in floral designs and representations of landscapes by well-known contemporary painters.

It was not until after 1800 in England that wallpaper became less costly and gradually available in quantity. By 1830 it was being made in continuous rolls and in the 1840s machine-printing had begun to replace hand-printing. In the second half of the century the reduced cost of wallpaper made it once more practicable to paste it on to the wall (this had been done with the early small wallpaper squares but the Chinese papers were so expensive that they had to be protected from damp and dirt and so were mounted on wood frames backed by linen and paper). Later in the century heavy embossed and washable papers such as Lincrusta became popular (see LINCRUSTA).

WARDROBE: until the late 17th and early 18th

Mahogany wardrobe
c.1750

Inside the carved stand and doors are drawers and adjustable shelves

Sheraton wardrobe design
with shelves and drawers
in central section and full-length
hanging-space in end sections
with sham drawer fronts
1793

Large painted
mahogany wardrobe
with plate glass mirror
1867

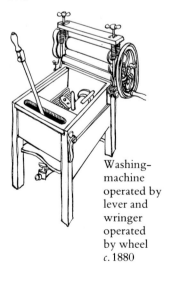

Washing-
machine
operated by
lever and
wringer
operated
by wheel
c. 1880

centuries 'wardrobe' usually meant either the range of clothes which a person possessed or a room (often next to the bedchamber, a kind of dressing-room) in which garments were kept: a similar usage to **garderobe** (see GARDEROBE). Clothes were stored during the early Middle Ages in **chests** which could be taken around on journeys (see CHEST)'or, after about 1500, in a **clothes press** fronted by doors behind which were shelves, drawers and pegs for hanging garments (see CUPBOARD, PRESS).

During the 18th century the word 'wardrobe' was used for a piece of movable furniture which contained clothes, but this had no hanging space. It was a fine piece of furniture, often of mahogany, and standing on short cabriole legs (see CABRIOLE LEG). Behind the full-length doors were shelves and drawers. Towards the end of the century the idea of hanging clothes, especially ladies' gowns, became accepted. In **hanging wardrobes** the centre portion was devoted to shelf space and this was flanked by hanging cupboards. In the lower part of the wardrobe were large drawers. This type of wardrobe appears amongst Sheraton's designs. Victorian wardrobes steadily became more massive with deep drawers and shelves and ample hanging space. By 1850 there was a full-length plate-glass mirror fitted to the central door.

WASHBOARD: a typically 19th-century aid to wash day. The board was made of wood and stood on legs. The zinc-covered front was corrugated so that clothes could be rubbed against these ribs to loosen the dirt.

WASHING-MACHINE: during the second half of the 19th century many designs of washing-machine were manufactured but they were all powered by human energy. The filling and emptying had to be done by hand and, in most models, the water had to be heated first. Soap was chopped up by hand and added to the hot water.

The design of these 19th-century machines varied considerably but they were all based on a mechanical means of imitating the traditional method of washing, using a dolly stick and washboard (see DOLLY STICK, POSSER, WASHBOARD). The mechanisms which were devised to achieve the agitation of the water varied from a machine which could be rocked by the foot like a cradle to one which incorporated a dolly stick attached to the lid or base of the tub; in others the washing was churned around by paddles or pegged wooden rollers. Apart from the rocking model, the motive power was provided by a lever operated by hand. Many designs had corrugated interior walls and floors to simulate the washboard action. Most were made of wood and shaped like a tub or box. Metal was used for stands and fittings.

By the 1880s a few machines were designed which could heat the water in the tub; gas jets were used for this, alternatively a coal-fired boiler. The first electrically powered machines were produced in the USA soon after 1900. In early models the existing machine was adapted to the addition of an electric motor which was usually sited beneath the tub – a dangerous proceeding as many tubs leaked and machines were rarely earthed.

It was the late 1920s before the American washing-machine was redesigned to take full advantage of electrical power and to meet the needs of a mass market. An all-metal tub replaced the wooden one and this was then enclosed in an enamelled metal cabinet. There were two chief methods of creating the washing action. One agitated the water by a revolving disc fitted with fins mounted in the base of the tub and operated by a driving mechanism beneath. The other was a perforated cylinder which was driven to rotate, first in one direction, then in the other.

Such machines were imported into Britain in small numbers in the 1920s and 1930s but it was not until after the Second World War that they were being manufactured and sold in quantity. The automatic washing-machine with programmed cycles of washing, rinsing and spin-drying became a widespread success in the 1960s. Since then models have steadily become more sophisticated, including a choice of programmes to suit different fabrics and biological washes; some now have microprocessor control (see ELECTRONIC CONTROL OF DOMESTIC APPLIANCES).

WASHSTAND: a piece of furniture fitted to contain the means for personal washing, introduced for bedroom use from the mid 18th century: before this an ewer and basin had been kept on a chest or cabinet. In 1750–60 the washstand was a wooden tripod stand fitted with a small ceramic basin at the top while lower down were small drawers containing soap and toilet articles. Later in the century more complex washstands in different designs were available. Some had built-in mirrors,

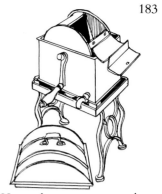

Howarth patent steam washer heated by gas jets beneath boiler with metal drum for the washing turned by handle 1889

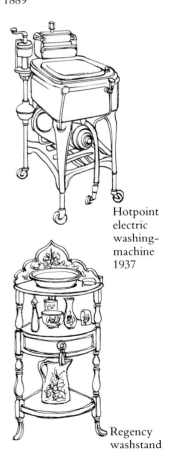

Hotpoint electric washing-machine 1937

Regency washstand

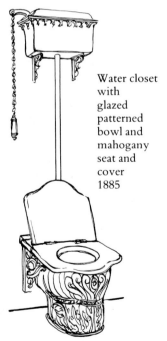

184

Washstand designed by William
Burges:
carved, painted and gilt
with marble top,
bowl and soap dishes
1880

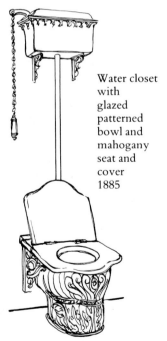

Water closet
with
glazed
patterned
bowl and
mahogany
seat and
cover
1885

several drawers and shelves, and some were
designed to fit into corners.

During the 19th century the washstand became
larger. Victorian designs had marble tops and tiled
splashbacks. Into the circular holes in the top were
fitted two florally decorated basins: jugs, jars and
soap dishes were in sets matching the basins. Later-
19th-century washstands were even larger and
more ornate. They included capacious drawers and
cupboards. With the advent of more bathrooms
with running water in the 20th century, the need
for bedroom washstands gradually waned.

WATER CLOSET: the inventor of the WC in
1596 was a godson of Queen Elizabeth I, **Sir John
Harington**, whose valve closet was constructed at
Kelston near Bath. This closet had a pan with a
seat, and a cistern above. He described it in his
Metamorphosis of Ajax: A Cloacinean Satire ('Jakes'
was current slang for a privy).

Unfortunately, due to lack of good water supplies and drainage systems, 179 years were to pass
before the first WC was patented by a London
watchmaker **Alexander Cumming**. This also
was a valve closet with overhead cistern; when a
handle was pulled up, the valve opened to empty
the contents of the pan into a waste pipe and water
entered to flush the pan. This was designed on
the principle common to subsequent WCs but its
sliding valve was inefficient and remained unsatisfactory until, three years later in 1778, **Joseph
Bramah** improved the valve and so produced a
WC which was the best standard pattern for a
hundred years.

Bramah's closet represented an important contribution to domestic hygiene but its usefulness
was restricted by the inadequacy of current water
supplies and sewage disposal methods. Its introduction actually increased health hazards. Closets
were tucked into corners of rooms, or even
cupboards, with little or no ventilation. The waste-
pipe emptied into a cesspool and foul gases returned to enter the house via this pipe. It was not
until the 1840s that town cesspools were outlawed
and later still before their sewage systems were
improved.

Cheaper closets such as the **long hopper closet**
and the **pan closet** were widely used. These were
inadequately flushed and became very soiled. It
was not until the 1870s that new designs replaced
these early closets. The model which became the
standard type was **Twyford's washdown closet**

in which water was always present in the pan and a strong flush was supplied.

WATER LEAF: a carved broad leaf decoration used in 12th-century Gothic capitals (see CAPITAL).

Water leaf decoration c.1200

WHATNOT: a piece of furniture with shelves in tiers supported by decorative posts used for the storing and display of books, papers and ornaments. Especially to be seen in Victorian homes.

WICKERWORK (BASKETWORK) CHAIR: a traditional type in which the back and sides were made in one continuous piece of construction. Made since before the time of the Roman occupation.

WIG STAND: stood by the bedside during the late 17th and 18th centuries to carry the wig. The usual designs were of wood, in tripod or pedestal form, often including drawers for wig-dressing materials. Some stands of wood and leather were in the shape of dummy heads.

Mahogany whatnot c.1810

WINDOW: medieval windows were of casement type (see CASEMENT WINDOW). Early examples were narrow **lancets** (see LANCET), either single or grouped under one arch head. Window glass was rare in the early Middle Ages but windows were fitted with wooden **shutters** which could be barred across at night (see WINDOW GLASS). As time passed and the need for defence became less acute, windows became larger. The pointed arch became wider (see EQUILATERAL ARCH, FOUR-CENTRED ARCH, POINTED ARCH) and the window head was ornamented with **tracery** (see TRACERY), and also, in some cases, with coloured glass. By the 15th century some windows were square-headed. **Bay** and **oriel windows** were characteristic of larger houses (see BAY WINDOW, ORIEL WINDOW).

In Elizabethan times the window area in a house increased markedly in proportion to the wall, rather as it had a century earlier in ecclesiastical building. The country was peaceful, defence and fortification had become superfluous and advances were being made in the production of window glass (see WINDOW GLASS). This notable change prompted the contemporary jingle that at **Hardwick Hall** (Derbyshire) built in the 1590s there was 'more glass than wall'. The tall bay and oriel designs seen in the 15th century were being intro-

Wickerwork chair

Mahogany wig stand c.1750

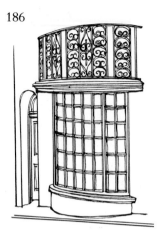

Balcony and bow-fronted window of a sea-side Regency house *c.*1820

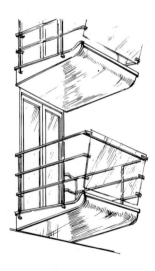

Modern glass, concrete and metal balcony and steel-framed window 1960

duced into more houses. **Mullions** were closely set and there were several crossing **transoms**: carved, moulded stone or wood was used for these. By the early Caroline period (see CAROLINE), with larger panes of glass, there were fewer mullions and generally only one or two transoms (see MULLION, TRANSOM). In all these 16th- and 17th-century large window designs, parts of the framework were made to open in casement fashion.

The **sash window** made its appearance in the late 17th century (see SASH WINDOW) and by the middle of the following century such sash designs were large and beautifully proportioned with slender glazing bars. **Bow-fronted windows** were characteristic of Regency houses (see BAY WINDOW), at which time (see REGENCY), the sash windows were often very tall, extending from picture rail nearly to the floor. Victorian windows were still large, many designs then made without glazing bars as large panes of plate glass had become more readily available (see PLATE GLASS). **French windows** were introduced at this time, leading into a conservatory or garden.

The casement window was re-introduced in Edwardian times and, during the 20th century, both types – sash and casement – have been available. Metal-framed windows were introduced: first steel (which needed painting); then, in the 1930s, aluminium (see ALUMINIUM). In the years since the Second World War 'picture window' and sealed double-glazed window units have become popular. See also DORMER WINDOW, LIGHTS, OCULUS, OGEE, VENETIAN WINDOW.

WINDOW GLASS (see also GLASS): windows were glazed in countries occupied under the Roman Empire: for example, Egypt, Syria, Greece, Italy, Gaul. In many Romano-British houses windows were glazed also. But after the departure of the Romans, domestic window glass became a rare luxury in Britain until well into the 15th century, enjoyed only by kings and wealthy citizens. Many kinds of substitutes were used in the small medieval window openings: thin sheets cut from horn or alabaster, oiled linen, mica or paper and parchment soaked in gum arabic.

British domestic glass was in more general use by the 16th century but it was still so costly that windows were usually protected by wooden lattices and, when the great house owner went away for some time, the windows were removed to preserve the glass. This English glass was in very small panes. It was not of good quality, being neither transparent, colourless nor flat. Coloured glass was imported, therefore expensive. Most glass was made by the **cylinder** method (see CYLINDER GLASS) and this was only replaced by the costlier **crown glass** in the 18th century (see CROWN GLASS). 19th-century demand led to the further development of **plate glass** and **sheet glass** (see PLATE GLASS, SHEET GLASS) and these processes were only superseded in the 1950s by the revolutionary method of **float glass** which was of such high quality of brilliance, exactitude and transparency (see FLOAT GLASS).

WINDSOR CHAIR: an essentially country chair devised and made by village turners and wheelwrights which developed from the early 18th century onwards into a popular and more fashionable design. Many types of Windsor chair evolved over the years; its popularity has continued unabated until today. It is basically a stick-back chair, easy to make, comfortable and conveniently light to carry.

The **comb-back** design was the earliest type. This has a shaped top rail into which the sticks (turned spindles) are socketed. It is so-called because the back resembles a hay rake or comb. By 1750 the **hoop-** or **bow-back** had been introduced in which the arched back is of one continuous piece of wood. Soon too came the **Gothic** version with pointed arch back, the decoratively carved splat and the cabriole leg.

Fashionable influences produced a number of variations on these forms during the 19th and 20th centuries, from the simple **kitchen Windsor** to the more complex **treble splat** (see SPLAT) or **wheel-back** designs. Some had arms, some none; some had straight turned legs, some cabriole (see CABRIOLE LEG). In all cases the members were splayed or angled, and the legs and turned back sticks were all socketed into the saddle-shaped seat. This seat was generally made from elm wood, the turned sticks from beech, and the bent arms and rails of ash or yew.

WING CHAIR: an upholstered armchair with side pieces.

WIRELESS: see RADIO.

WORK TABLE: a dainty table made from the late 17th century onwards in varied and elegant

Comb-back Windsor armchair 1740–50

Bow-back Windsor armchair c.1765

Bow wheel-back Windsor armchair c.1825

Gothic-back Windsor armchair c.1770

Upholstered wing chair c.1715

designs to contain materials for sewing, painting or reading.

WRITING-CHAIR: see LIBRARY CHAIR.

WROUGHT IRON: see CAST IRON, IRON AND STEEL.

Papier mâché
work table
c. 1845

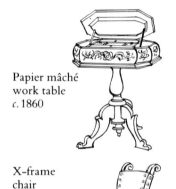

Papier mâché
work table
c. 1860

X-frame
chair
c. 1580

Velvet-
covered
upholstered
X-frame
armchair
c. 1615

X-FRAMED CHAIR, STOOL: a traditional design with a long history dating back to ancient Egypt. These antique forms of seating were folding pieces of furniture. The two X-frames, with connecting stretchers at sides or front and back, were made of wood or metal, elaborately decorated and painted. The seat was of leather or fabric.

The X-frame design was in use all through the Middle Ages but by the late 14th century it was becoming a fixed structure and no longer folding; chairs had high backs. Both chairs and stools were widely used in the 16th century and the X-frame stool reappeared at intervals over the years, seen particularly between 1770 and 1820 (see STOOL).

ACKNOWLEDGEMENTS

The illustrations in this book have been drawn from my own sketches and notes made over a period of many years in houses and museums all over England. I should like to express my gratitude for the courtesy and generous assistance shown to me at all times by the staff of the museums and houses listed on the following pages.

SOURCES OF INFORMATION

LIST OF SELECTED HOUSES

The houses listed below display interiors and contents of particular interest. For some of them, details of charges, times of opening, parking, etc., appear in Historic Houses, Castles and Gardens in Great Britain and Ireland *published annually by ABC Historic Publications. Other of these houses are not generally open to the public but admit parties by special arrangement.*

MEDIEVAL: 1300–1500
Athelhampton, Dorset – medieval and later.
Bradley Manor House, Newton Abbot, Devon – 15th century.
Cotehele House, Calstock, Cornwall.
Glastonbury Abbey, the Abbot's Kitchen, Somerset – c.1320.
Great Chalfield Manor House, Melksham, Wiltshire – moated house, c.1480.
Great Dixter Manor House, Northiam, Sussex – half-timber, 15th century.
Haddon Hall, Bakewell, Derbyshire – medieval and later.
Ightham Mote, near Sevenoaks, Kent – moated medieval manor house.
Lower Brockhampton Manor House, Leominster, Hereford and Worcester – 15th century, half-timber with gatehouse.
Lytes Carey, Somerton, Som. – 14th/15th century manor house with chapel.
Markenfield Hall, Ripon, Yorkshire – 14th to 16th century manor house.
Old Soar Manor House, Plaxtol, Kent – solar block of knight's dwelling, c.1290.
Oxburgh Hall, Swaffham, Norfolk – 1482.
Paycocke's, Coggeshall, Essex – merchant's house, 1490–1500.
Penshurst Place, Tonbridge, Kent – 1340 onwards.
Rufford Old Hall, near Ormskirk, Lancashire – 15th and 16th century.
Shute Barton Manor House, near Axminster, Devon – c.1400 and later.
Smallhythe Place, Tenterden, Kent – yeoman's home, from 1480.
Stoneacre Manor House, Otham, Kent – c.1480, half-timber.

TUDOR: 16th CENTURY
Barrington Court, Ilminster, Somerset – c.1530.
Burghley House, Stamford, Northamptonshire – Elizabethan.
Cadhay, Ottery St Mary, Devon – Elizabethan.
Cobham Hall, near Rochester, Kent – c.1594 onwards.
Compton Wynyates, Warwickshire – c.1490–1530.
Cothelstone Manor House, near Taunton, Somerset – c.1590.
Hardwick Hall, near Chesterfield, Derbyshire – 1591–7.
Hengrave Hall, Bury St Edmunds, Suffolk – c.1525.
Levens Hall, Kendal, Cumbria – Elizabethan.
Little Moreton Hall, Congleton, Cheshire – 1559–80.
Longleat House, Warminster, Wiltshire – 1550–80.
Montacute House, Yeovil, Somerset – 1588–1601.
Speke Hall, near Liverpool – half-timber, Elizabethan.
Sulgrave Manor, near Banbury, Oxon – Elizabethan manor house.
Trerice, St Newlyn East, near Newquay, Cornwall – Elizabethan.

STUART: 1600–1714

Aston Hall, Birmingham – Jacobean, 1618–35.
Audley End, Saffron Walden, Essex – Jacobean and later.
Bateman's, Burwash, Sussex – 1634.
Belton House, near Grantham, Lincolnshire – 1684–7.
Blenheim Palace, Woodstock, Oxon – 1705–22.
Blickling Hall, Aylsham, Norfolk – Jacobean, 1619–25.
Castle Ashby, near Northampton – early 17th century.
Castle Howard, North Yorkshire – 1699–1726.
Chastleton House, Moreton in the Marsh, Oxon – Jacobean, 1603–12.
Chatsworth, near Bakewell, Derbyshire – 1686–1707.
Dyrham Park, Avon – 1698.
Felbrigg Hall, near Cromer, Norfolk – 17th and 18th centuries.
Fenton House, Hampstead – late 17th century.
Ham House, Richmond, Surrey – Jacobean and Restoration Stuart.
Hanbury Hall, near Droitwich, Hereford and Worcester – c.1700.
Hatfield House, Hertfordshire – 1607–12, Jacobean.
Kingston Lacy, Dorset – 1663–5.
Knole, Sevenoaks, Kent – Jacobean from 1607.
Mompesson House, Salisbury, Wilts – 1701.
Old House, Hereford – half-timber, 1620s.
Petworth House, Sussex – 1688–93.
Quebec House, Westerham, Kent – c.1625.
Sudbury Hall, near Uttoxeter, Derbyshire – 1660–80.
Tintinhull House, near Yeovil, Somerset – early 17th century.
Uppark, near Petersfield, Sussex – c.1690.
Weston Park, near Shifnal, Shropshire – 1670s.
Wilton House, near Salisbury, Wiltshire – c.1650 and later.

GEORGIAN: 1714–1837

Ashridge Park, near Berkhamsted, Herts – early Gothic Revival, 1806–13.
Attingham Park, near Shrewsbury, Shropshire – c.1784.
Basildon Park, near Pangbourne, Berkshire – 1776–83.
Bath, 1 Royal Crescent – 1767–74.
Bristol, 7 Great George Street (The Georgian House) – 1789–91.
Chiswick House, London – 1727–36.
Clandon Park, near Guildford, Surrey – 1729–31.
Dodington House, Chipping Sodbury, Avon – 1798–1817.
Harewood House, near Leeds, West Yorkshire – 1759–71.
Heveningham Hall, near Halesworth, Suffolk – 1775–1800.
Holkham Hall, near Wells, Norfolk – begun 1734.
Houghton Hall, near Kings Lynn, Norfolk – designed 1721.
Ickworth, near Bury St Edmunds, Suffolk – 1794–1830.
Kedleston Hall, near Derby – 1758–68.
Kenwood House, London – 1767–8.
Marble Hill House, Twickenham, Middlesex – begun 1724.
Moccas Court, Hereford and Worcester – 1775.
Moor Park Mansion, Rickmansworth, Hertfordshire – reconstructed 1727.
Nostell Priory, near Wakefield, West Yorkshire – 1735–70.
Osterley Park House, Middlesex – from 1761.
Peckover House, Wisbech, Cambridgeshire – 1722.
Saltram House, Plymouth – 18th century.

Shugborough, near Stafford – 1745–1806.
Stourhead House, Stourton, Wiltshire – 1722.
Syon House, Brentford, Middlesex – from 1762.
Woodhall Park, Watton at Stone, Hertfordshire – 1778–82.

VICTORIAN: 1837–1901
Carlton Towers, near Goole, Yorkshire – remodelled 1871–7.
Cragside, near Rothbury, Northumberland – 1870–84.
Hughenden Manor, near High Wycombe, Buckinghamshire – remodelled 1862.
Knightshayes Court, near Tiverton, Devon – 1869–71.
Osborne House, Isle of Wight – 1844–8.
Prestwold Hall, near Loughborough, Leicestershire – remodelled 1842.
Somerleyton Hall, near Lowestoft, Suffolk – 1844–51.
Standen, East Grinstead, Sussex – 1891–4.
Waddesdon Manor, near Aylesbury, Buckinghamshire – 1874–89.
Wightwick Manor, near Wolverhampton, Staffordshire – 1887–93.

LIST OF SELECTED MUSEUMS

The museums listed below contain collections of period rooms, furniture, fittings and artefacts. For details of special exhibits, contents, charges, times of opening, parking, etc., consult the booklet Museums and Art Galleries in Great Britain and Ireland, *published annually by ABC Historic Publications.*

Banbury (Oxon) – The Banbury Museum
Barnard Castle (Co. Durham) – The Bowes Museum
Birmingham (West Midlands) – City Museum and Art Gallery
Bristol (Avon) – Blaise Castle House Museum
Carlisle (Cumbria) – Museum and Art Gallery
Cheltenham (Glos.) – Art Gallery and Museum *and* Holst Birthplace Mus.
Chester (Cheshire) – Grosvenor Museum
Colchester (Essex) – Colchester and Essex Museum
Dawlish (Devon) – the Dawlish Museum
Exeter (Devon) – Rougemont House Museum *and* St Nicholas Priory
Gloucester (Glos.) – City Museum and Art Gallery
Great Yarmouth (Norfolk) – Elizabethan House Museum
Halifax (West Yorkshire) – Bankfield Museum and Art Gallery
High Wycombe (Bucks) – Wycombe Chair and Local History Museum
Hove (East Sussex) – Museum of Art
Ipswich (Suffolk) – Christchurch Mansion
Kendal (Cumbria) – Abbot Hall Museum of Lakeland Life and Industry
Kings Lynn (Norfolk) – Museum of Social History
Leeds (West Yorkshire) – Abbey House Museum *and* Temple Newsam House
Lewes (East Sussex) – Anne of Cleves' House Museum
Liverpool (Merseyside) – Croxteth Country Park
London – Geffrye Museum, Kingsland Road, E2.
       – Science Museum, South Kensington, SW7.
       – Victoria and Albert Museum, South Kensington, SW7.
Manchester (Greater Manchester) – City Art Gallery
                   – Heaton Hall, Prestwich
Norwich (Norfolk) – Strangers' Hall Museum of Domestic Life
Oxford (Oxon) – Museum of Oxford *and* Woodstock Museum

Reading (Berks) – Museum of English Rural Life
St Helen's (Merseyside) – Pilkington Glass Museum
Salisbury (Wilts) – Salisbury and South Wiltshire Museum
Singleton (West Sussex) – Weald and Downland Open Air Museum
Stanley (Co. Durham) – Beamish North of England Open Air Museum
Telford (Shropshire) – Ironbridge Gorge Museum Trust
Torquay (Devon) – Torquay Museum
Totnes (Devon) – The Elizabethan House Museum
York – The Castle Museum

SELECTED BOOK LIST

Agius, P., *British Furniture 1880–1915*, Antique Collectors' Club, 1978
Airs, M., *The Making of the English Country House*, Architectural Press, 1976
Amery, C., *Period Houses and their Details*, Architectural Press, 1974
Aronson, J., *The Encyclopaedia of Furniture*, Batsford, 1977
Barley, M. W., *The House and Home*, Studio Vista, 1971
Barnard, J., *The Decorative Tradition*, Architectural Press, 1973.
Cesckinsky, H., *English Furniture, Gothic to Sheraton*, Bonanza Books, New York, 1968
Clifton Taylor, A., *The Pattern of English Building*, Faber, 1972
Cook, O., *The English Country House*, Thames & Hudson, 1974
Curl, J. S., *English Architecture, Illustrated Glossary*, David & Charles, 1973
Fleming, J., and Honour, H., *The Penguin Dictionary of Decorative Arts*, Allen Lane, 1977
Girouard, M., *Life in the English Country House*, Yale U.P., 1978
——— *The Victorian Country House*, Yale U.P., 1979
Gloag, J., *Guide to Furniture Styles*, A. & C. Black, 1972
Hayward, H., *World Furniture*, Hamlyn, 1981
Hussey, C., *English Country Houses, 1715–1840* (3 vols), Country Life, 1958
Joy, E. T., *Chairs*, Country Life, 1980
——— *Country Life Book of English Furniture*, Country Life, 1964
——— *English Furniture 1800–1851*, Ward Lock, 1977
——— *Getting Dressed*, HMSO, 1981
Lambton, L., *Temples of Convenience*, Gordon Fraser, 1978
Lloyd, N., *History of the English House*, Architectural Press, 1976
Moody, E., *Modern Furniture*, Studio Vista, 1966
Peel, J. H. B., *The Englishman's Home*, Cassell, 1972
Robertson, E. G. and J., *Cast Iron Decoration*, Thames & Hudson, 1977
Savage, G., *Concise History of Interior Decoration*, Thames & Hudson, 1966
Sutcliffe, A., *Multi-Storey Living*, Croom Helm, 1974
Waddell, R., *The Art Nouveau Style*, Dover Publications, 1977
Wright, L., *Clean and Decent*, Routledge & Kegan Paul, 1960
——— *Homes Fires Burning*, Routledge & Kegan Paul, 1964
Wheeler, J., and others, *The History of Furniture*, Orbis, 1982
Yarwood, D., *The Architecture of Britain*, Batsford, 1980
——— *The British Kitchen*, Batsford, 1981
——— *The English Home*, Batsford, 1979
——— *English Houses*, Batsford, 1966
——— *Five Hundred Years of Technology in the Home*, Batsford, 1983
——— *Robert Adam*, Dent, 1970